A Family Guide to

WASTE-FREE
Living

Lauren & Oberon Carter

For Audrey, Xanthe and Maisie, who constantly inspire us to question, learn and create positive change. May the contents of this book be useful to you when you leave the nest, if not before. We hope it goes a little way towards helping to create a cleaner and healthier planet for you and your children. Love, Mum and Dad xx

A Family Guide to

WASTE-FREE
Living

Lauren & Oberon Carter

plum.   Pan Macmillan Australia

Foreword

This handbook is a yarn. A really honest and transparent yarn for that matter. It is the story of a family and their choice to make some changes to their habits and lifestyle. It was a conscious choice. It was open-ended from the beginning and remains open at the conclusion. Hang on – doesn't a book start with an introduction and finish with a conclusion? Herein lies the beauty of this book: there is no set destination and outcome! We, the readers, get to follow the authors' footsteps all the way to a point which feels just right for us. There is nothing contained within or proposed by this book that any one of us can't have a go at. If the most difficult aspect of any change is the getting started, then all you need is the starter and their starter's pistol to be fired. Lauren and Oberon Carter have mounted the stand and fired the pistol, so dive in!

> Never before in history have we had access to so much information on a daily basis. The incessant current is coming at us from the moment we wake up to the moment we go to sleep.

Never before in history have we had access to so much information on a daily basis. The incessant current is coming at us from the moment we wake up to the moment we go to sleep. Our access to, and ability to connect on, more and more platforms makes it almost impossible to escape the tidal wave of words 24/7 via email, text message, Facebook, Instagram, Periscope, Facebook Live, Instagram Live, Linkedin, Twitter, Twitter Live, Snapchat and did I mention the old telephone? I feel tired just reading the options! But with so many choices as to how we access information and who we believe comes a whole new challenge in itself. Who do we turn to and work with when it comes to the challenges that we face? The tone and quality of our incoming information needs to be digestible and, happily, *A Family Guide to Waste-free Living* is beautifully pitched and delivered. This is a family leading us on their intrepid attempt to navigate the world without the waste from the day-to-day convenience and consumption paradigm that most of us have been sold into.

I cannot overlook the fact that the completion of this gorgeous handbook flows seamlessly with the ongoing ABC *War on Waste* television series as well as the expertly compiled and years-in-the-making book, *Retrosuburbia* by permaculture co-founder David Holmgren, in which he deploys decades of research, expertise and practical application to look to a future where we can reduce consumption and uplift our communities by retrofitting the suburban environment. Lauren and Oberon write in tandem with these realities, directing their focus on their family, their home and how their actions can make a difference. A real difference to the big picture of a regenerative future by illustrating and crafting the change as a waste-reduction project across the family's daily life. By looking at the world today from a linear economy point of view, Lauren and Oberon interrogate the recycling economy and find a future filled with solutions within a circular economy. They begin the journey by knocking the lid off their rubbish bin and diving in head first. Their success lies within the audit, the honest and totally truthful acceptance of the statistics they uncover around and within their waste. Data does not lie! Within the data lies the opportunity. Being realistic about the contents and its reach is where this book hits its sweet spot. This is where *A Family Guide to Waste-free Living*'s believability, its applicability and its achievability will win over even the harshest of non-caring consumers. It is undeniable because of the honesty and simplicity of the discovery that we make alongside Lauren and Oberon and their family.

A Family Guide to Waste-free Living is an access-all-areas approach to setting out on a more sustainable lifestyle. It ticks boxes that were not even there to tick. It does not demand you go 'zero waste' and turn your life on its head. It uses non-intimidating but very specific language that enables it to walk a tightrope between being an easily understood and digestible record of a journey, as well as a very well-crafted and structured manual for change. By making it a family project that people can undertake together, it points no fingers and passes no judgements, but allows for a transition to begin and steps to be taken towards moving into a slightly different lifestyle.

From canvas bags to buying in bulk, fresh produce to preserving, beeswax wraps to unwrapping the packaging, personal care to clothes repair, gatherings to gifts, from nature to your neighbours; no area in our lives is left unvisited. It's our house and our lives that we get to see from a new perspective and this is what makes this book compelling. A concept or change is proposed and a recipe or action is provided. Lauren and Oberon have done the hard work so we get to apply it in our context and at our own pace. The familiarity of Refuse, Reduce, Reuse, Recycle and Rot goes the next step to Reframe: meaning a shift in the way we see the world and act within it.

This book provides the ingredients to create a new normal.

This book provides the ingredients to create a new normal. It's all about a personal, family project to do and share together. To grow in ways that you didn't realise you could grow or flex or change. Real change is felt; it is believed. Lauren and Oberon share their stories in a way that you want to hear again like a song that becomes an ear worm. Each note, each tune creates the big picture, but you get there by humming the chorus, the bridge and all the verses along the way. *A Family Guide to Waste-free Living* will quickly make its way onto your best-of playlist. A classic hit that you will replay and share long into the future!

Costa Georgiadis

Contents

5.
CELEBRATE
&
VENTURE
OUTSIDE
Gather without
waste
219

6.
CHANGE
Foster a
waste-free
community
275

'At first people refuse to believe that a strange new thing can be done. Then they begin to hope it can be done. Then they see it can be done. Then it is done and all the world wonders why it was not done centuries ago.' – Frances Hodgson Burnett

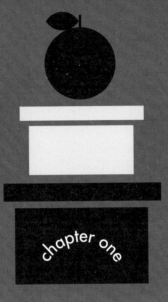

chapter one

THE BASICS

An introduction to waste-free living

Before we get started, let us tell you a little bit about ourselves and how we came to be interested in reducing the waste we make. We'll guide you through the ins and outs of waste, talk about some of the tricky things, and set you on the path to working out how to reduce the waste your family makes, in a way that feels right for you.

At its heart, waste-free living is simple

— It requires you to do just one thing: to make a conscious decision to avoid making waste, then apply that approach to as many facets of your life as you can. Once you've made that conscious decision, the doing part becomes much easier. The way to avoid or reduce some types of waste is not always immediately apparent, so, to help you along, we have compiled some of our favourite methods for waste-free living. It would be impossible to include absolutely every waste-reducing hack there is in this book, because, as you will soon learn, waste-free living filters into every aspect of life. So we've focused on what works well for us.

In the following pages, we impart some practical know-how and offer the reasoning behind our suggestions. We reckon that most people can make changes to reduce their own waste, without having to compromise their finances or standard of living. In fact, we've found that living waste free makes life so much richer and more rewarding.

In our busy, consumer-based society we can forget that it's possible to live happy and productive lives without endlessly and mindlessly consuming. Through our attempts at waste-free living and, supported by a framework of permaculture-based and ecological thinking, we aim to share what we think is a means to reconnect; bringing us back in touch with nature and helping to meet our own and our community's needs, in a sustainable way.

We reckon that most people can make changes to reduce their own waste, without having to compromise their finances or standard of living.

It is our hope that in years to come, waste-free living will be the norm, rather than the exception. Kerbside rubbish collection and landfill pits will be lost to antiquity. We'll work with our local environmental conditions to nourish ourselves, efficiently and without pollution or social harm. Our communities will be resilient and supported by diverse local food systems and social networks that facilitate the sharing of food and other items to meet local needs. The sooner the better!

Waste-free living has the potential to become normalised as more people build connections within their community, by engaging in conversations with retailers and each other and by being resourceful through growing food, bartering goods, sharing ideas and swapping resources. We can each make a positive difference to the planet we inhabit and create a new normal for our children. We think many families can make that conscious decision to reduce their waste and if they do, we will be more likely to provide a healthier, cleaner and better future for our planet and future generations.

We know how easy it is to feel overwhelmed when it comes to tackling environmental issues, feeling that *it's all too big*. We can feel like small fish in a big pond, or like our individual actions are inconsequential. But if inaction on waste leads to environmental and social harm, then conversely, our positive actions can have great benefit. Your choices around consumption and waste can make a positive difference and might encourage others around you to change their habits, too. Reducing waste in our homes is something we can all do, because it is an area where we have a lot of control and choice, and we're here to help guide you as you make some of those choices.

Just your average family ...

━ We are, on paper, what you might call a fairly average family of five. We live in a smaller-than-average-sized, 1950s-built, suburban house. Our mortgage costs us a little more than what the average Tasmanian family pays on housing. Our family income is close to the Australian average, but our weekly food budget, both before and after switching to waste-free living, is below what the average family of four would spend.

Bringing children into the world and seeing it through their eyes strengthened our resolve to care for the earth in the best ways we can.

We're fortunate to have good health and we've had many opportunities to work towards a life that feels good and honest and provides what we need. We're luckier than many, which is why we feel it's our responsibility to care for the planet we leave for our grandchildren. There are a few things that steered us towards waste-free living. Lauren has been keen on gardening since making mud pies and helping her grandfather tend gardens as a child. Her mum always cooked amazing food from scratch and was spectacular at refashioning old clothes for dress-up days, so practical stuff and making-do are things that she knows well. Oberon loves all things nature and is a trained ecologist who has worked in nature conservation for twenty years. He is interested in the way humans are connected to (or disconnected from) earth's ecosystems and waste provides an interesting focal point to address those interactions.

Bringing children into the world and seeing it through their eyes strengthened our resolve to care for the earth in the best ways we can. One of the easiest and most practical ways for city folk, like us, to connect with nature on a regular basis is to keep a garden. Since shacking up in the late 1990s, we've always had a veggie patch in each house we've lived in and delighted in growing some of our own food, as well as composting scraps. Along the way, we dove deep into learning about permaculture and the way we had been living and interacting with nature seemed to make more sense.

We've been slowly implementing a permaculture design for our home ever since, while sharing our knowledge of permaculture with our children. Permaculture is a design framework devised by Bill Mollison and David Holmgren in the 1970s. It provides a set of useful ethics and principles for people to live and thrive in a way that is nourishing, whilst caring for the planet and each other. The ethics of 'Earth Care', 'People Care' and 'Fair Share' really struck a chord with us and are in our minds with most decisions we make.

THE BASICS

A few years ago, we knuckled down and focused on the permaculture principle 'Produce no Waste', spurred on by a challenge set by a local community group to live as sustainably as possible for a couple of weeks. Now, we figured we were already living pretty sustainably, so how could we improve our baseline? All our food was composted or fed to the chooks. We recycled. We thought we were pretty environmentally aware and *doing the right thing*. Surely there couldn't be much more we could do that would make a difference, could there? We set out to see.

We set ourselves a target to produce no waste at all for the following fortnight. We made a conscious decision to avoid all single-use products. We lived as though such items no longer existed and it became a bit like a game. Plastic bags, bottled drinks, single-use straws and cups – and even metal cans – just disappeared off our radar, unless we had to actively refuse them. Suddenly, supermarkets weren't part of our weekly shopping trip and our idea of what was necessary in our daily lives changed.

Living waste free has made us think and act in new ways, grow more food, learn lots and importantly, it has been much easier and more fun than we expected.

We developed a habit of remembering our reusable water bottles, shopping bags, coffee cups and straws, if we thought we'd need them. Even the kids were totally on board with it and so a waste-free life became very achievable. We were amazed. During the fortnight we accumulated no rubbish or recycling. Not one piece! And we did it without having to compromise on our standard of living. We knew we could never go back to the way we lived before.

We had previously been blind to much of the waste we generated. Like many households, we weren't particularly concerned that our bin was full every week. The rubbish truck would take the waste away and it wouldn't exist in our world anymore. We learned that much of the waste we produced does not really go *away*, instead, it lingers and could harm the environment for many generations to come. Australians produce an average of 2.7 tonnes of waste per person every year, and we think there is a lot that can be done to reduce that.

Living waste free has made us think and act in new ways, grow more food, learn lots and, importantly, it has been much easier and more fun than we expected. Aiming to live without producing waste involves a shift towards a simpler life. But it does not have to mean going without. We've found abundance without excess packaging: it has helped deepen our understanding of food production, the seasons and the natural world.

What is waste?

— Waste is the stuff that we throw away when it is no longer useful or functional.

Waste can include food, plastics, fabric, metal, chemicals, building materials, glass, wood, electronics and more. It is not limited to the things put in rubbish bins or down the toilet; waste can be produced when resources or items are extracted, produced, transported, packaged, marketed, used, recycled and disposed of.

The vast proportion of household waste ends up in landfill at the local rubbish tip, which is usually a relatively out-of-sight hole in the ground that gets filled with waste over many decades. Landfill sites can leach toxins into soil and groundwater and contribute to greenhouse gas emissions. Once filled, the rubbish heap might get capped with soil and planted with trees. Unfortunately, many of the things we acquire, use and discard (for example, plastic straws and glitter), pollute other parts of the environment before they even reach the tip.

In nature, waste tends not to be a problem. This is because most of the nutrients lost by one part of an ecosystem, via dead or decaying matter, are utilised by fungi, worms and other critters and then made available for use by other species. Nutrients move through native ecosystems in cycles; nature is pretty nifty like that. However, humans extract, modify and redistribute extremely high amounts of nutrients and resources (e.g. oil, coal, metal ores, wood, meat and grain) and this has led to waste being a huge problem for a large number of species, including our own. Nature is out of whack. Modern society's waste production and management far from emulates the efficient cycling of nutrients in nature.

What is waste-free living?

— For us, waste-free living means bringing nothing into our home that we can't consume, compost or repurpose. It means not contributing to landfill, or to giant floating islands of plastic that accumulate in the oceans. It means little to no recycling (more on that later). It means not being complacent about where our waste goes. It means thinking. Lots of thinking. And refusing stuff that we can't put to good use. We want to take responsibility for everything we bring into our home and anything that leaves it. This means focusing both on what items we will refuse and reduce, as well as those items that we *can* make good use of that won't create excessive waste, once used.

Instead of asking, 'is it landfill?', or 'is it waste?', we ask 'is it compostable?' Earth is losing soil at a rapid rate, so anything we can do to help build it up, such as composting and keeping carbon in the soil, helps. It is important that we take good care of our own land and live in a way that does not harm others. Minimising waste is part of that aim.

A commonly associated term is *zero waste*. Put simply, this is a philosophy for living that involves not producing or contributing to excess or needless waste, both in the home and elsewhere, such as in shops, factories or the workplace. Whilst the term has its origins in the industrial sector, the zero waste label was popularised by waste-free living proponent and writer Bea Johnson in her book *Zero Waste Home*. Since then, many individuals and businesses have adopted the term, although interpretation has varied somewhat. In this book we consider zero waste and waste free to be interchangeable terms.

In the term *zero waste*, the word *zero* is a bit of a misnomer. Through the manufacture and production of most things in our waste-free home, there is inevitably waste. We visit the bulk food shop, where products may have been transported in large plastic bags which go on to be repurposed or recycled. There's *less* packaging and we only purchase exactly what we need, but there's still waste. Plus, there is waste in the transport we use to go to the shops, in our impact on the roads and paths we travel, in the light and heating of buildings and spaces. When household items break beyond repair and have outlived their usefulness, if they're not compostable, they are recycled or sent to landfill. There's still waste. Unless we're growing every single thing ourselves and doing it in a highly efficient way, there will be waste. But does that mean we shouldn't strive for zero?

Even amongst the most die-hard of zero-waste campaigners you will still find that 'jar of waste' which has been collected over time, containing waste items that just seem unavoidable. Plastic-coated paper parking tickets, plastic wrappers for medicines, Blu-Tack, broken plastic buttons and other miscellaneous things. You'll be surprised at just how often you will be left with items that have no practical future use, beyond maybe a short-lived craft activity. These reflect some of the physical wastes that are accumulated, but even these do not portray the hidden wastes that are created to provide many of the goods and services we use. Remember that *zero waste* is an aspiration rather than an absolute reality. This will continue to be the case until our societies, including our governments and the populace, embrace waste-reduction actions in all aspects of life.

We're not doing anything radically new here. Many of the concepts and recipes in our book are similar to those our grandmothers and great-grandmothers used in raising their families. In fact, a couple of the recipes we've shared here came directly from our grandmothers' handy hints books. When we imagine the family who grew up in our home before we lived here, we wonder, did they fill the small pantry shelves with preserves, too?

What we're embracing in these pages is a return to slower, simpler times. To making things by hand, growing our own, slow fashion, preserving, fermenting, mending, buying locally and supporting our local farmers. A gentle shift from the broad-scale industrialised agriculture and mass consumerism that fuel our economy and fill our homes, towards smaller, local, resilient economies and self-reliance.

We recognise that *waste* means different things to different people and each person's own circumstances will determine what is practically achievable in terms of waste reduction. Reducing waste by a small amount every now and then can be easy, but reducing most, or all, household waste will require a change of habits and most likely a change of attitude. We prefer to think of the switch to waste-free living as a decision, rather than a journey. As such, waste-free living is achievable with just small shifts in preparation, motivation and perspective. And, of course, some encouragement and support is invaluable for everyone along the way.

We'd recommend not focusing too much on the *zero*. It can lead to feeling like you're missing out on something. Focus on the things you do have access to, as this can help create and maintain a feeling of abundance. We prefer the term waste free for this reason. It evokes the idea of breaking free of the shackles of waste, so we can get on with the job of living!

DIVE INTO YOUR TRASH –
ARE YOU GAME?

Just before bin night, try putting a tarpaulin on the ground and emptying your rubbish and recycling onto it. Facing up to the sum of your week's waste can be confronting, especially to those in the family who either don't pay much attention to what goes in the bin, or who have not yet jumped on board with the notion that reducing waste is something worth doing. You might feel moved to take a photo of yourself or your family surrounded by the week's worth of waste you've collected. How do you feel looking at the waste that your family creates in an average week? Is it surprising? Keep the photograph of this scene for later comparison.

The waste hierarchy

— The waste hierarchy is a way of ranking actions that are intended to reduce waste. Various waste hierarchies are used in industrial and commercial contexts and more recently in zero-waste thinking for individuals. A popular waste hierarchy for businesses, government and people going waste free is known as the *five R's*; from most to least beneficial, the relevant actions include *Refuse, Reduce, Reuse, Recycle* and *Rot*.

IN OUR HOME

You might read elsewhere about extensions to the five R's, using other words starting with the letter R. One of our favourites is *Reframe* – this reminds us that waste-free living requires a shift in the way we perceive the world and act within it, by making a conscious decision to avoid waste, where possible.

- Refuse – Consider whether you really need that thing. If not, refuse it! The strongest way to minimise waste is to abstain from purchasing it.

- Reduce – So you decided you really need that thing, but how much do you need? Only buy or use what you need instead of creating waste in buying surplus.

- Reuse – After you've finished with an item, can you repurpose it? There are many ways to repurpose general household items. They can be repaired, or even rehomed (see page 184).

- Rot – Rot refers to the decomposition of organic materials into a form that is useful for other things. This can include compost, worm farms, backyard poultry or other animals that can help you recycle the nutrients. We reckon home composting is a much more beneficial action in this hierarchy and would tend to favour it above recycling.

- Recycle – Most cities offer recycling collection services. This might include paper, glass, plastics and green or organic waste. Recycling is likely to be a better option than having items go directly to landfill. (Note, this is usually fourth in the waste hierarchy but we think it's less effective than composting).

THE BASICS

Principles for waste-free living

— Throughout this book we talk about different types of waste and offer solutions for avoiding or reducing it. Some solutions will work for you, but others might not apply, depending on your own personal circumstances. Not every source of waste will have an obvious waste-free alternative. But we think that recalling a few broad principles on *how* to live waste free might be useful to help you to refocus when things get difficult. We've distilled waste-free living into the following principles:

MAKE A CONSCIOUS DECISION TO AVOID WASTEFUL THINGS

- *Be flexible* in the way your needs can be met. Recognise that waste-free living does not require one-for-one substitutions for everything you currently consume.

- *Grow* what food you can and otherwise source local and organic.

- *Create* a new normal when shopping (e.g. carry reusable bags and containers).

- *Talk* with your local makers, growers and retailers to find waste-free solutions.

- *Learn* how things are made, to better understand their benefits and harmful impacts. If you must consume a wasteful item, consume less of it.

- *Reconnect* with nature and rediscover the mutually beneficial connections between humans and natural ecosystems.

These are the principles that have guided us since we decided to try and live without waste. You might like to keep some of these principles in mind as you work towards reducing your own waste. This is not an exhaustive list and you may very well find you can add to it.

THE BENEFITS

Waste-free living doesn't have to be about going without things you love. Here are some of the perks we enjoy and you can look forward to:

• An abundance of locally grown, fresh food.

• Delicious home-grown produce. Meals tend to be healthier. We'd say the way we value our food has changed and we're definitely focused on the good stuff.

• The marvels of composting! Everything we use will one day provide a valuable resource for our garden, helping to grow food to feed ourselves and nourish our community.

• A pantry full of food and devoid of advertising! When we unpack the shopping, our food is already in the jars or containers that we intend to keep it in for freshness, so we just pop it straight in the cupboard, fridge or on the bench. It saves time!

• The convenience of not having to put out your rubbish bin. No more late-night or dawn bin runs and one less thing to remember each week.

• We're more mindful of what comes into our home. There's no waste to deal with.

• Slowing down. We're saving time and life's getting simpler. It's feeding into other areas of our lives where we're thinking minimally and simply.

• Enjoying products that are designed to last. We appreciate things that are crafted with care and time.

• A lifestyle that supports nature conservation and a cleaner local environment.

• Our soils are improving! By focusing on what we can compost, we're staying mindful of things that feed and nourish the soils, which in turn nourish the plants that nourish us. Which may lead us to the next frontier of waste … humanure! (see page 142 for more information).

• Opportunities to support local business. Frequenting different shops (as opposed to buying all our food from one monolithic supermarket) means we're engaging with our community more. We have conversations with people to find out more about where our food and other stuff comes from, which is a definite win. Shopping is friendlier and more enjoyable. It's quicker, because once you hit your waste-free groove, there are fewer choices and fewer decisions to make. There is no advertising or excess packaging to deal with. Once you've got it sussed, you save time and shopping is generally more pleasant.

• Making financial savings. We thought shopping this way would be more expensive but, surprisingly, it's not. We have managed to stick to our budget and feed ourselves well. We've found there are actually savings to be made on certain items we've always bought. And we're not paying for packaging or advertising, which makes up part of the cost of most pre-packaged foods. Awesome.

THE BASICS

Waste-free living on a budget

— One of the biggest roadblocks many families and individuals face when moving towards living waste free is cost. We get it. Living hand-to-mouth each week and struggling to make ends meet makes it difficult to change your routine. It may also mean that some suggestions in this book are not possible for you right now. That's okay. Work with what you can.

In saying that, we have discovered that embracing waste-free living wholly is what makes it affordable. That cheap packet of pasta may cost less than the organic pasta you can buy in bulk, but that deodorant you're now making saves money. Or maybe you'll find time to make your pasta by hand. And buying second-hand clothes could make some room in your budget for groceries. The jam you make from scratch saves you some more. There will be swings and roundabouts, but all the little savings add up and provide for other areas where spending might increase. You might also give thought to the *amount* of certain products you're consuming and reduce them or make some shifts there. The things you value most may also change.

It's no surprise to us that many of the ideas in these pages are also tips shared by budgeting experts, and even our grandmothers, for ways to stretch money further. When you approach these ideas in a wholehearted way and take on as many as possible, they make for a comfortable and affordable way of living. You may even find there's a little left over to put towards other things that matter.

Other constraints

— Money may not be the only thing preventing you from making lifestyle changes. Physical disability, impairment or illness can limit the ability to prepare some waste-free alternatives, or may mean that some packaged goods are necessary. Community can go a long way in assisting with this. Likewise, if your demands are location- or time-based, then working with others can alleviate some pressure. This is particularly relevant for single-parent families, or families living in remote areas. We talk more about finding your community in the Change chapter (see page 275). We recognise that we all have different circumstances, but everyone can find individual ways to reduce waste and make a positive difference. Look for ways that work best for you. Remember that this is not a competition and we are all, in our own way, working towards a healthier planet.

GET STARTED – AUDIT YOUR WASTE

A helpful reality check on your own waste production is to simply count the number of waste items you place in your bin. See if you can keep a record of all the rubbish and recycling you throw out during one whole week. Make sure not to change your habits just yet! Record your normal usage so you have a baseline level to improve upon.

• Starting on your next bin night, take two pieces of paper and mark one for rubbish, with space for food, packaging and any miscellaneous items you might be discarding. Mark the other piece of paper 'recycling' and make space for paper, plastic, metal and glass.

• Place the worksheets somewhere prominent – maybe in the kitchen where most household waste is produced and used. The fridge door is a good spot, or perhaps a wall near your rubbish bin.

• Every time you put something in the rubbish bin or the recycling, mark it on your worksheet. The value in this is that it creates a mindfulness habit as your awareness grows. It's challenging to maintain regular habits whilst remaining fully accountable for them every single time you throw something out, but the slow nature of this process really brings awareness to your actions.

• How much do you throw out each week? Each day? Keep a tally of every item of rubbish and recycling you throw out for one day, a weekend or one whole week. Are you surprised by the amount of waste your family generates? Take some time to reflect on the exercise and think about how you could regulate your waste production. Meet up for a family conference and chat about your findings.

Developing your family's approach to waste

— A particular challenge for families moving towards waste-free living arises when attempting to bring children and other family members along with the changes. Perhaps your child has a favourite cereal that comes in a plastic bag, or enjoys occasional treats that come wrapped in plastic. Perhaps your partner thinks that the changes we make as individuals are inconsequential. There are many ways that people resist or argue against the benefits of reducing waste. You may not get traction with the rest of your family until you lead by example. Show them the way!

You may like to encourage other members of your family to participate in waste-reducing strategies and to brainstorm solutions for different types of household or individual waste. You could also show documentaries, videos or websites that explain waste problems in a convincing way. No doubt some of that information will be confronting, but it might also be surprising, motivating or even enlightening. You may also like to undertake a little research and analysis of your own, work out what resources you have to hand, set some goals and work out how to choose what is right for your family. You may like to approach it very slowly and incrementally, or all at once.

For us, doing a little research and then making a very quick transition away from packaged, plastic and single-use products worked better on a budgetary and motivational level. We all made a pact together to reduce our waste and so decisions on what we'd consume, or choose not to consume, were very clear cut and easy to make. We hope you will discuss things openly and frankly with your children and find encouragement in the fact that you're taking practical steps to create change. Yay, you!

We have found one of the best ways to keep everyone on board with waste-free living is to hold regular family conferences. These can be as formal or relaxed as you like and are really about checking in with each other and how you are going. In our home, conversation flows best over food, so we usually discuss things around the dinner table. Some of the concepts around waste-free living may be intuitive to your child, so try to give them space to talk about and explore those ideas. You may find your children have clear and surprising insights into waste and waste reduction. Try to come up with some practical solutions together. Go with the flow and see where the conversation leads.

Including children in discussions around waste is hugely important, but giving children the space to be *practically* involved is also vital. It's one way they can be involved in making a direct positive difference to their environment. Help them take responsibility for their own decisions. Involve them in activities, shopping and family decision-making as much as possible so they feel just as invested in reducing waste as you and gain skills to become great earth-stewards in the future.

IN SUMMARY

- Nature doesn't create waste. Be like nature!

- Take responsibility for the waste you create.

- Look for compostable products.

- Look to past generations and how they managed life before plastic.

- Embrace a slower pace of living.

- Examine and audit your rubbish.

- Learn and follow the waste hierarchy when making decisions and designing systems for your home.

- A whole lifestyle shift makes waste-free living more affordable.

- Encourage open and honest discussion in your home about waste and take everyone's needs and ideas into account.

'This magical, marvellous food on our plate, this sustenance we absorb, has a story to tell. It has a journey. It leaves a footprint. It leaves a legacy. To eat with reckless abandon, without conscience, without knowledge; folks, this ain't normal.' – Joel Salatin

chapter two

FOOD

Close the loop

Food waste makes up the greatest proportion of all household waste, so it's a great place to start. In this chapter, we take things right back to where food comes from and look at how to grow it, how to make the most of it, how to preserve and forage for it, and how to compost it to feed your growing garden.

■ Cast your mind back to what life was like a few hundred generations ago, and chances are your ancestors spent a large portion of their days hunting, gathering and possibly farming food, simply to survive. Food was, as it is now, vital to survival. But obtaining food took *work* by almost everyone and, as a result, it was likely treated as something precious, valuable, useful and necessary. Wasting food would have been highly inefficient and could have led to hunger, sickness and death. Wasting food most likely meant there was a short-term glut that could not be consumed (e.g. more berries or fish than people could eat), or if food was scarce, it might suggest they weren't going to live very long.

Advancements in agriculture, particularly over the last century, have led to the conditions we have today, where most food is produced in factories, often a long way from home. Some of the big leaps occurred with the invention of synthetic nitrogen-based fertilisers in the early twentieth century, the widespread use of pesticides, the development of high-yield crops (c. 1940s onwards) and the industrialisation of agriculture in the mid-to-late twentieth century.

We need to slow down, enjoy the food we eat and even fall in love a little with how it's grown and prepared.

Industrialised agriculture enabled more people to be fed, which influenced rapid population growth. But it also created huge amounts of waste, through polluting fertilisers and pesticides, such as DDT, and the prevalence of non-renewable energy sources that power different agricultural land uses. Whilst food is now often cheap, there are hidden economic, social and environmental costs of production. For example, the cost of waste management is not factored into the cost of the food we buy.

We see a great need to recalibrate our consumption of and connection with food and better reduce and manage any food waste we create. We need to slow down, enjoy the food we eat and even fall in love a little with how it's grown and prepared. In this chapter we offer suggestions for avoiding waste in the growing, transportation, preparation and disposal of food. Part of the answer lies in better understanding where food comes from and how it is grown, and in applying techniques to make the most of the food that is acquired. By growing your own food and then composting the scraps, you can create something close to a closed-loop nutrient cycle in your own home, which is comparable to nutrient cycles that occur in natural ecosystems. Rather than seeing organic waste as something you send to the tip, view it as a valuable resource.

FOOD

The problem with food waste

— With food and other organic material comprising up to 40 per cent of waste put into kerbside bins, food makes up the largest proportion of household waste by volume. And this is on top of the 20–40 per cent of fruit and vegetables that are rejected on farms prior to reaching retailers, due to their odd shapes or blemishes that do not meet cosmetic standards. It follows that finding solutions to eliminate food waste will go a long way towards reducing the overall amount of waste we produce.

It is estimated that Australians throw out nearly $10 billion worth of edible food every year, which equates to more than $1,000 per household. But food waste bears more than just a huge economic cost. Food and other organic waste in landfill is less likely to receive the adequate moisture, air and bacteria required to decompose into available nutrients. Under these anaerobic conditions, there is likely to be an increase in emissions of greenhouse gases, such as methane and carbon dioxide. Whilst greenhouse gases regulate the temperature of the earth's surface, human activities have increased chemical concentrations in the atmosphere to levels that are resulting in a dangerous warming of the earth and other impacts of climate change.

It is clearly a big problem when so much edible or otherwise nutrient-laden food (organic matter) is wasted and sent to landfill, seemingly without awareness of the impacts to the climate or to the back pocket. But a lack of understanding around the damaging impacts of food waste is unsurprising, given the noticeable detachment between people and the source of their food and the energy that goes into its production. With the combination of a highly efficient kerbside waste removal process and the relative affordability of many foods, the problems of food waste becomes less obvious to those who aren't looking deeply at the issue.

Food scraps are commonly discarded to the rubbish bin in *bite-sized* quantities and each scrap appears to carry very little environmental impact, because hey, they're just food scraps, right? That waste is collected weekly or fortnightly in the wee small hours and all we have to do is remember to put the bins out. Most bins rest conveniently on sturdy wheels, so that even a full bin is pretty easy to move out to the front kerb. We just don't have many in-your-face reasons to consider where food waste goes or to be motivated enough to be accountable for any impacts caused by discarded food. The spreading out of waste collection into small but frequent trips narrows our perception of the enormity of the waste that we produce over long periods of time. Placing food scraps directly into the bin can seem a benign process; a habit; *normal*. If we could see or recognise that households discard, on average, 345 kg of food per year, then maybe we'd think twice about sending food scraps to the bin.

We can do so much to reduce food waste, but where it is unavoidable (e.g. when food becomes spoiled), there is still good sense in seeing that organic matter as a highly useful resource. Food and garden scraps can be utilised so that they benefit us and our community, helping to build our soils to feed more plants, to grow more food to eat.

Composting

— Composting is one of the best ways to prevent food waste from entering landfill. Instead of wasting food scraps (and money on wasted food), you can make good use of the scraps and concoct a soil-like compost mixture that will help feed your garden and, in turn, feed you! In this way, you can work towards closing the nutrient loops and reducing waste.

Compost is one of our favourite substances. This lush, organic material is made when food scraps or other organic matter decompose, through the action of worms, fungi, bacteria, oxygen, moisture and heat. Compost acts as a fertiliser that helps other plants to grow, which is super helpful if you're trying to grow food in your garden. There are lots of ways to compost at home and the best method for you will depend on your living situation.

Home composting emulates the processes that occur in natural ecosystems.

If you live in an apartment or small space, then you might like to look into Bokashi – this method was devised in Japan and it ferments your kitchen scraps using a culture of microorganisms in a reusable plastic bucket, providing you with a compost tea. Apartment dwellers might also make use of the compost bays at their local community garden or at a friend or neighbour's house, and there are some services that will collect home scraps for commercial composting.

If you are lucky enough to have a yard with some space, then there are many options for composting. The most common method is called *cold composting* and we've provided a tutorial for that over the page. Other composting methods that you might like to research include hot composting, worm farms (see page 212), worm towers, industrial composting, mechanised turning-unit compost systems, sheet composting, or trench composting (which we call the dig-a-shallow-hole-fill-with-food-scraps-and-cover method). All these methods do much the same thing, but use a different container to get the job done.

One of our favourite smells is the fresh smell of decomposition on the floor of a wet eucalypt forest – it is nutrient-cycling in action, with all the fungi, worms and microscopic critters hard at work converting fallen trees, leaves and other organic materials into available nutrients that contribute to fertile soil. Home composting is about emulating the composting process that occurs in native ecosystems; we are just trying to create conditions to help speed things up!

WHAT YOU'LL NEED

- Somewhere to place or contain your compost pile. A compost bin, a designated corner of the garden, a hole in the ground – all of these can work well.

- Carbon-based waste material. As a general rule, things that are brown are higher in carbon. This might include straw, dried leaves, sticks, paper and cardboard.

- Nitrogen-based waste material. Food scraps and green things are higher in nitrogen. This might include fresh grass clippings, kitchen scraps, chicken poo and green leaves – even hair!

COLD COMPOSTING

Cold composting is a simple method of breaking down waste matter that allows bugs, worms and microorganisms to do most of the work. It operates at a cool temperature that worms and larger insects can tolerate and takes a little while to break everything down. Cold compost heaps don't require turning or much maintenance, other than feeding and keeping an eye on them to keep them healthy. They may like to be aerated with a garden fork every few weeks or so. They're suitable for small home gardens and for taking care of your kitchen scraps.

If you live on a large property, or have lots of organic material you'd like to break down quickly, you might also like to have a look into hot composting. It requires a bit of turning, being careful around small children (it can burn) and a bit of knowledge about timing, but it can provide good, fast results.

Make sure that anything you add to your bin is broken into small pieces so the worms and other organisms can munch through it faster. Only put a small amount of citrus in there and maintain a vegetarian compost heap to keep pests away, otherwise try placing mesh at the base. Meat, citrus and onions will slow the composting process. Coffee grounds and nutrient-dense leaves from plants, such as the herb comfrey, are wonderful treats for your compost heap. In a few months' time you should be able to begin collecting the beautiful compost at the bottom of the bin where decomposition happens first. With this material you can feed your garden for free!

STEP 1

Find the best spot for your bin – ours is situated beside a fruit tree. As the bin slowly fills up, nutrients leach down into the soil and fill the tree. We allow the contents to fill up and break down, then we remove the bin and spread the compost around. We then place the empty bin beside a different tree so nutrients from the compost can feed that tree next. If you have access to two compost bins, you can use them in rotation, spending six months to build one up, then six months composting while the other bin is filling up. It's a great way to slowly spot-feed your garden.

STEP 2

Start by placing a layer of woody material at the base of your compost heap. Some sticks, twigs, bark … this will give it good drainage and help everything break down.

STEP 3

Add a good layer of carbon material. Straw or similar (about 10 cm-deep) is ideal. Now add a layer of nitrogen-based material. Manure (about 2 cm-deep) would be a fabulous beginning.

STEP 4

Water your compost before continuing to add to it in equal measures. Anywhere between 75 per cent carbon to 25 per cent nitrogen and 50 per cent carbon to 50 per cent nitrogen will work. If your compost heap starts to get a bit stinky or overrun by flies, it's likely you need a little more carbon material.

Grow your own

— We reckon that the absolute best thing that you can do to reduce your family's overall waste is to grow your own food. With food at your door there is no packaging and zero food miles. Plus, you have the incalculable satisfaction of knowing exactly where the food came from! A productive food garden can be established without creating waste, on a very minimal budget and even utilise items that might be considered waste.

You can build a no-dig garden bed using cardboard, compost and mulch. You can swap or buy seeds in compostable paper bags. Manures, compost and mulches can be purchased by the trailer (or boot/scoop) load. You can swap or share tools with a neighbour and reuse or repurpose punnets and bags. You can make your own compost using organic waste from around your home, or collected nearby. You might have a friend or relative who has plant cuttings or seeds they are willing to share with you, or maybe some animals, whose poo you can put to good use.

Think about what foods you love to eat. If they suit your local climate and soils, try your hand at growing them yourself. Food can be grown just about anywhere and setting up a garden can be done very cheaply, so why not have a go?

ACTIVESMART
TECHNOLOGY

WHAT YOU'LL NEED

- 2 tablespoons of sprouting seeds, such as chia, alfalfa, buckwheat, kale, lentil, sunflower, radish, pea and broccoli. Bulk food shops often stock seeds for sprouting

- 1 clean glass jar, some old stocking or cheesecloth and a rubber band, or a purpose-built sprouter or mesh cover for a Mason jar lid

SPROUTING SEEDS

Growing your own food can start as small as sprouting a jar of seeds on your kitchen bench. Home-grown sprouts are a great way to add flavour and nutrition to your meals, without any plastic waste or fuel, and to make use of some common household items.

STEP 1

Add the seeds to the jar.

STEP 2

Cover the jar with stocking/cheesecloth and a rubber band, or mesh-covered lid.

STEP 3

Half-fill the jar with clean water, then tip the jar upside down to strain out the water.

STEP 4

Half-fill the jar with water again andplace in a cool spot out of direct sunlight, overnight. We like to leave ours by the kitchen sink.

STEP 5

Drain the water out and place the jar on its side to allow further drainage and air-circulation.

STEP 6

Rinse the seeds with water twice a day until they look ready to eat. There should be some green baby leaves and a little stalk. Have a little munch to taste them if you're unsure whether they are ready.

STEP 7

Store your sprouted seeds in a clean jar in the fridge.

WHAT YOU'LL NEED

- plant material – weeds, seaweed, dynamic accumulator plant leaves (see below)
- mesh bag (e.g. an orange bag or hessian bag), or a piece of hessian and string
- bucket or garbage bin
- large rock
- watering can

LIQUID FERTILISER TO FEED YOUR GARDEN

This is a great way to make the most of garden waste. See what you can gather around you – perhaps weeds, seaweed or leaves from a dynamic accumulator plant, such as comfrey or dandelion. Dynamic accumulators are plants that gather certain micronutrients, macronutrients and minerals from the soil and store them in their leaves. You can use the liquid fertiliser to feed your garden beautiful nutrients and improve the health and growth of your plants for minimal effort, increasing your yield.

STEP 1

Grab a handful or two of the plant matter and place it in the mesh or hessian bag. You are essentially making a giant tea bag here, so make sure the top is secured so the plant material can't fall out.

STEP 2

Place the mesh bag in the bucket and place a rock on top of it.

STEP 3

Fill the bucket with water and leave it for 4–5 weeks – it'll get pretty stinky so leave it somewhere you don't need to visit often!

STEP 4

Pour the fertiliser into a watering can and apply it to your plants every couple of weeks.

FOOD

WHAT YOU'LL NEED

- cardboard boxes or old newspapers

- wheelbarrow (optional)

- garden fork

- additional carbon-based material – straw, lucerne hay, composted wood chips, shredded paper or even dry autumn leaves. Some tree loppers will happily deliver a load of wood chips to your house for free

- nitrogen-based material – composted manure, sheep poo or rock dust/minerals work well and can be sourced in bulk from local nurseries and farms

- organic compost – we like mushroom compost. Mushroom farms provide a good source for this, or you can make organic compost at home (see page 32)

- seeds or seedlings

START A NO-DIG GARDEN

Sheet mulching an area of lawn or disused land is a wonderful way to let natural processes and microbes do the hard work of soil improvement for you. With this simple method of layering materials, bit by bit, you can grow a garden as large or as small as is manageable for your family. It's a great way to turn a backyard of lawn and other available resources (e.g. garden clippings, cardboard boxes or old timber), into a productive edible garden.

STEP 1

Start by marking out the area where you'd like your garden. Consider edging it with timber, straw bales, old bricks, or even broken-up concrete paths. An edge is not essential, but it can be helpful for weed control. If the area you've chosen is lawn, mow it down low.

STEP 2

Soak the cardboard or newspaper in water – a wheelbarrow is helpful for this – and you can water plants with the leftover water when you're done.

STEP 3

Use a garden fork to make holes in the ground to help integrate the existing soil and the layers you will add, and to encourage microbes and nutrient flow.

STEP 4

Place a thick layer of wet cardboard or thick newspaper on the base of the garden bed. Make sure every bit is covered, with no gaps, to suppress weed growth.

STEP 5

Top with a layer of carbon material (about 20 cm deep), followed by a sprinkling of nitrogen material, and repeat until the bed is the desired height (around 30 cm high).

STEP 6

Finish with a layer of carbon material, then place little pockets of organic compost (about 10 cm deep) where you intend to plant your seeds or seedlings.

STEP 7

Plant the seeds or seedlings in the garden bed. By the time your first crop has finished, the garden bed should have composted and created lovely, lush soil. You can top it up for the new season's planting with some compost and mulch, before planting again.

Box Car Willie

Big Rainbow

Japanese Black Trifele

Russian red

Saturn

Olueovic

Indian moon

Red fig

Lady red

Matt's Cherr

SEED SAVING

Seed saving is a great way to grow a garden without waste and with minimal cost. Once you have your hands on some seeds, you can keep those plants growing in your garden season after season. Maybe you have let some strong, healthy plants go to seed in your garden. Or you might spy some in a neighbour's garden. Maybe you could save the seeds from inside a particularly yummy tomato or other organic vegetable. Generally, just about any seeds collected well after the fruit or vegetable has ripened or dried will have gone through the processes needed to save the seeds and keep them healthy. If your seeds need to dry out, try placing them on a plate or piece of paper to dry completely before storing in an airtight jar.

Keep your seeds in envelopes, bags or containers, away from direct sunlight and moisture. Make sure to label them well and include the date when they were collected. They should last for a few years – even longer if you store them in your freezer – but we reckon plant them out again next growing season and continue the cycle. Save lots so you can swap some with friends!

FOOD

Buy locally and know your farmer

▬ We live in a society in which large supermarket chains dominate the food industry. Many fruit, vegetable and dairy producers are beholden to the supermarket giants who demand exclusivity and want the option to receive huge volumes of goods, even though they may not end up ordering them. This situation has led to unacceptable instances where farmers are left having to waste a large proportion of their yield because supermarkets decided to purchase a smaller volume.

The farmer may not have the option to sell the remainder elsewhere. This means perfectly edible food rotting on the ground unless food charities have the means to collect it from farmers for free. Food waste may be created at the farm or factory, due to rigorous aesthetic standards imposed by supermarkets (e.g. size, shape, colour, ripeness, number of blemishes) forcing rejection of edible food. In addition, we think a system that results in such high volumes of food waste is not beneficial for society in the long-term and it is certainly not good for the environment.

Depending on the supply chain and the type of food, the distance between us and where our food is grown or produced (referred to as *food miles*) can be huge. Large quantities of food are imported from overseas, particularly processed foods. Buying locally and from smaller-scale shops can mean more control and choice over how your food is packaged and sold to you. There will inevitably be fewer food miles. Plus, you're more likely to get to know your food suppliers and have conversations with them. Such conversations can lead to a better understanding of food-waste issues and you might find you can help influence positive waste-free practices beyond your front door. You'll also be supporting the local economy.

You might like to try only buying food that is grown locally, and you may find you are eating more seasonally when you purchase food in this way. In our efforts to pay more attention to food miles, we realised that our primary culprits for very high food miles were tropical fruits (e.g. banana, pineapple, mango) that don't grow well in our Tasmanian climate and sweeteners including sugar and maple syrup (from Canada). Increasing the proportion of local fruits (such as apples), and more often opting for local honey instead of sugar or maple syrup, were small changes we adopted to try to reduce some of the detrimental impacts of our food choices.

Try supporting your local farmers' market, small grocery stores or farmers directly. How easy is it for you to access locally grown or made food? Do you have to change your buying habits or the way you eat in order to buy locally? Look for seasonal bulk food opportunities and if you can't preserve the surplus, share it with friends and family.

FOOD

Eat seasonally

—— Keeping an eye on what Mother Nature is up to can help you eat well, save money and reduce waste. When you pay particular attention to seasonal cues, you become aware of food that's available near you and often at a cheaper bulk price than buying out of season. Sometimes food bought in this way is fresher, meaning it is more nutritious and lasts longer before going bad. There's also a nutritional benefit in following the seasons for your own body's needs. For example, sweet, juicy fruits are more readily available in the warmer seasons when we're more active and burning energy, as opposed to the cool, dark winter, where food often comes in the form of leafy greens and protein, and venturing outside is less likely.

We like to keep an eye on gardens, local farms and the farmers' market to see what's available to eat and grow as the seasons progress. We take advantage of seasonal availability and plan ahead so we can harvest a good crop later on. For example, where we live, we need to be organised to plant garlic in April so we can harvest a year's supply in December. Sometimes we buy extra fruits and veggies, such as berries or tomatoes, in bulk, when they're at their cheapest and yummiest, then we can enjoy our food fresh and tuck any extra away as preserves (see overleaf) for the winter when those foods are less readily available.

FOOD

Preserving

—— Preserving and storing food surplus is a marvellous way to reduce your waste. Gather foods while they're in season and prepare them in bulk so you'll have them ready when your local options are limited at other times of the year. It's an economical way of reducing your carbon footprint while still being able to enjoy out-of-season foods. Bottling, fermenting, pickling, freezing and dehydrating are all wonderful ways to preserve the surplus, plus preserving is a great way to make use of any jars you may have collected. You could try drying herbs, storing a garlic crop, making tomato sauce, fermenting cabbage to make kimchi, cooking jam or bottling fruit so you can enjoy a little bit of summer in the depths of winter. If we collect an over-supply of food when it is most abundant, we can then store it for use at a later time. Preserving is a great way to do that. Over the next few pages you'll find some of our favourite recipes for bottling seasonal produce that are sure to brighten the cooler months.

MAKE THIS

WHAT YOU'LL NEED

- 1½ cups coconut sugar (or other sugar/sweetener of choice)

- 6 x 750 ml jars (or equivalent smaller jars)

- spices, such as cloves, star anise, cinnamon bark or vanilla pods

- 3 kg plums, halved, quartered, or left whole, depending on how you like to eat them and with pits removed if you prefer

PRESERVED SPICY–SWEET PLUMS

Plums are often abundant in late summer, hanging heavily on backyard fruit trees and in public spaces. If you don't have a plum tree, why not ask your friends or neighbours to share some of theirs, or go foraging for local fruit trees around your neighbourhood (see more on foraging on page 247). These spiced plums are super yummy over ice cream, porridge, yoghurt, muesli, in crumbles, or just by themselves.

FOOD

STEP 1

Place the sugar and 2 cups of water in a saucepan over medium heat.

STEP 2

Simmer and stir until the sugar has completely dissolved.

STEP 3

Remove the pan from the heat and add another 2 ½ cups of water. Set aside to cool.

STEP 4

Prepare the preserving jars. We wash our jars thoroughly in hot, soapy water, rinse well and dry but you may prefer to sterilise your jars first (see page 49 or use the recommended method for your particular preserving jar system).

STEP 5

Drop some spices into the jars.

STEP 6

Pack the plums on top of the spices and then pour the sugar syrup over the top, to about 1 cm below the rim. Remove any air bubbles by sliding a blunt knife between the fruit and the sides of the jars, or by tapping the jars gently on your workbench.

STEP 7

Seal the jars and place them in a large stockpot of simmering water for an hour or so, ensuting that the water doesn't boil. This pasteurises the contents of the jars for a longer shelf life.

STEP 8

Remove the jars and place them on a wooden board to cool and stand, untouched, for 12 hours or more.

STEP 9

Store the jars of plums in a cool, dark cupboard for up to 1 year – try and hold out until winter!

MAKE THIS

WHAT YOU'LL NEED

- 1.25 kg rhubarb, trimmed and sliced into 2 cm pieces
- 400 g berries (or thereabouts)
- 1 kg sugar – we use organic raw sugar, but feel free to try a sugar that suits you
- 1 vanilla bean, or a dash of vanilla extract
- juice of 1 lemon
- pinch of salt
- 6 x 250 ml jars

BERRY, RHUBARB AND VANILLA JAM

If you're lucky enough to have some summer berries, picked fresh or in the freezer (as we often do), you might like to make this jam. It's delicious over ice cream, yoghurt, in sandwiches, baked in jam-drop cookies, sponge cakes or decadent jam tarts – or eaten with a spoon!

FOOD

STEP 1

Place the rhubarb, berries and 1 cup of water in a large saucepan.

STEP 2

Bring to a simmer, stirring, until the rhubarb is tender.

STEP 3

Add the sugar and the vanilla bean or vanilla extract. You can use old vanilla beans that have had the seeds scraped out, so as to make the most of the lingering flavour.

STEP 4

Add the lemon juice and salt and simmer until the jam has thickened.

STEP 5

While the jam is simmering, sterilise the jars. Place the clean jars on a rack in a preheated 120°C oven for 10–15 minutes, or in a large stockpot of boiling water for 10 minutes, then drain on a tea towel.

STEP 6

To test the jam, place a saucer in the freezer and, when you think the jam might be ready, drop a teaspoon of jam onto it. Return the saucer to the freezer for a couple of minutes and then check to see if it wrinkles a bit when you nudge it. If it wrinkles, it's ready.

STEP 7

Transfer the jam to the sterilised jars and screw the lids on.

STEP 8

To keep the jam for longer than 6 weeks, follow the pasteurising process for the spicy–sweet plums on page 46.

FOOD

MAKE
THIS

WHAT YOU'LL NEED

- 1 jar
- 1 cabbage, sliced – wombok (also called napa or Chinese cabbage) is traditionally used, but other cabbages will work, too
- 2 cups grated daikon radish – or other radishes if you can't find daikon
- 1 carrot, grated
- 1 beetroot, grated
- 1 bunch of spring onions (we've also used baby leeks and garlic tops before with great success)
- 3 cm piece of ginger, grated
- 4 garlic cloves, crushed or finely chopped
- dried chilli flakes, to taste
- 2 tablespoons sea salt

SUPER-EASY BEETROOT KIMCHI

Fermented foods offer great nutrients and probiotics to complement the rest of your diet. When Lauren travelled to South Korea, she was lucky to sample a traditionally fermented kimchi that had been buried underground for three months and she was instantly hooked. This is our super-simple and kid-friendly (mild) version of kimchi. The process for making it is similar to sauerkraut. We like adding beetroot because it makes the kimchi pink and sweet, but you can experiment with all sorts of veggies – it's a great way to make the most of your garden or seasonal surplus. We swear by this dish for keeping us healthy and happy all winter. Serve a little with meals, or eat it by the forkful, straight from the jar!

FOOD

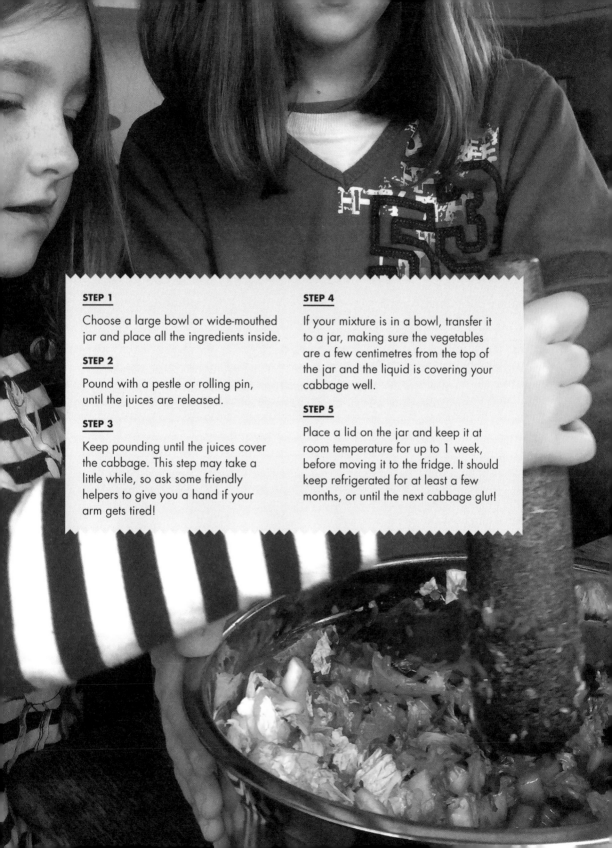

STEP 1

Choose a large bowl or wide-mouthed jar and place all the ingredients inside.

STEP 2

Pound with a pestle or rolling pin, until the juices are released.

STEP 3

Keep pounding until the juices cover the cabbage. This step may take a little while, so ask some friendly helpers to give you a hand if your arm gets tired!

STEP 4

If your mixture is in a bowl, transfer it to a jar, making sure the vegetables are a few centimetres from the top of the jar and the liquid is covering your cabbage well.

STEP 5

Place a lid on the jar and keep it at room temperature for up to 1 week, before moving it to the fridge. It should keep refrigerated for at least a few months, or until the next cabbage glut!

Planning ahead

— One of the easiest ways to prevent food waste is to work out what food your family will need through meal planning. If you're not a planner, that's totally okay. We tend not to stick to a plan either, but setting aside some time to think, and writing down what meals you might expect to eat during the week, fortnight, month or even year, can definitely help to avoid waste, excess packaging and extra trips to the shops.

PLANNING FOR THE WINTER

Have a think about foods that are staples in your house – the foods that you reach for each week and always pop in your shopping basket, without fail. Many people have become accustomed to eating food out of season and rely on commercial jars or cans of food to keep them going through the winter months. One example of such a food is tomatoes. A key ingredient in dishes from many cuisines, particularly hearty, wintery dishes. People often rely on canned or bottled tomatoes to keep pasta sauces, curries and casseroles full of flavour at a time when fresh tomatoes are scarce or flavourless. So how do you prepare for tomatoes to get you through the leaner months? Working backwards from your meal plan, or list of favourite winter meals, you can calculate roughly how many jars of tomatoes you'll need each week. Multiply that by the number of weeks where tomatoes are out of season near you. Where we live, we need to have tomatoes stored between mid-April and late December. Then, come the late summer and early autumn months, you'll know how many tomatoes you'll need to store. Perhaps you have a local farm where you can buy tomatoes by the box. Or, maybe you want to take it a step further and grow your own. It may take you a few seasons to refine the quantities needed, but it is well worth the effort. The cans of processed tomatoes thrown into your supermarket trolley during your weekly shop pale in comparison to the sense of satisfaction you get when looking into a pantry filled with bottles of summer tomatoes.

> Have a think about foods that are staples in your house.

- Think about your favourite meals, consider your budget for the week and the meals you want to prepare, and take into account what's seasonally available and locally produced.

- Now list meals for each day of the week, plus snacks. Doing this can help you write a shopping list and ensures you buy only what you need. A good shopping list can also reduce the likelihood of impulse purchases and, thus, save money. Based on the recipes you plan to cook, make a shopping list and, if necessary, think about what quantities you need of each ingredient. Then you're ready to tackle your shopping.

- Alternatively, you may like to do your shopping first and then write up a meal plan based on what you have sourced locally and in-season. Or, maybe you have a handful of recipes in mind that are your go-to meals, so you don't really need to plan. Go with what works for you. We've found it really helpful to focus on the rhythm of our weeks. We make note of the busiest days and days when we'll be home late, with less time for food preparation. Then we identify the quieter days and plan to cook things that need a little more time and attention.

- We're big fans of cooking once and eating twice, so we'll cook a double batch of something we can freeze on one day every week. Then there's at least one meal covered for the following week.

- We regularly use a slow cooker to prepare big batch meals, and we generally cook a roast once a week, so we always have plenty of leftovers to make use of (see what we do with them on page 59). Each family's rhythm will be different and yours, like ours, may change several times each year. Being aware of days you're able to do more makes the days you're able to do less much easier. It also means there's time for some of the extra work you may come across when shifting towards waste-free living.

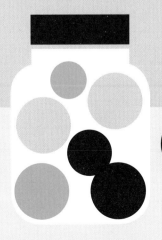

MAKE THIS

WHAT YOU'LL NEED

- tomatoes – we tend to prefer smaller heirloom varieties because they plop into the jars without the need for further preparation

- jars – you can re-use old sauce bottles, or invest in a bottling system (either second-hand or new). Clean them in hot, soapy water before you begin

- fresh herbs – these make a lovely addition for bottling away the flavour of summer. Basil and oregano are our favourites

- sea salt

SUPER-EASY RUSTIC
BOTTLED TOMATOES

We're all about doing things the quick and easy way when it comes to preserving food in bulk, like our tomato harvest. This means that sometimes our food is a little more rustic, but it's certainly not lacking in flavour. One of the easiest ways to store your tomatoes for winter use is to freeze them. They become like pleasant-sounding billiard balls rolling around in containers in your freezer, and although they can go a little mushy when defrosted, they cook beautifully. If you're short on freezer space, though, jars are a great option. Clear out some space in a cupboard or on a shelf for your harvest – it'll soon become your pride and joy. This recipe is one that we've used many times over the years for our home-grown tomatoes.

We slowly chip away at preserving tomatoes through the harvest season, popping a half-dozen jars or so away each week. When it's time to use the tomatoes, we just open the bottle and pour them into the saucepan, squashing them a bit with the back of a wooden spoon, for a lovely, sweet, flavour-filled sauce base.

FOOD

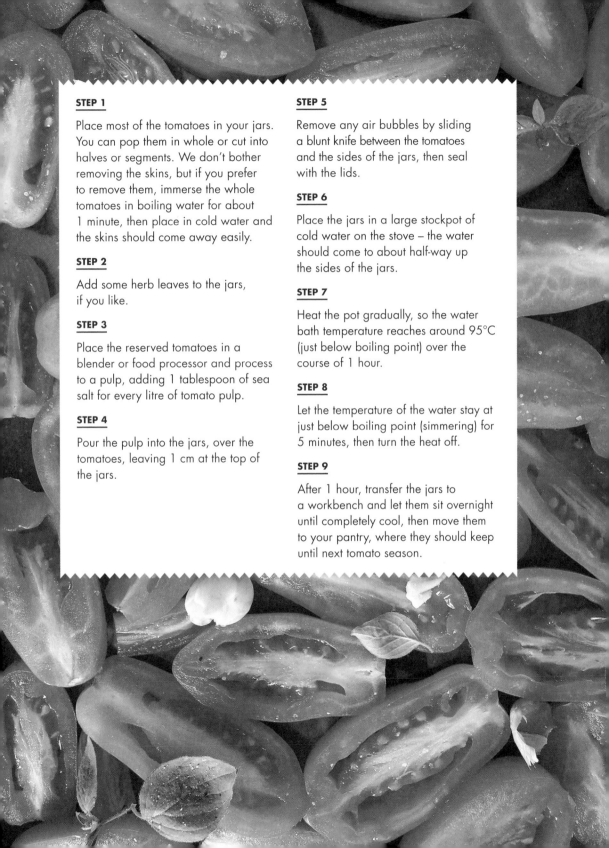

STEP 1

Place most of the tomatoes in your jars. You can pop them in whole or cut into halves or segments. We don't bother removing the skins, but if you prefer to remove them, immerse the whole tomatoes in boiling water for about 1 minute, then place in cold water and the skins should come away easily.

STEP 2

Add some herb leaves to the jars, if you like.

STEP 3

Place the reserved tomatoes in a blender or food processor and process to a pulp, adding 1 tablespoon of sea salt for every litre of tomato pulp.

STEP 4

Pour the pulp into the jars, over the tomatoes, leaving 1 cm at the top of the jars.

STEP 5

Remove any air bubbles by sliding a blunt knife between the tomatoes and the sides of the jars, then seal with the lids.

STEP 6

Place the jars in a large stockpot of cold water on the stove – the water should come to about half-way up the sides of the jars.

STEP 7

Heat the pot gradually, so the water bath temperature reaches around 95°C (just below boiling point) over the course of 1 hour.

STEP 8

Let the temperature of the water stay at just below boiling point (simmering) for 5 minutes, then turn the heat off.

STEP 9

After 1 hour, transfer the jars to a workbench and let them sit overnight until completely cool, then move them to your pantry, where they should keep until next tomato season.

Stretching your food further

— How resourceful can you be? Traditionally, mothers, grandmothers and great-grandmothers shared all sorts of handy hints to make food and resources go further. Some have been forgotten with time, notions of convenience and access to good food, but it's well worth looking to old family recipe books and knowledge to see if there are any food-stretching recipes in your family already. We discovered our own grandmothers' notebooks in amongst family documents and old photo albums and they're full of recipes for using up leftovers and creating flavourful meals from basic rations.

Women who lived through world wars, the Great Depression and times of food rationing needed to be masters at making ends meet and using up leftovers. People were encouraged to grow their own food in what were called 'victory gardens'. In the United Kingdom, pig clubs and keeping chickens were encouraged as a way to add extra nourishment to diets, whilst saving and redistributing any food waste collected by family, friends or neighbours. Waste was illegal and heavily penalised. Women shared recipes and kitchen hints with each other and the government circulated information on ways to stretch food further.

After World War II came a push to boost the economy through purchasing consumer goods. People embraced this with enthusiasm after long years of frugality. Technological advancements led to refrigeration, frozen meals and processed food, while broad-scale agriculture and machine-based transport made a wider range of foods available year-round and highly accessible. Unfortunately, in just one generation, due to the easy accessibility of consumer goods, much of the knowledge that had been essential during the Great Depression was forgotten. Looking back to those old handy hints and thinking about stretching food resources further, can help us make smarter choices and create less waste – and it's even easier with the information and technology we have now.

● Quince surplus for cooking and sharing

● Bottled tomato sauce for winter pies

● Dried herbs for teas and herbal remedies

● Preserved fruit for crumbles and desserts

MAKE
THIS

VARIATION

Add a dash of alcohol, such as rum or Grand Marnier, and some toasted slivered almonds in the final stages of cooking the jam, for extra fanciness. Lauren's mum sometimes gives a version of this as Christmas gifts.

WHAT YOU'LL NEED

- 1 kg dried apricots
- juice of 1 lemon (reserve the squeezed lemon halves)
- 700 g sugar
- 8–10 jars

DRIED APRICOT JAM

There may be times where you've gobbled through all your summer goodies and are left without treats like jam for your morning toast. Dried fruit can be a mid-winter saviour at times like these. This dried apricot jam is deliciously sweet and full flavoured, and comes in at under $2 per jar. This recipe will make enough for 8–10 jars of jam, depending on the size of your jars.

STEP 1

Preheat the oven to 220°C.

STEP 2

Place the apricots in a large saucepan with 2 litres of water, the lemon juice and the two lemon halves (the rinds add flavour, nutrients and pectin to help the jam set).

STEP 3

Bring to the boil, then reduce the heat, cover and simmer for 30 minutes, or until the apricots are tender.

STEP 4

Add the sugar and stir until dissolved.

STEP 5

Bring to the boil again, then reduce the heat and simmer, uncovered, until the mixture thickens.

STEP 6

While the pot is simmering, sterilise the clean jars by placing them on a rack in a 120°C oven for 10–15 minutes. Alternatively, place the jars in a large stockpot of boiling water for 10 minutes, then drain on a tea towel.

STEP 7

To test the jam, place a saucer in the freezer and, when you think the jam might be ready, drop a teaspoon of jam onto it. Return the saucer to the freezer for a couple of minutes and then check it to see if it wrinkles a bit when you nudge it. If it wrinkles, it's ready.

STEP 8

Ladle the jam into the sterilised jars, then screw the lids on. Store in a cool, dark cupboard or pantry for up to 1 year.

IN OUR HOME

Often, families, particularly those with young children, will find they have leftover or uneaten food. It's great if you can make that food go just a little bit further. Good for reducing food waste and good for your pocket, here are some suggestions for reusing cooked food, scraps and leftovers.

- Mix leftover porridge with your favourite pikelet, cake or muffin batter to make a heartier, more sustaining snack.

- Use leftover cooked pasta to make a pasta bake or pasta salad.

- Save cooked veggies and fry in butter with mashed potato and onion for bubble and squeak.

- Juice fruit that's over-ripe, then use the pulp in baking.

- Save any raw vegetable scraps (e.g. onion and carrot tops and celery leaves) in a container in the freezer for making stock.

- Use leftover roasted or steamed vegetables for a delicious salad, curry, frittata, pizza topping, or mash with spices and wrap in pastry to make veggie sausage rolls.

- Save leftover mashed potato to make cottage pie or shepherd's pie, or add to rissoles and veggie burgers.

- Use bread crusts to make crumbs for schnitzel or homemade nuggets.

- Use apples with one small bite out of them to make muffins or crumble, or cut them up for a fruit platter (minus the teeth marks).

- Freeze over-ripe banana slices to add to smoothies, or throw them in a food processor to whip into banana ice cream.

- Collect eggshells and dry them in the oven while the oven is switched off but still warm after baking a cake or cooking dinner. Brown the eggshells to make them more brittle, then crush them up into a course powder. This can be fed to your chooks as shell grit, or sprinked over the garden. Lemon trees love a bit of extra calcium, as does your compost. Eggshells can keep snails away, too. Grind them down into a fine powder to add calcium to other products, such as toothpaste (see page 122) and pet food (see page 214).

- Save orange peels and dry them out to make excellent firelighters or Orange Cleaner (see page 175).

- Clean out the crisper drawer for a fabulous vegetable curry or soup.

- Make nut or oat milk, then use the leftover ground nuts or oats in baking, or lightly toasted and sprinkled over yoghurt or muesli.

- Give leftover food to the dog or chooks! Or save some to add to your homemade dog food (see page 214).

- Use leftover coffee grounds to make a facial scrub, or in your garden for adding nutrients and keeping slugs away from your plants.

WHAT YOU'LL NEED

- 2 cups plain flour (or gluten-free plain flour), plus extra for dusting
- 1 tablespoon baking powder
- pinch of salt
- ½ cup rapadura/coconut sugar (or raw sugar if you like, but you might like to use less honey), plus extra for sprinkling
- 100 g butter, plus extra for greasing
- 1 tablespoon honey
- ¾ cup milk
- 1 egg (2 if you're going gluten-free)
- 1 cup leftover porridge
- 1 teaspoon cinnamon
- 2 small apples or 1 large apple, grated (the apples that children like to leave with single bite marks in them are perfect!)
- rolled oats, for sprinkling

LEFTOVER PORRIDGE MUFFINS

These muffins make a delicious snack during the autumn–winter porridge season, when the apples, spices and honey are overflowing in our Tasmanian kitchen. Adding the leftover porridge makes them a little heartier than a regular muffin. We like to eat them fresh from the oven and still warm, but they make a denser, nourishing snack the next day. This recipe makes 12 muffins.

FOOD

STEP 1

Preheat the oven to 220°C.

STEP 2

Sift the flour, baking powder and salt into a large bowl and mix through the sugar.

STEP 3

In a saucepan, melt the butter and stir in the honey. Remove from the heat and beat in the milk and egg.

STEP 4

Tip the porridge, milk and egg mixture, cinnamon, apple and any variations (see opposite), into the bowl with the flour and sugar. Fold together gently.

STEP 5

Place spoonfuls of the mixture into buttered and floured muffin tin holes or reusable or compostable patty pans.

STEP 6

Sprinkle the extra sugar and oats over the top, and pop in the oven for 12–15 minutes, or until the muffins are golden brown and spring back when pressed gently in the centre.

STEP 7

Remove the muffins from the oven and allow to stand in the tin for 2–3 minutes before lifting them out to cool on a wire rack.

VARIATIONS:

If you like, you could try adding any of the following ingredients when folding in the fruit and porridge:

- 1 small handful of sultanas
- 1 small handful of sunflower seeds
- 1 small handful of cranberries

You could omit the apple, cinnamon and honey altogether and add one or two well-ripened mashed bananas and some dark chocolate chips. Use up what you have on hand.

ONE ROAST CHOOK, FIVE PEOPLE, THREE MEALS, ZERO WASTE

Harking back to childhood, when there would be a roast every weekend, we now do the same. It sets up our week with full, happy bellies and a bunch of meals already begun for the week ahead. It's an economical way to use an entire animal and make the most from it. Here's our chook rhythm and how it all works:

We start by roasting one large chicken, always free-range, local, preferably organic and pasture-fed. We keep some of the juices for gravy and pour off some oil for the next day's cooking. We also roast up a load of veggies (a little more than we need) to go with it and that's our first meal of the week. Afterwards, we remove all the remaining meat from the bones and pop the meat in the fridge for another meal. Soup, fried rice, chicken pie, a quick stir-fry, curry, pizza, pasta, risotto, salad and chicken sandwiches are all favourites made with leftover roast chicken. After we've removed all we can from the roast chicken carcass, we make chicken stock. We get about 2 litres of stock, which usually makes two serves for our family, enough for soup and to add to a casserole or other tasty dish.

HERE'S HOW WE MAKE STOCK

STEP 1

Place the leftover chicken bones in a slow cooker with leftover frozen veggie scraps, an onion chopped in half (skin and all), some garlic, a carrot, a few celery stalks, peppercorns and a bay leaf.

STEP 2

Cover with water and add a good slosh of apple cider vinegar.

Set over low heat and leave to bubble away for up to 24 hours, popping some parsley leaves in towards the end.

STEP 3

Strain the stock through a sieve into a large bowl or jug and then transfer the stock to large clean jars, leaving a 2 cm gap below the rim.

STEP 4

Once the jars have cooled, place them in the fridge or freezer, ready to make another meal or two.

SO WHAT TO DO WITH THE LEFTOVER STOCK BITS AND BONES?

After 24 hours of cooking, the chicken bones become so brittle they crumble to a paste in your fingers. This can be spread around the garden – our fruit trees love it!

When mashed up with a fork or processed in a food processor, the bones make a lovely, mineral-dense treat for dogs and cats. Remove the onions before mashing and ensure the bones crumble rather than splinter, as splintery bones are dangerous for animals to consume.

MAKE THIS

Try this recipe using different kinds of fruit scraps, such as pears, plums, berries, pineapple skins and grapes.

WHAT YOU'LL NEED

- apple scraps – peels, cores, leftovers
- 1 large, clean jar
- sugar – 1 tablespoon per 1 cup of water
- cooled, boiled water – enough to completely cover your apple scraps

SCRAPPY APPLE CIDER VINEGAR

FOOD

Living with children and with a garden full of young heritage apple trees, we tend to end up with lots of apple scraps. By autumn you'll usually find us dehydrating and preserving apples, making apple jelly and apple crumbles, leaving lots of apple peel and cores spare. Rather than throw these straight into the compost, we make sure we make the most of them first – making scrappy apple cider vinegar is one of our favourite ways to use them up. This vinegar can be used in salad dressings, cleaning products and almost any other place you might use a regular apple cider vinegar.

STEP 1

Place apple scraps in the jar until it is about three-quarters full.

STEP 2

Dissolve the sugar in the cooled, boiled water.

STEP 3

Pour the water into the jar so the apple is just covered.

STEP 4

Place some fermenting weights, or a smaller jar filled with water, on top of the apple, to press it down. You want to make sure the apple isn't exposed to the surface because it can become mouldy.

STEP 5

Cover the jar with cheesecloth or a breathable fabric, secured with a rubber band or string. A large beeswax wrap will also work.

STEP 6

Leave out of direct sunlight in a place with a stable room temperature. We use a dark corner of our kitchen bench, but a cupboard or pantry will work well. Now it's ready to ferment!

STEP 7

Check in on the fermenting process every few days. It can take up to a month, depending on how warm it is where you live. Ours typically takes about 3 weeks to do its thing.

STEP 8

The liquid should bubble and form a little foam – if your apples are really sweet it can bubble over, so do keep an eye out. When the bubbling begins to subside, strain the liquid into a large jug and feed the apple to the chooks or compost.

STEP 9

Clean your jar and pour the fermented liquid back into it. Cover and leave for a week or two. During the second fermentation, it's a good idea to taste the liquid until you get the vinegary flavour you prefer – this can take from a week to a few months. A little note here: we've forgotten about our vinegar and skipped the second fermentation on more than one occasion and still ended up with a useful vinegar – it's quite a forgiving process.

STEP 10

You may notice a cobweb-like substance floating in your vinegar after a little while. This is called the mother or SCOBY (Symbiotic Community Of Bacteria and Yeast). It's a helpful part of the fermentation process and an indicator that things have gone well. You can remove the mother if you like, or keep it and transfer it with a little vinegar to your next batch, for healthy and faster fermenting.

STEP 11

Store the vinegar in a clean jar or bottle with a lid. Store in a cool, dark place, such as a cupboard or pantry.

POTATO SKIN CHIPS

Foods that families may miss when living waste free include packaged favourites, such as potato chips and crackers. There's something about the taste of a salty, crunchy snack while waiting for dinner or watching a movie. For those times, we might reach for homemade buttery popcorn, but one of our favourite snacks uses up leftover potato skins to make chips. They're quick to make, super delicious and a completely waste-free food that you might otherwise throw out or compost.

Save the peelings when you cook with potatoes. You can store them in the fridge in an airtight container for a couple of days if you don't intend to use them right away.

STEP 1

Preheat the oven to 200°C.

STEP 2

Place the peels on a baking tray and drizzle with olive oil.

STEP 3

Sprinkle the potato skins with salt. You can also add herbs, such as rosemary or sage, spices, such as paprika, or nutritional yeast for a cheesy flavour.

STEP 4

Massage the oil and salt (and herbs/ spices if using) into the potato skins.

STEP 5

Bake in the oven for 10 minutes, or until golden brown and crispy.

STEP 6

Store the chips in an airtight container for later. We find this step impossible because we usually gobble them up as soon as they're cool enough to touch.

VARIATION:

Kale chips – take a handful of kale and remove the centre vein from each leaf using a sharp knife. Cook in olive oil and sea salt, as per the potato skins. These are super yummy and crispy, and a great way to eat your greens!

STORING FOOD

Making sure your food is correctly stored is a sure-fire way to reduce food waste in your home. It can be so disheartening to find a crisper drawer full of limp veggies or a box full of green potatoes that haven't lasted as long as you needed them to.

HERE ARE SOME TIPS TO MAKE SURE YOU ARE GETTING THE MOST OUT OF YOUR FOOD

Make sure foods stored in the fridge have plenty of airflow around them and adequate ventilation. Foods that are stored too closely together tend to go off faster.

Meat should be stored in a well-ventilated container, preferably sitting on a rack to allow full airflow. The exposed surface dries out to prevent microbial activity. Keep for up to 5 days under 3°C.

Store fruits and vegetables separately. Some fruits produce a high amount of ethylene gas, which acts as a ripening agent and can make vegetables (and some fruits) ripen too quickly.

Food storage guide

- **Apples** – store in a cool spot on your kitchen bench for 2 weeks. For longer storage, wrap in paper and place in a box or the fridge.

- **Avocados** – place in a paper bag and keep on the kitchen bench until ripe.

- **Bananas** – store in a well-ventilated spot on the kitchen bench.

- **Beetroot, radishes, parsnips and carrots** – remove any leafy green parts to maintain flavour and moisture. Save the greens for a salad! Wash and store the roots in a container or crisper covered with a damp cloth.

- **Berries** – store in a paper bag in the fridge and only wash immediately before eating.

- **Bread** – store in a linen bread bag, airtight container or beeswax wrap on the kitchen bench.

- **Broccoli** – wash and wrap in a damp cloth in the fridge.

- **Cabbage** – store in a cool spot on the kitchen bench for up to 1 week, then keep in the fridge.

- **Capsicums** – store in a cool room for up to 2 days. Place in the crisper for longer storage time.

- **Celery** – place in a cup or bowl of water on the kitchen bench.

- **Cheese** – store in a container or beeswax wrap in the fridge.

- **Cherries** – keep in a sealed container in the fridge. Only wash immediately before eating.

- **Citrus** – store in a cool, well-ventilated spot.

- **Cucumber and zucchini** – store in a cool spot on the kitchen bench for a couple of days, or wrap in a damp cloth for fridge storage.

- **Garlic** – store in a cool, dark place.

- **Green beans** – place in a container draped with a damp cloth.

- **Leafy greens** – place in a jar of water on the kitchen bench (like cut flowers), or wrap in a damp cloth and store in a container in the fridge.

- **Leeks** – place in a jar with a tiny amount of water at the base, on the kitchen bench. Or wrap in a damp cloth in the fridge.

- **Lettuce** – store in an airtight container in the fridge.

- **Melons** – whole melons will keep for a few weeks if stored out of the sun. Once cut, store in a container in the fridge.

- **Onions** – store in a cool, dark, well-ventilated place (don't store with potatoes because the ethylene released by the onions will make your potatoes sprout!).

- **Potatoes and sweet potatoes** – store in a cool, dark, well-ventilated place, or a paper bag. Never store in the fridge or with onions.

- **Spinach** – store in a container in the fridge.

- **Stone fruit** – keep in a well-ventilated spot and then move to the fridge when ripened.

- **Tomatoes** – keep for up to 2 weeks on the kitchen bench, then freeze to maintain nutrients. Never refrigerate.

REMOVE YOUR KITCHEN BIN

When we first eliminated our food waste, we realised our kitchen bin was no longer soggy and smelly. We ditched plastic bin liners in favour of a couple of large pieces of newspaper placed in the bottom of the bin, which we would wrap up any waste in before taking it out to our kerbside bin. After a while, we decided to stop using bin liners altogether. Our council accepts waste without liners, but some don't, so check first if you decide to stop using bin liners, too.

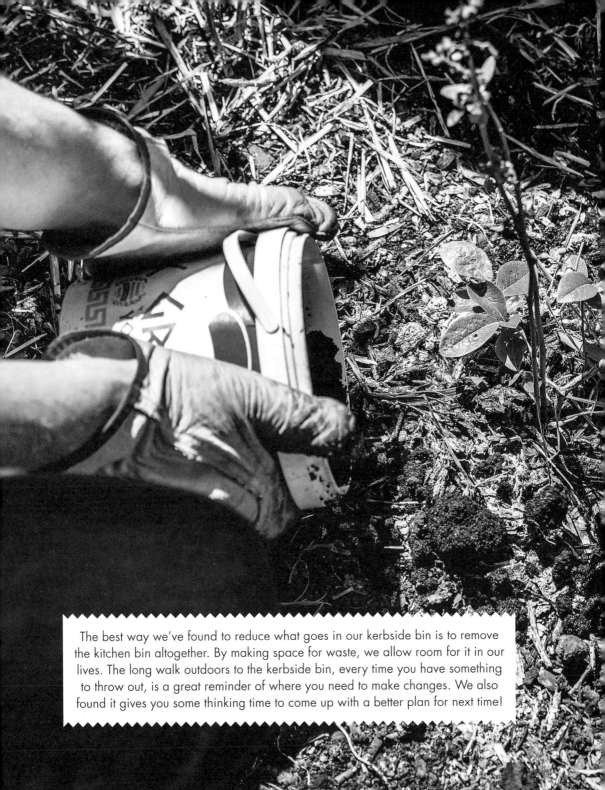

The best way we've found to reduce what goes in our kerbside bin is to remove the kitchen bin altogether. By making space for waste, we allow room for it in our lives. The long walk outdoors to the kerbside bin, every time you have something to throw out, is a great reminder of where you need to make changes. We also found it gives you some thinking time to come up with a better plan for next time!

IN SUMMARY

- Food waste accounts for a large proportion of most household rubbish bins.

- There are many ways to reduce food waste. Consider food scraps as a resource, rather than as waste. Scraps are useful! By composting scraps and organic material, you can help build soil that helps grow more food. Avoid landfill and close the loop.

- Buy only what you need, stretch your food further, preserve your excess and plan meals to use what you have.

- Get to know who makes your food and how they make it, in order to make better-informed food choices.

- You are now well on your way to not needing a bin at all!

'Dear future generations: Please accept our apologies. We were rolling drunk on petroleum.' – Kurt Vonnegut

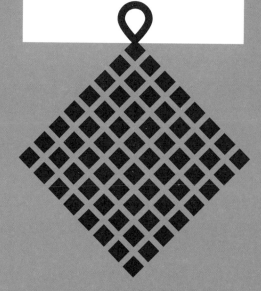

chapter three

PACKAGING

Unpack your life

Let's look at what our food, and the other things we bring into our home, are wrapped in. We take a good close-up look at what packaging is made from, the nitty-gritty on recycling it and offer some great solutions on avoiding it, from making your own beeswax wraps and personal care products, to bulk food shops.

Nearly every item that is available to buy, whether online or at a bricks-and-mortar shop, is packaged, or was packaged at some time before reaching you. Just take a stroll down your supermarket's aisles and pay attention to what items are packaged in – mostly plastic, metal, glass and paper. That packaging exists for various reasons: hygiene (e.g. avoiding germs), physical protection (of the product or of you), economic efficiency (e.g. lightweight packaging is cheaper and requires less fuel to transport) and to make products look more appealing so you will be enticed to buy them. Packaging has become the norm; a universal practice in modern, consumerist societies.

Packaging may be designed to engender trust in people that food is fresh and goods are not tainted, spoiled or damaged. This is important as we have a deep-set instinct to avoid eating things that we think will injure us or make us sick. Packaging can help relieve potential anxiety that comes with buying or receiving goods from an unknown source. But have we taken things too far? We tend to think so.

Plastic

—— Before mass production of plastic kicked in during the 1940s, our ancestors got by making stuff and packaging things with materials, such as metal, wood, paper, ceramics and fabric. But plastic proved to be super versatile and useful and has been applied to almost every facet of modern life.

The flip side is that plastic has caused and continues to cause a lot of damage. Much of the harm relating to plastic occurs during the extraction of crude oil and natural gas, as well as in the factory production of plastics. Plastic manufacturing uses approximately 6 per cent of global oil and gas consumed each year (this figure is projected to rise to 20 per cent by 2050), releasing harmful greenhouse gases, such as carbon dioxide, into the atmosphere, which contribute to global warming.

Almost all the plastic ever produced remains on or near the surface of the earth, often degrading into tiny pieces called microplastics. Plastic just never really goes away. Once discarded, plastic products can leach chemical pollutants from rubbish dumps into other areas. Plastic and its pollutants commonly find their way into waterways and are having a huge negative impact on marine life.

Lots of waste ends up in expansive areas of marine debris, such as the Great Pacific Garbage Patch, a swirling soup-like mass of plastic bits covering more than 20 million square kilometres. There are also human health concerns in relation to the chemical Bisphenol A (BPA) and other potential toxins found in some plastics. In addition, there is evidence of microplastics in waterways and even within the drinking water of many countries.

So many everyday products are made with plastic or come in plastic packaging: toothpaste tubes, straws, coffee cups, bags, toys, stationery, health and hygiene products, makeup, food packaging, drink bottles and plastic wrap, to name but a few. Each of these on their own appear inconspicuous and benign, but all are causing problems given the mass quantities produced, used and discarded.

You can minimise the amount of plastic and other packaging that you accept into your home by taking your own reusable bags and containers to the shops, or by making products from scratch using ingredients bought loose in reusable containers. Later in this chapter (see pages 106–112), we detail how to go about buying food in bulk and without single-use packaging – this is one of the easiest ways to greatly reduce plastic consumption.

PACKAGING

WHAT ABOUT BIOPLASTICS?

With increasing awareness of the harmful impacts of plastic, new products are constantly appearing on the market that are made with non-petroleum-based ingredients or may be BPA-free. Bioplastics are made from a wide variety of substances including, but not limited to, vegetable fats and oils, corn flour, sugarcane, algae and even microbiota (microscopic organisms). Many bioplastics are promoted as biodegradable and compostable. Often, the substances used are by-products of agriculture, such as sugarcane pulp that would otherwise be waste or of little use. Bioplastics generally need less fossil fuels to make and they produce fewer greenhouse gas emissions than oil-based plastics, with all other manufacturing energy sources being equal. But these products are not without waste.

We don't think bioplastics, especially the single-use kind, form an important part of waste-free living. In many cases, bioplastics still use fossil fuels during all steps of production. It is easy to forget that the energy consumed in the *making* of a thing often derives from fossil fuels and to instead focus on the end product. Many bioplastics appear environmentally friendly, with their *green* labelling and use of words like *bio* and *eco*, which can lull us into a false sense of security that the product is without environmental impact.

> In landfill, bioplastics will most likely produce methane greenhouse gas emissions, as per oil-based plastics.

Many bioplastic packaging products are touted as compostable, but to meet the Industrial Composting Australian Standard, would require industrial composting facilities that provide high temperatures and regular turning. Unfortunately, such facilities are not yet common in many places where bioplastic takeaway packaging is offered. It is somewhat misleading to promote products as compostable in areas that do not have suitable commercial composting facilities.

To add to this, many products claim to be compostable but do not specify on their product whether this requires commercial or home-composting systems. Commercially compostable products that are placed into home-composting systems may not break down for many, many years, if ever, due to temperatures being too cold. If there are no suitable composting facilities nearby, bioplastics will likely end up in landfill where they may or may not biodegrade (i.e. be broken down by microbes into carbon dioxide, water, biomass and mineral salts). In landfill, bioplastics will most likely produce methane greenhouse gas emissions, as per oil-based plastics. It is reasonable to expect that in the future there will be a greater proportion of bioplastics processed in refineries powered by renewable energy and which are transported by efficient cars also powered by renewable energy. This will be an improvement to the carbon footprint of bioplastics, but the same could be said for most manufactured products. However, we are not there yet! We wish we could say that bioplastics offer a silver-bullet solution to the plastic problem. And proponents of bioplastics might argue that they do. On face value, they offer an alternative for people to access takeaway food without oil-based packaging. But we'd say that most of the time, there are less wasteful alternatives to bioplastics, especially the single-use varieties.

WHAT YOU'LL NEED

- 50 g beeswax or 30 g candelilla wax for vegan wraps

- 30 g pine rosin (this form of refined tree sap can be made or sourced from specialty shops), crushed

- 1 tablespoon jojoba or coconut oil

- 1 clean jar or can

- squares of fabric, cut to size with pinking shears. Squares with sides 20–45 cm long are useful. A 45 cm square will cover a loaf of bread

- flat paintbrush

BEESWAX WRAPS

Beeswax cloth wraps have been in use since ancient Egyptian times for food preservation, and they have many applications in modern kitchens. Use them in place of plastic wrap, foil or waxed paper. A large piece will keep bread fresh, while small pieces are wonderful for cheese. You can use beeswax wraps to cover a wide variety of things, such as leftovers, ferments, sandwiches, baked muffins and desserts, or cut fruit and vegetables, such as melons and avocados. Beeswax wraps are made with a combination of wax, oil and tree resin. The wax forms a seal that keeps food fresh, while the oil makes the wraps malleable. The tree resin provides tackiness, so your wraps cling, like plastic wrap.

When choosing ingredients for making your wraps, see what can be found locally to you. Maybe you have a local beekeeper who can supply you with some beeswax. You may find coconut oil easier to source than jojoba (jojoba is the top pick for oil because it is a liquid wax with a long shelf life and it won't melt as easily in warmer climates.) Olive oil will work, too, and might be a good locally grown option for you, but it may oxidise sooner and start to give off a stale sort of smell after about 12 months. Coconut oil is more likely to melt and may not last quite as long as jojoba, but should still last well. It's easy for us to find nearby, so we tend to use that. Your wraps can last anywhere from 12 months to 5 years.

PACKAGING

STEP 1

Turn your oven to the lowest setting.

STEP 2

Half-fill a small saucepan with water and bring to the boil.

STEP 3

Place the beeswax, rosin and oil in the jar and place the jar into the saucepan of water, making a double boiler.

STEP 4

Melt and mix the ingredients in the jar using a spoon or wooden chopstick. The rosin may take a little longer to melt than the other ingredients, so make sure it is well mixed and not blobby.

STEP 5

Place some baking paper on a baking tray, then place your first fabric square on the paper.

STEP 6

Drizzle some of the melted beeswax mixture onto the fabric and use your paintbrush to spread it around. Work quickly! Add more wax mixture as needed. The fabric needs to be well saturated and will take on a darker, more translucent appearance when ready. Try not to spread it too thickly. If this happens, take another prepared square of fabric and use it to blot any excess wax mixture.

STEP 7

Place the baking tray in the preheated oven for 1 minute.

STEP 8

Remove the tray from the oven and, if necessary, use the brush again to distribute the beeswax evenly. Put the wrap back in the oven if you need to repeat this step. Remove after 1 minute.

STEP 9

Using tongs (or your hands if it's cool enough to touch), lift the fabric square and wave it around to cool a little.

STEP 10

Hang the fabric square to dry on a clothes horse, clothes line or pegged to a coat hanger.

STEP 11

If you have any leftover beeswax mixture, you may like to pour it into a mould and keep it for another time. It can be grated directly onto your fabric square, placed straight into a just warm oven to melt and then spread with a paintbrush before hanging to dry.

STEP 12

The tree resin scent in your wraps may be a little strong to begin with. It should settle after a few days. To care for your beeswax wraps, clean them in cool soapy water and dry them flat. You can revive your wraps by placing them on a lined tray in a warm oven – it should help the stickiness come back a little. You can also re-coat them with the above blend of ingredients.

Metal

— Canned foods and drinks remain a staple in the diet of many people in Australia. We churn through approximately 3 billion metal cans each year. These cans are mostly made from aluminium or steel, whose raw materials are extracted from destructive surface mining. The subsequent refining and smelting processes demand huge amounts of energy and often involve high fuel consumption to transport materials long distances to the next stage in production.

For example, single aluminium smelters in Victoria and New South Wales use approximately 10 per cent of each state's energy supply. And that's only the smelting stage. Those cans are also likely to have an inner lining made from petroleum-based epoxy resin or other plastic polymer, to prevent corrosion of the can and maintain the quality of the contents.

These products offer convenience, but can often be avoided, reducing waste considerably.

Aluminium foil is another common single-use metal product, which can come in the form of sheet foil, barbeque or takeaway trays, or wrapping for things, such as butter and chocolate. These products offer convenience, but can often be avoided, reducing waste considerably.

Since going waste free, we have only directly used one single canned product, which happened to be a small can of cat food for our elderly cat who was near death – an old favourite for what was her final meal. For other items we've found alternatives or slightly shifted our diet. In our pre-waste-free days we would churn through roughly six to twelve cans per week, equating to 312 to 624 cans per year!

We'd rip through cans of tuna, tomatoes, coconut cream, corn kernels and beans each week, without a thought. For these items, we have since shifted to local, line-caught fish bought from local fishmongers and put into our reusable containers, home-grown (and preserved) tomatoes, bulk coconut milk powder, fresh corn cobs and dried beans bought at the bulk food shop and transferred into our own bag. Minor changes, but we are still nourishing ourselves and with less reliance on a particular resource (in this case, aluminium) that we can do better without.

For any small pieces of aluminium that you collect (Easter egg foil, butter wrappers etc.), remember to scrunch them up into a large fist-sized ball before putting them into kerbside recycling, otherwise they may not be captured by the recycling machinery.

Glass

— Glass has been used for centuries and remains a common packaging material. Glass bottles and jars are made primarily from sand, soda ash and limestone. These raw ingredients are all found in nature, from non-renewable resources, albeit in plentiful supply. Mining of raw materials, such as sand, can damage local ecosystems. Glass production is energy intensive in terms of electricity consumption, as large amounts of gas or oil-powered energy are required to heat the glass mixture to over 1,500°C in a furnace. Glass is relatively heavy, weighing roughly seven times more than equivalent containers made from aluminium or plastic, resulting in higher fuel consumption during transport of goods.

Glass bottles and jars often come with a metal lid which has a polyethylene (plastic) lining. The metal lids are recyclable, however bear in mind that the plastic part of the lid is likely to be 'melted off' during the metal recycling process. Also, the glass container will often have a sticky label made from paper, plastic or a mixture of both. We've noticed more plastic-based labels sneaking onto jars of food, so watch out for those (and try to avoid them if you can). Check your local council website to see if they have guidelines about how to prepare your bottles and jars for recycling, if you do intend to recycle them.

On one hand, it's easy to disparage glass containers for their high embodied energy, their considerable weight, their fragility and the fact that they originate from non-renewable sources. However, glass bottles and jars have attributes that garner way more eco-street cred. Those credentials come from the capacity for glass jars and bottles to be reused. Jars are great for refilling with your store-

bought dry or wet foods, or for other prepared foods and even for freezing foods (see page 88). They can also be reused to store stuff besides food.

If you are compelled to buy something in a glass container, consider how that container might have a practical reuse. We've found some jars to be better than others for reusing and we maintain jars of a variety of sizes. In general, look for jars with a wide mouth, or without a complicated shape. These are easier to clean and find more uses. Bottles can be reused if you plan on making your own cordials or other beverages. If you take good care of your glass jars, bottles and containers, they can last for generations. Make sure to check for any chips and cracks and to keep your lids in good condition, replacing them if needed and recycling the steel.

Eventually, you may reach saturation point; when you've acquired the maximum number of glass containers that you can practically reuse, beyond which you're just stockpiling and the jars are gathering dust. For us, we started waste-free living with a small batch of jars and after two years we have maybe 50 or so jars of various sizes and we've reached saturation point for most jar sizes. As our garden grows and we increase our store of home-preserved food, we might allow the occasional new jar to come in.

For those at, or near, jar saturation point, it is worth considering ways to avoid new glass containers. One option to reduce glass consumption is to buy drinks that are available on tap (some breweries and pubs offer this). Alternatively, some breweries now offer the option to refill glass 'growlers' (c. 1.9 litre bottles). Also, some dairies offer a service where customers can return glass bottles and jars used for milk, cream or yoghurt, so they can be cleaned and reused.

HOW TO FREEZE FOOD
IN GLASS JARS

Glass has a bad reputation for breaking under extreme temperature conditions, which can be off-putting. The last thing you want when trying to create no waste is a broken jar full of food you can't eat and have to throw in the bin. But we've been using jars for years now and they're one of our favourite ways to store food in convenient serving sizes in our freezer.

STEP 1

Clean your jar in hot, soapy water and rinse well before use. If you have a dishwasher, this will do the trick. You can let it cool a little. A warm jar is a good idea if you're pouring hot food or liquid into it.

Make sure the food you place in the jar is not colder than the jar. If you've sterilised or washed your jar in really hot water and then pour cold liquid or food into it, the jar will crack.

STEP 2

Choose a wide-mouthed jar where possible. If your jar has a curved neck (most do), fill it to just below the curve. When the food or liquid freezes, it will expand, so giving it a little room will make sure the jar doesn't crack.

STEP 3

Make sure your jar can stand up in the freezer and won't fall over or be battered around. Our freezer is fitted with drawers that are well designed to handle jars so it works well for us. Your freezer set-up may be a factor in how well jars work for you.

STEP 4

One of our favourite tools for storing food in glass jars – whether it's stock, jam, pet food, leftovers, or dried goods – is a jam funnel. These stainless steel funnels have a wide opening and fit into the mouth of most jars so you can pour food into the jar without spills – great for reducing waste and for keeping your jars clean and your hands safe from hot liquids.

STEP 5

Take your jar out of the freezer and let it defrost slowly. If you plunge a frozen jar into warm, or even cold, water it will crack. It's also likely to crack if you attempt to reheat it in a microwave. This means you need to think ahead a little because it can take a few hours for the contents of your jar to defrost.

Paper and cardboard

—— It's easy to assume that paper is relatively waste free, or that it's always fine to use, given that the material is natural and compostable. However, paper and cardboard come from primary resources (trees) and require chemical inputs and energy in the form of electricity, fuel, water and human effort. In Australia, approximately 127 kg of paper is consumed per person per year, and a single kilogram of paper needs 9,000 litres of water to be produced. One sheet of A4 virgin paper uses 2 to 13 litres of water. Approximately half of the paper and cardboard produced in Australia comes from recycled materials, with one-quarter from plantations, eight per cent from native forests and the rest from various sources including imports. Recycled paper and cardboard saves trees, uses two-thirds of the amount of water, halves the need for fossil fuels and demands only one-quarter of the bleach used to make office paper. Remember, using products made from recycled materials uses fewer resources than virgin products (and that's good!), but there are still resource demands. Once used, most paper products should be able to avoid landfill, having the advantage of being compostable.

IN OUR HOME

We favour recycled paper products over non-recycled paper. This reduces the demand for virgin materials and encourages the manufacture of items made from recycled materials.

- Scrap paper and toilet rolls are used to help start our wood heater.

- Paper bags are used over and over again before feeding our compost.

- Cardboard is used as sheet mulch to help suppress weeds in the garden, helping to build more productive soils or growing food and other plants.

- Single-sided printed paper is reused for note-taking, before being used for fuel for the fire or compost. You may prefer to add paper to your kerbside recycling, especially glossy magazines and non-recycled paper (e.g. printer paper), but the choice to compost or recycle will depend on your home set-up, and the recycling considerations offered on page 94.

- Some paper can be reused as wrapping paper and paper calendars can be reused in future years. For example, your 2019 calendar will line up correctly in 2030 and 2041 – now that's planning ahead!

TIPS WHEN CHOOSING PAPER OR CARDBOARD PRODUCTS:

- Favour paper products from sustainably derived sources – consider certification labels on your products and critically examine assurances made about sustainable farming and land management.

- Consider the origin of the product – if no information is provided to indicate that the item is derived from sustainably grown or forest-certified timbers, then consider what ecosystems may be impacted by wood harvesting in that country.

- Look out for hidden materials in your products that make recycling more difficult or impossible where you live. For example, many single-use 'paper' coffee cups have a thin polyethylene lining. Many recycling facilities will not adequately separate and recycle the separate materials in these cups and so many will end up in landfill.

- Look for unbleached paper. Traditionally, elemental chlorine-based bleaches were used to brighten pulp and create whiter paper, and these emit toxic dioxins that pollute waterways and harm humans. Since the 1990s there has been a transition towards chlorine-free bleaching in some countries (mostly in Europe), but chlorine bleaches are still commonly used in Australia.

- If you have the option, consider the reuse potential of paper bags – thicker bags can be reused many times if carefully handled. Where possible, try not to treat paper bags as single-use items.

- Consider compostability – shiny, glossy and heavily inked papers may be less suited to composting or burning because of the pollutants they emit or leach. Traditionally, mineral oil-based inks are used, which contain petroleum hydrocarbons and use hazardous heavy metals to make colour pigments.

- Watch out for greenwash marketing of paper products. For example, labels that say 'recyclable' are moot, as all paper is recyclable!

- Consider tree-free papers that may use fewer resources in production. Alternatives include paper made from bamboo, recycled denim, hemp, other plant by-products and even animal poo! Note that not all these may be suitable for recycling with tree-based papers.

PACKAGING

What about recycling?

━━ It may come as a surprise to you, but we do not consider kerbside recycling to be an important part of waste-free living. As far as the waste hierarchy goes, recycling is way down the list of actions for producing less waste. We reckon that it is more worthwhile to focus on how you can *refuse* certain packaged items and *reduce* the use of others. Kerbside recycling should be a second-to-last resort. Last would be sending waste to landfill.

Kerbside recycling is an industry, as opposed to an altruistic activity for the environment. It involves transporting, usually via diesel-fuelled trucks, a portion of our waste to local depots, where it is sorted, often added back to landfill (e.g. the bits that are not collected by the sorting machinery), or moved on (often overseas) and sold to companies who purchase and repurpose it as a raw product. Recycling processes require the addition of varying amounts of energy, fuel, water and raw materials; the amounts of each depends on where you live and what recycling services are provided. Look for solutions that avoid the energy consumed in the recycling process.

Have a look in your kerbside recycling bin just before collection day.

Recent changes to recycling in China sparked conversation in the media about the fate of Australia's recycling. In 2014–15 China accepted around 30 per cent of Australia's recycling exports (ironically, much of the plastic exported to China was being recycled to make plastic rubbish bins!). However, in 2018 China imposed restrictions on a variety of recyclable materials for import. This meant that many Australian local governments were faced with the dilemma of either stockpiling collections of kerbside recycling, seeking new locations to export to, or sending recyclables to landfill. This dilemma was dubbed Australia's recycling crisis. But for us, the restrictions strengthened our belief that our society needs to take responsibility for its own waste, and avoid recycling if possible. It was another not-so-subtle reminder that there really is no 'away' and that what we face is actually a consumption crisis, rather than a recycling crisis.

Have a look in your kerbside recycling bin just before collection day. What sort of materials and items are you currently recycling? Are there items you could substitute for package-free alternatives? Maybe you can swap canned goods for fresh ingredients, canned meat for butcher-bought meat in reusable containers, or milk in cartons for milk in returnable glass. Maybe you can reduce the quantity of some items and maybe you can find other reuses for others (e.g. using newspapers as sheet mulch). You may notice resources in your kerbside recycling that you can put to some other good use at home.

PACKAGING

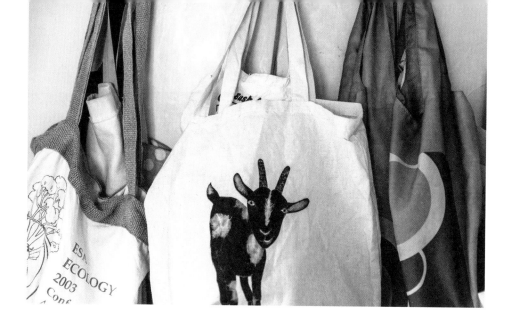

HERE ARE A FEW THINGS TO CONSIDER WHEN IT COMES TO RECYCLING:

- **Distance** – The longer the distance to the recycling facility, the more fuel that is consumed in transport. Remember, the local waste-management centre is not necessarily the same place your waste gets recycled. For us in Tasmania, most kerbside recycling items are baled up and shipped to the mainland or overseas. While this may appear to be convenient, being out of sight and out of mind, the process wastes fossil fuels through transport on diesel-fuelled ships and the final fate of those items is uncertain.

- **Efficiency** – Whilst aluminium can be recycled infinitely, the recycling process itself uses lots of energy via transport, material separation, washing and re-smelting, and so we prefer to minimise waste by using alternatives to single-use aluminium (refer back to the refuse part of the waste hierarchy on page 19). If you do use cans or foil, then recycling is a sensible option, because it requires much less electricity to produce a new can from

recycled aluminium than to make metal products from virgin materials.

Also, when plastic items are returned for recycling, they are usually downgraded to lower forms of plastic. So a plastic milk bottle doesn't become a new plastic milk bottle, it becomes something else and eventually becomes a low-grade plastic of limited use. There is just too much plastic being consumed, and forecast to be produced, for the earth to make use of it all in a sustainable way without enormous damage to the atmosphere and our living planet. At present the vast majority of plastic you see in shops is not made from recycled plastic.

In some areas, glass may be accepted for kerbside recycling, but that glass might not be sent for recycling into new glass containers. Glass is a relatively heavy material and is, therefore, an expensive material to ship to far-away recycling facilities. Instead of recycling, some councils use kerbside recycled glass to make secondary products, such as sand substitutes or part of the mixture in concrete pavers and for car parks. Such secondary products are also used when recycled glass is contaminated, such as with incompatible glass types or fragment sizes. We consider the use of glass in these secondary applications to be a type of once-off upcycling. Whilst preferable to landfill, the single reuse of discarded glass for secondary products is not an efficient use of the embodied energy in glass.

- **Demand** – What is the retail demand for the recycled end product? There is not much use in recycling if the recycled product is not saleable. For example, only a tiny proportion of plastic-wrapped products are made from recycled plastics. At present, recycling rates of plastic in Australia are low at around 12 per cent.

The majority of plastics in Australia end up as landfill and are likely to remain at or near the surface of the earth for hundreds of years, along with all the other plastics that have been produced over the last century. For plastic recycling to be viable there needs to be demand for recycled plastics, however often there is not, or those recycled plastics get converted to local council playgrounds or street furniture, and those plastics still continue to pollute as they degrade. A less wasteful approach is to seek solutions that avoid the need for recycling in the first place.

Remember, using products made from recycled materials uses fewer resources than virgin products (a good thing), but there are still resource demands. Avoiding certain materials in the first place, whether they are recyclable or not, is going to be less wasteful than consuming and recycling them. Avoid 'wish cycling', where non-recyclables are placed in the recycling bin in the hope that they will magically get recycled anyway. This can contaminate the recycling stream and lead to higher rates of landfill.

RECYCLING OPTIONS NEAR YOU:

- Check your local council's website for recycling and waste programs and get in touch by email or phone. Find out the location of your nearest recycling centres for paper, glass, metal and organics (green waste). You might like to organise a visit, or just ask someone in the know.

- Find out what can be disposed of or recycled in your area. Does your council have a commercial composting or green waste collection?

- Ask about what happens to the products you send for recycling. Do they travel far for recycling? Are they actually recycled, or do a percentage of them end up in landfill?

- Finding out what happens to your waste may help you figure out what choices you are comfortable with.

PACKAGING

Avoiding packaging

━ Consider that all packaging has to come from somewhere. Raw materials are extracted, then processed, formed and transported, ironically, usually in more packaging! Understanding the large amounts of energy and resources required to produce packaging, and learning the basics of packaging production, can motivate us to avoid certain materials, to use certain types sparingly and to try to make them last.

It can be easy to trust that what we are presented with in supermarkets and other stores is necessary, not harmful and is even good for us. Advertisers have spent decades working to convince us to have trust in their products. It can be easy to consume without question, especially when something is provided in attractive packaging. But some packaging is unnecessary, harmful and downright unhealthy, to us and to the broader environment. All the more reason to consider alternatives.

We think packaging should be considered on an as-needs basis. We've found that most of our needs can be met without any single-use packaging at all, especially at the retail end of production. Not buying packaged products may mean making your own instead. One of the benefits of this, aside from saving on packaging waste, is that you get to understand and choose exactly what goes into what you consume. You may find there are health, financial and ethical benefits to being able to choose. Many of the things we purchase regularly are actually really easy to make from scratch. We've included in these pages some of the recipes we make and have incorporated into the running of our household. There are many simple ways to meet the majority of routine needs without harmful and unnecessary packaging. So let's unpack.

PANTRY AUDIT

A quick way to get a good overview of just how much packaging waste you regularly create is to look in your pantry. Taking the time to evaluate the contents can help you decide if you need to make any changes to your shopping habits.

Look through your cupboards and fridge and pull out everything that is in a single-use plastic or cardboard packet or container. You may wish to take a photo of your pantry (or your single-use packaged goods) to use as a marker of your progress at a later date.

If you consume dairy foods, you might like to consider what packaging they arrive in. If you're lucky to receive reusable glass bottles, that's excellent! If you consume milk in cartons or plastic bottles, decide whether you feel you can justify your level of consumption and what you will do with the cartons or bottles when you are finished with them. Recycle? Repurpose? Or will you reduce your consumption? Perhaps you'll make yoghurt from scratch rather than purchase it in containers? Think about what feels comfortable for you.

If you are keen to see what your zero-waste pantry might look like right away, you could empty out some of those single-use packages and put the contents into glass jars or containers for storage and repurpose them or dispose of the packages as thoughtfully as possible.

Make a list of which items you need to find a good local source for, especially if there are no waste-free alternatives at the supermarket. List where to find waste-free options and the quantity you need.

Assess what can be replaced with bulk foods, bought in your own jars or bags. Decide what can be let go of and what can be replaced with food made from scratch.

Compile your lists and your kit and shop when you feel ready.

School (and work) lunches

—— This is an area where you can provide waste-free options, preferably in discussion with your child, to ensure that you are offering something that they are going to happily eat. We realise this can be easier said than done! Sturdy lunch boxes and bento-style lunch boxes go a long way to making lunches diverse and exciting for kids, as well as easy to pack for themselves. Schools can encourage a changing culture around waste and school lunches. Some schools have adopted package-free lunch days, which promote change while regularly alleviating the school rubbish bins. Other schools have taken it a step further and request package-free lunches five days a week. You may like to suggest to your school that they consider a weekly 'waste-free day', encouraging all parents to provide their child's lunch and snacks without single-use plastic packaging. This could lead to a change in policy to encourage all days to be waste free. We've heard from some parents that package-free lunches are easier to maintain, so you may like to suggest it at your school, or make a commitment to try it for your family and lead by example.

IN OUR HOME

Of course, these same considerations can easily be applied to packed lunches for work, too. Here are some of our favourite ideas for package-free school and work.

We recommend having occasional cook-ups where you prepare some of these things in advance, so they're ready to pack and go – see if you can add more:

- banana bread
- bliss balls
- chocolate-zucchini cake
- corn chips – made from homemade tortillas, or some Mexican restaurants make their own and will sell them to you directly. Ask your local!
- corn on the cob
- cubes or slices of cheese
- dip and veggie sticks
- dried fruit and seeds (some nuts, too, if your school allows)
- dried fruit leather
- fresh fruit
- hard-boiled eggs
- homemade muesli bars

- homemade muffins or biscuits
- homemade tortilla wraps with yummy fillings
- homemade yoghurt with a dollop of honey or jam
- kale or potato skin chips (see page 66)
- leftover dinner – homemade falafel and cold pizza are among our faves
- meatballs
- pikelets – our all-time favourite!
- popcorn
- raw veggies – snow peas, carrots, cherry tomatoes, beans, cucumber
- sandwiches
- zucchini fritters

WHAT YOU'LL NEED

- ½ cup black tahini
- ¼ cup tamari
- 2 tablespoons nutritional yeast
- 1 tablespoon apple cider vinegar
- 1 jar

SESAMITE

Our eldest has always been a big Vegemite fan, and this was one of the first things that she missed when we switched to waste-free living. Using simple ingredients we found at our local bulk food shop, we made this alternative, which is not only delicious on toast, sandwiches or homemade scrolls, it's full of nutritional goodness. It's super easy to make, too!

STEP 1

Place all the ingredients in a small bowl, blender or food processor.

STEP 2

Blend the ingredients in the blender or food processor, or if you don't mind a slightly rougher texture, mix together with a fork.

STEP 3

Transfer to a clean jar. This should keep in a cool place for a few months.

PACKAGING

WHAT YOU'LL NEED

- 1 cup plain flour (gluten-free plain flour works, too), plus extra if needed

- 1 cup yoghurt, plus extra if needed

- ½ teaspoon baking powder

- olive oil or melted butter, for drizzling

FLATBREAD

Many families consume wraps for lunches, snacks and dinners. This simple recipe is one older children can make with ease, for their own lunches or snacks, or when cooking dinner for the family. It's a super easy recipe to increase, too, using equal parts of flour and yoghurt. You can freeze cooked flatbreads for later use if you decide to cook them in bulk. Or cut them up, drizzle with oil, season with salt and pepper, then toast under the grill to make a great cracker alternative with dips.

STEP 1

Place the ingredients in a bowl and mix until well combined and dough-like. Add more flour if it feels too wet, or more yoghurt if the dough feels too dry.

STEP 2

Dust a work bench with flour, then tip the dough out onto the bench and knead until the ingredients are well combined.

STEP 3

Divide the dough into five or six pieces.

STEP 4

Take one piece of dough and roll it on a floured work surface, or on a floured piece of compostable baking paper (this might be easier for gluten-free flour, which can get a little sticky).

STEP 5

Heat a large frying pan over high heat, then drizzle in the oil or butter.

STEP 6

Place the rolled flatbread in the pan and cook for 1–2 minutes on each side, then transfer to a plate.

STEP 7

Repeat with the rest of the dough pieces until you have a delicious pile of flatbread ready to eat!

PACKAGING

The convenience myth

—— Retailers and product marketers have been telling us for decades that their products will make our lives easier. Recognising that people work longer hours and have less time to prepare food or repair broken items, retailers have built an industry that feeds our vulnerabilities and our need to feel nurtured and rewarded for all the hard work we do. Items of supposed convenience are often badged as being healthy for us, easy to use and simple to discard.

Being mass-produced and with value adding, these items often seem cheap! However, the rows upon rows of convenience products come at a high cost to the environment in terms of pollution to land, sea and air (especially via oil-based plastic packaging and disposable items) and from high non-renewable energy use along the production and distribution chain. There is also a run-on effect to our own health. Not to mention the fact that these *convenience* foods may not actually be saving time in the kitchen!

Happy, waste-free living can mean seeking joy in preparing simple, healthy meals from locally grown ingredients, without packaging. You can find abundance and satisfaction in accessing the foods and handmade products that do not cause environmental harm. There can be joy in making things yourself, from a handful of items already in your pantry.

There are other truly convenient things we've noticed about waste-free shopping, such as shorter shopping trips, less advertising and fewer distractions while shopping (helpful when shopping with kids!), buying exactly the amount of food we need, placing food in our own jars at the store ready to put straight into the pantry, and not having to remember to put the bins out. No more kerbside dashes at dawn in your pyjamas, with your heart racing and the bin trailing clumsily behind you. You may start to question which lifestyle is really more convenient!

PACKAGING

RESEARCH YOUR LOCAL RESOURCES

The more you know about what is in your neighbourhood, the better equipped you will be to access food without packaging. Whatever you can't grow at home will need to be brought in from elsewhere. If you're new to the concept of waste-free living, it might help to take on the role of super sleuth, to learn about how you might realistically be able to meet your food needs without relying on the normal, wasteful supermarket shop. Try these:

- Visit your local store, bulk food shop, butcher, bakery, community co-op and/or farmers' market. See what you can buy without waste at the shops you frequent regularly. Have conversations with shopkeepers. You might like to leap into shopping right away, or take your time, scoping things out. Either approach is okay! You might find some businesses will happily accept reusable bags, jars and containers right away while others do not, and discovering that is what this activity is all about.

- If you eat meat, try approaching your local butcher and asking them if they're comfortable with putting your purchase into a container you've brought from home.

- What if there are limited options where you live? Try scoping out local farms, organise community swaps and maybe consider starting your own bulk food co-op with friends. More on this later (see page 112).

- Look at how fruit and vegetables are packaged and presented at your supermarket, farmers' market or greengrocer.

- Have a think about your pantry audit (see page 98) and whether you can replace any of the items in your pantry with things you can buy without packaging.

- Consider whether any dietary changes might be necessary and whether that's something you're willing or able to do.

- Think about the distances food has travelled to reach you and look for local options, where possible.

- Find out how your food arrives to the shop and what the hidden packaging and transport waste might look like.

HERE'S A LIST OF THE TOOLS THAT WE'VE FOUND MOST HANDY FOR HELPING TO AVOID EXCESS PACKAGING:

- **Reusable produce bags –** There are a variety of options for bags to collect your loose fresh produce in: nylon mesh bags work well for almost everything except fine flour. Silk bags, organic cotton or re-purposed cotton or linen fabric can be even better as they are compostable. You may like to have a range of different bags to carry a range of different products. Make sure to keep spares with your grocery bags, so you're ready for anything!

- **Large jars –** These can be found second hand, or bought new. Gather a range of sizes to suit what you think you might need for your kit. For our family of five, we have approximately 10 extra-large jars (used for rice, pasta, flour and cereals), 20–30 medium-sized jars (for nuts, spreads, sugars and other bits and pieces) and two bottles each for olive oil and apple cider vinegar. We don't bring all our jars for every shopping trip (that would be pretty hard to carry!), but jars for liquids and things, such as peanut butter, along with some of our larger jars, are always helpful.

- **Containers or bottles** – Use these for shampoo, conditioner, hand soap and dishwashing liquid. Buy something long-lasting, or reuse old bottles until they are no longer useful.

- **Containers for meat and fish** – If you eat meat or fish, you might need to gather some containers to take to your butcher, deli or fishmonger. Many will be happy to help weigh and tare using your containers made from reusable plastic, stainless steel or glass (see Meat and Dairy on page 114).

- **Reusable grocery bags** – Cloth bags are a readily available, plastic-free option for carrying groceries. Be sure to keep some in your car, your handbag, or near the front door so you don't forget them when you're on your way out shopping. You could repurpose old clothing or fabric and make some for your kit.

Your responsibility as a waste-free shopper

— We live during a time where the number of people striving to keep their waste to a minimum, is in the minority. This means that any individual trying to live without waste, has a responsibility to avoid doing things that would give waste-free lifestylers a bad name amongst the broader populace. Consider that being a responsible waste-free shopper is part of enacting a broader positive influence. Here are a few ways to uphold the principles of being a responsible waste-free shopper:

- Be polite to your shopkeeper.

- Be clear about your expectations with shop owners, to help them understand that you want to shop without creating unnecessary waste. Sometimes the transaction can go awry, but keep trying to be clear so the shop assistant can understand what you mean. The classic example we've experienced is when you request a loaf of bread be put in your cloth bag, only to have the shop assistant put on a single-use plastic glove to grab the loaf, put it in your bag and then proceed to discard the plastic glove after only a few seconds of use! In those instances, we suggest persisting with the assistant (if only in preparation for the next transaction), by phrasing your needs as a problem that the shop assistant can help solve. In the bread example, this might be by saying something like, 'Can you help me to get that loaf of bread into my bag, without using the plastic glove?' They might suggest tongs, or using the bag-as-a-glove trick.

- Make sure you are well-equipped with enough bags and containers, to meet your own package-free needs. Carry clean and appropriate containers and keep your cloth bags clean and in good condition.

- Understand that it is the right of businesses to refuse your reusable containers, but also that it is your right to gently explain your preference.

- Let wasteful businesses know (in person or in writing) about the waste that you don't accept and offer solutions to reduce or avoid harmful waste – that feedback can be helpful.

> Support shops and businesses that support your choices – let others know about them.

Bulk food shops

— Bulk food shops can be wonderful resources for buying the foods you need without bringing them home in plastic packaging. Food is usually stored in large quantities in tubs, bins or large jars or buckets, so you can use scoops provided to place the food you need into your own containers, or the bags provided. Do keep in mind that while much of the food you buy from bulk food shops will have arrived there in plastic, it is usually in larger quantities, so less packaging is used in the process. It's well worth asking your favourite shop about how their products arrive and what they do with the packaging, so that you can make an informed choice about how you buy your food.

If you have coeliac disease or allergies, cross-contamination may be an issue for you, so discuss processes with the shop manager. Sometimes these challenges can be overcome by locating flours in different areas of the shop, keeping scoops in food bins and making sure food is handled carefully when refilling. Most bulk food shops sell most things that you'll need (in terms of dry foods, raw ingredients for baking and other condiments etc.), but if your local store is lacking something you need, then ask the manager and they may be able to stock that item for you.

HOW TO SHOP AT A BULK FOOD SHOP

• Visit your bulk food shop with your shopping kit in hand. If you're unfamiliar with shopping at bulk food shops, spend some time observing other shoppers and finding out how things work. Get comfortable and have conversations with the shopkeepers if you need to. They're often used to helping customers who are a bit unsure about the process and are quite happy to run through it.

• Find the scales where you can weigh, measure and tare your jars or containers. To do this, place your jar on the scales and mark the weight on the bottom of the jar. Most bulk food shops will have a marker or sticker system ready for you to use.

• Find the tubs or containers for the products you need and, using the scoops provided, fill your jars and bags as you shop.

• Think about what products you regularly use that you might need to substitute, and locate those items.

• You might like to take along a regular weekly shopping receipt and compare prices of your favourite products. We'd encourage you to attempt a whole week's shopping and not focus on the individual price differences of some products, as shopping across the board will give you a clearer indication of your savings.

• Involve your children as much as possible. Help them to scoop or measure out products and locate what you need. Older children might like to weigh, mark and fill jars. Have fun with it together! If shopping with children is totally impossible in your situation, you might like to ask them if there's anything they'd especially like, so they can be part of the process, too.

• Save receipts for the first week or so, so you can work out whether the way you are shopping is cost-effective, or whether you might need to find a compromise (e.g. you might choose to cook with more vegetables and pulses rather than meats) or replace some items with others.

PACKAGING

Food cooperatives

—— Another approach to weekly shopping is to stock up on larger quantities of particular foods at certain times, when they're seasonally available or as the family budget allows. This can be a good way to make buying some of your favourite foods more affordable. Buying in bulk quantities directly from food suppliers and distributors can also be a way that families in remote or regional areas, as well as cities, can make shopping with less packaging more affordable.

You might like to gather some friends or neighbours together and see whether forming a co-operative buying group is viable for you. Your order will most likely arrive in larger plastic bags, but for total surface area, waste will be reduced and larger bags may even be useful for reuse by members of your community. It means you can take full responsibility for what happens to your food packaging and there is no *hidden* waste.

IN OUR HOME

Things you can find in bins or on tap at most bulk food shops include:

- **Cereals** – oats, muesli, gluten-free muesli, rice puffs, corn flakes, quinoa flakes

- **Condiments and pastes** – tamari, tahini, peanut butter, apple cider vinegar, spices, salt

- **Cleaning** – dishwashing powder, laundry powder, fabric softener, liquid detergents, bicarb soda, Epsom salts

- **Dried fruit and nuts** – apricots, sultanas, apple, coconut, cashews, almonds, hazelnuts

- **Flours** – wholemeal, plain, baking, gluten-free, rice, potato, buckwheat, rye

- **Grains and seeds** – jasmine rice, brown rice, wild rice, quinoa, buckwheat, barley

- **Oils** – olive oil, sunflower oil, coconut oil

- **Pasta** – organic, gluten free

- **Personal care** – shampoo, conditioner, liquid soap

- **Pulses** – lentils, kidney beans, cannellini beans, chickpeas

- **Snacks** – dark chocolate, milk chocolate, popping corn, rice snacks, trail mix, tea

- **Sweeteners** – raw sugar, rapadura, coconut sugar, honey, maple syrup, rice malt syrup

BEANS FOR WEEKS!

It's so easy to grab a can of lentils, chickpeas or beans and whip up a quick dinner. But it's less wasteful, more economical and really easy to cook up a large batch of your favourite package-free dried beans or pulses and have them on hand to use in multiple ways for quick, cheap meals and snacks. For example, we really like cannellini beans, so once every couple of months we buy a bulk lot of beans, soak them overnight and cook them up in a big pot. We'll use some for a meal right away – it might be a quick baked bean dish or cannellini bean hummus. The remainder will go into jars to be stored in the freezer until needed for other dishes, such as cannellini bean mash, minestrone and salads.

The leftover bean water is known as aquafaba and can (if it's a good, thick consistency after cooking) be used as a plant-based egg-white replacement, which is wonderful for sponge cake, pavlova or meringues! It can also be used to water and nourish pot plants, or your garden.

Meat and dairy

— The meat and dairy industry gets a lot of attention in relation to waste. Rightfully so, as broad-scale industrialised animal agriculture is a major contributor to global greenhouse gas emissions – largely from the methane in cow farts (called enteric fermentation), but also from many other aspects of production.

Regardless of any ethical stance in relation to direct slaughter of animals for meat or their products, it is worth giving attention to the origin of meat and dairy products that you may consume to better understand any potential waste impacts. Not all farms are equal. Some farmers seek to adopt ethical practices and make efficient use of inputs (e.g. sourcing local feed) as well as outputs (e.g. composting manures). Grazing and feeding methods, breeding strategies, processing, distribution and packaging methods can all vary and will influence the amount of waste (or other harm) that results from a particular cut of meat or dairy product. When shopping for meat or deli goods, try to buy from reputable businesses who know their stuff, including where products originated and how they were processed (if at all). If your butcher or delicatessen is receptive, you can provide clean, reusable containers to eliminate the additional plastic wrapping that would otherwise occur at the retail end. In a typical transaction, the butcher tares the container on their scales (so that you don't pay for the weight of it) and places the meat directly into the container. Upon payment, the butcher hands your container back, which is then placed in a reusable bag for transporting away. (Note that some by-laws require meat products to be double bagged, so a reusable bag to carry your containers home in is important.)

> When shopping for meat or deli goods, try to buy from reputable businesses who know their stuff, including where products originated and how they were processed (if at all).

The above transaction reflects a typical visit to our butcher after developing a rapport with them – the butcher knows us, knows our containers, knows the sorts of meats we buy and knows that we want it without excess plastic packaging. However, your first interactions with a butcher might not go as smoothly. Couch your initial conversation as a problem-solving exercise that your butcher can help with. Some may be initially hesitant when confronted by a request to work outside their usual processes, but may be more receptive to solving the plastic-free problem with you or for you, given time and customer demand.

Dairy options can be a little trickier. The dairy industry is highly regulated and so reusable options and buying direct from the farmer will not always be possible, depending on your location. Going for larger packaged quantities, or buying directly in catering or bulk sizes and sharing with friends, is one option. When we started living waste free, we located a delicatessen that was happy to sell us slices of cheese off a wheel into our own container. But after a little discussion we realised this meant they'd throw out a huge sheet of plastic wrap each time! This created more packaging waste than if we bought it by the packet. Then we looked at buying waxed cheese and repurposing the wax. But we discovered the paraffin wax was just as bad as the plastic, and although we could reuse it to make firelighters, we didn't want the toxic fumes it emitted in our home or the environment.

Nowadays, we're extremely lucky to have access to an organic dairy which provides milk, cream and yoghurt in glass bottles that we can return at the farmers' market each week. They also make soft and hard cheeses that we place in our own containers, without any plastic involved in the transaction at all. They've encountered lots of red tape along the way, but with patience, care and customer support, a dairy like this is testament that it can be done. Premium products like this don't come cheaply, of course.

As a family, we've adjusted our thinking around how much milk, cheese and meat we consume. We've done this with consideration for the production and the cost involved in our consumption. Sometimes we'll substitute organic powdered milk in place of fresh milk for baking, or nutritional yeast where we might use cheese. We've reduced our dairy milk consumption significantly. Cheese is now a delicacy to be savoured, rather than something we chuck on a sanga. When buying any products, but especially meat and dairy, it's important to consider how much you consume, along with the waste it creates and decide what amount you are comfortable with. What quantity is really necessary?

WHAT YOU'LL NEED

- 1 litre milk
- 2 tablespoons powdered milk, if desired (it makes the yoghurt stretchier)
- 2 tablespoons natural yoghurt – with all the good bacteria in it! You can use a shop-bought yoghurt, or ask a friend for some. Your future batches will start with your own homemade yoghurt
- 1 clean jar

YOGHURT

Yoghurt is so easy to make yourself at home and can save you money. Like most fermented foods, it does require a certain rhythm to keep your supply constant and fresh, but the results are worth it for this simple and creamy food. It can also help to use up milk nearing its use-by date, thereby minimising food waste.

STEP 1

Place the milk and milk powder, if using, in a saucepan, whisk together, then heat until the mixture begins to foam.

STEP 2

Remove the pan from the heat. Cool for about 15 minutes, until you can tolerate holding a finger in the milk for the count of 20 – careful not to burn yourself!

STEP 3

Skim off any skin from the milk.

STEP 4

Place the natural yoghurt in a clean jar. Add a little of the heated milk and whisk.

STEP 5

Pour over the remaining milk and whisk again.

STEP 6

Seal the jar, wrap well in a towel and leave somewhere warm for 8 hours. We like to place ours in a box on the mantelpiece or on a sunny windowsill in winter, for extra warmth.

STEP 7

Refrigerate and serve when cold. Remember to save two tablespoons of yoghurt for your next batch!

MAKE THIS

WHAT YOU'LL NEED

- 1 cup raw nuts (e.g. almonds, hazelnuts, walnuts, cashews, macadamias) or oats

- generous pinch of sea salt

- natural sweetener, if desired (e.g. dates, maple syrup, organic raw sugar), to taste

- 1 large jar or bottle

NUT OR OAT MILK

Dairy milk may not be a very sustainable option for you, depending on where you live, where your milk travels from and what it is packaged in. Or you may choose not to consume dairy for other personal, health or ethical reasons. Nut, rice, soy and oat milks are alternatives that can be made at home with relative ease. Check where your nuts or grains come from and how much water and fuel are consumed in making them available to you. We've chosen to include nut and oat milk recipes here, because they're our best local options.

STEP 1

Place the nuts in a bowl and cover with water. Leave to soak overnight. If you're making oat milk you can skip this bit.

STEP 2

Drain the nuts and rinse well.

STEP 3

Place your nuts or oats in a food processor or blender with 1 cup of water and the salt.

STEP 4

Blend for up to 1 minute, until it forms a smooth paste.

STEP 5

Add another 2 cups of water and blend for a further 1 minute. Add a sweetener to taste, if desired.

STEP 6

Place a nut milk bag or muslin cloth over a bowl or large jug and pour the blended mixture into it, then gather up the corners and squeeze to strain out the milk. You can use the remaining pulp in cakes, in place of almond meal, or lightly toasted and served over muesli.

STEP 7

Pour the nut or oat milk into a large jar or glass bottle, keep refrigerated and use within 4–5 days.

PACKAGING

BUTTER

A little effort and patience will turn a jar of cream into a pat of butter and some buttermilk for scones. You can do this much faster in a food processor, but this is a good way to demonstrate the energy needed to create butter for your family. Place some (preferably organic) cream in a jar with a marble. The cream should fill the jar half-way. Now shake! This'll take some time and require everyone to take turns to get the job done. Eventually that small marble and your effort will turn the jar of cream into a jar of butter, with buttermilk on the side. Make a batch of buttermilk scones and cover with lashings of your homemade butter.

FLOUR

Personal care products

— Personal care products can create vast quantities of packaging waste. Tubes of toothpaste, hair-care products, beauty products, deodorant, insect repellent, make-up – there are supermarket and pharmacy aisles bursting with these products and all of them create waste. Many cannot be recycled in your kerbside recycling bin, although there are increasingly more recycling programs available for these products, which is wonderful if you truly do need them.

There is also a huge and increasing range of alternative products available, which you can buy in reusable or compostable packaging. Look at what you can find on tap at bulk food shops near you and don't be afraid to rethink your routine.

In many cases, there is a simple, homemade alternative that will work perfectly well and sometimes even better than a packaged product. Better still, you can tweak recipes to tailor them in a way you prefer and to suit your needs. You can also be assured that, being made from simple ingredients of your choosing, they are unlikely to harm you or the planet. We've included some of our favourite recipes over the following pages. Have a look and see if any will work for you and experiment to perfect them for your family.

DENTAL CARE

The dental aisle in any supermarket is like a sea of plastic, but there are many alternatives that work just as well. Plastic toothbrushes can be swapped for compostable bamboo brushes, which can be found at many bulk food or health food shops. If you have trouble finding them, ask your favourite shop to order some. If they have nylon bristles, try using pliers to remove them before popping in your compost bin.

PACKAGING

MAKE THIS

WHAT YOU'LL NEED

- 2 heaped tablespoons coconut oil
- 1 teaspoon bicarb soda
- 1 clean jar

- 15–20 drops essential oil (to taste) – essential oils, such as peppermint and rosemary, have proven antibacterial qualities and can act against oral pathogens

TOOTHPASTE

This is quite a versatile recipe that you can add ingredients to for different reasons, if you wish. It won't give you the same feel or flavour as a conventional toothpaste might, but you may start to notice other benefits. All ingredients have been chosen for their antibacterial, antifungal and re-mineralising properties, and all ingredients are less abrasive than regular toothpaste so should be safe to use in the appropriate quantities. We've noticed healthier gums, stronger teeth and reduced or slowed decay.

Our dentist is happy to recommend our toothpaste and has been impressed with the results, but if you have any concerns at all, do discuss it with your own dentist.

You could experiment with adding one or all of the following ingredients:

- Finely ground eggshells or calcium powder, for added calcium, gentle abrasion and re-mineralisation.

- Activated charcoal – reputed to have whitening qualities.

- Food-grade bentonite clay – antibacterial and alkaline, creating less favourable conditions for harmful bacteria in your mouth.

- Arrowroot instead of coconut oil if you prefer an oil-free toothpaste. Use it with a damp toothbrush.

STEP 1

Place all the ingredients in a small bowl.

STEP 2

Mix with a fork until well combined.

STEP 3

Place in a clean jar for use. Use as you would regular toothpaste.

TIP:

If you are intending to use this toothpaste for children under six years old, you may like to try cinnamon or orange oil, which are generally considered to be the safest oils for young children.

PACKAGING

WHAT YOU'LL NEED

- 30 g beeswax
- 1 tablespoon coconut oil
- 5–10 drops peppermint essential oil
- silk or cotton thread. Strands of embroidery floss separated from the skein or lengths cut from a spool (doubled over and twisted to make your desired thickness) work well. A 2-metre length of thread should do
- an old dental floss container, cleaned and spool removed

DENTAL FLOSS

Dental floss is a little tricky to find completely waste free, with many offering plastic floss in compostable packaging, or vice versa. There are some silk flosses available that come with refill options. Cotton or silk thread can also work well, taken off the spool or from reclaimed fabrics or garments. We sometimes prepare a little wax coating for ours to help it glide between teeth, while strengthening it a little so it doesn't break too easily.

STEP 1

Place the beeswax and coconut oil in a bowl over a saucepan of boiling water, creating a double boiler. Alternatively, heat the bowl in a microwave on high until the mixture is liquid.

STEP 2

Stir until melted and well mixed, then stir in the essential oil.

STEP 3

Take one end of the thread, then dip and pull it through the wax mixture, using the bowl to help guide it slowly. As you lift the thread out, the wax coating will dry.

STEP 4

Wind the new floss around your reused dental floss spool, slowly dragging the other end through the bowl of wax as you go. It can help to have an extra pair of hands here to make sure one end of the thread is dipping through the wax while you wind, but you should get the hang of it after a while.

STEP 5

Place the spool into your floss container and you're ready to use it as regular floss.

DEODORANT

Deodorant regularly comes packaged in single-use, non-recyclable, hard plastic bottles or roll-ons. Some people prefer long-lasting salt crystals, or even just bicarb soda sprinkled on after a shower. Remember the element that causes body odour is bacteria, so using antibacterial ingredients are helpful in preventing odour. Here are a couple of recipes that work well for us, using simple ingredients known to have antibacterial qualities.

MAKE
THIS

WHAT YOU'LL NEED

- 1 teaspoon bicarb soda
- 100 ml warm water
- 10–20 drops essential oil – lemongrass, tea tree, thyme, rosemary, lavender or geranium
- spray bottle

BICARB-FREE DEODORANT SPRAY

- spray bottle
- 1 part apple cider vinegar
- 1 part water

DEODORANT SPRAY

This recipe is handy if you prefer a lighter deodorant spray, or for less active days.

STEP 1

Place all the ingredients in a spray bottle. We use and refill an old deodorant bottle.

STEP 2

Shake until well combined.

STEP 3

Use a few squirts each day, or as needed.

WHAT YOU'LL NEED

- 2 heaped tablespoons coconut oil

- 1 teaspoon bicarb soda

- 10–20 drops essential oil – we love rosemary, lemongrass, lavender, thyme, tea tree or geranium

- some people like to add other ingredients, such as clay or arrowroot powder. Try experimenting to find a blend that works for you

- 1 clean jar

DEODORANT PASTE

This is actually very similar to our toothpaste recipe, which makes for compact travelling! We find this recipe works well for day-to-day use and more active days.

STEP 1

Place all the ingredients in a small bowl.

STEP 2

Mix with a fork until well combined.

STEP 3

Place in a clean jar for use. To use, evenly spread on fingers or palm and apply.

PACKAGING

SKINCARE

Skin is our body's largest organ, so it's understandable that we'd want to care for it well. We can tone, exfoliate, moisturise and nourish it with a plethora of products, but sometimes less is more. There's a tendency to over-treat our skin and drive it to need more and more moisture. Washing our skin too often can dry it out, too, so have a think about whether your day warrants that shower!

We're big fans of embracing your smile lines, as well as keeping it simple and natural by using what's on hand. Olive or coconut oil can make a wonderfully nourishing cleanser and moisturiser for some skin types. Masks can be made using natural ingredients, such as honey, avocado and egg. Of course there are some great products available in compostable packaging that will provide what you need. Often the best way to care for our skin is with good old soap and water, or just plain water! Here are some of our favourite recipes for nourishing our skin.

MAKE THIS

WHAT YOU'LL NEED

- 1 cup soap ends
- ½ cup olive oil, plus extra for oiling
- soap mould – a small glass baking dish works nicely

OLIVE OIL SCRAP SOAP

Lauren found this recipe noted in her grandmother's 'Kitchen Hints' notebook from the 1940s. It's a marvellous example of reusing and stretching products so they go further – something many of us could do well to remember.

STEP 1

Grate the soap ends and place them in a saucepan with water.

STEP 2

Place over medium heat and stir well until the soap fragments have dissolved.

STEP 3

Remove from the heat and add the olive oil, stirring well.

STEP 4

Beat well with a whisk and, while the mixture is still warm, pour it into an oiled dish or mould.

STEP 5

When the soap block is completely cold, turn it out onto a board and cut it into squares.

STEP 6

Leave your new soap bars to harden for a few days before using.

PACKAGING

OATMEAL SCRUB

STEP 1

Place all the ingredients in a bowl. Mix well.

STEP 2

Transfer to a clean, dry jar and seal the lid.

STEP 3

To use your new scrub, pour a little (about 1 teaspoon) into your palm and add a few drops of warm water. Mix the water into the scrub to make a sort of paste, then apply to your face or body, using small circular movements. Leave it on your skin for about 1 minute, then rinse off. We like to do this in the shower.

CHARCOAL AND CLAY MASK

This is a good cleansing mask that acts to draw excess oils, dirt and toxins from your pores, leaving it feeling smooth and fresh. It can be especially helpful for oilier skin types, although it can work for more delicate skin types, too.

STEP 1

Place both ingredients in a bowl.

STEP 2

Add a few drops of water and mix to form a smooth paste.

STEP 3

Apply to your face gently, using your fingertips. Avoid the area around the eyes.

STEP 4

Allow the mask to dry.

STEP 5

Remove with warm water. The shower is a great place to do this, because it can get pretty messy!

STEP 6

Follow up with a splash of cold water and your favourite moisturiser.

MAKE THIS

WHAT YOU'LL NEED

- herbs from the garden – calendula, lavender, mint, chamomile, rosemary, yarrow and thyme are all wonderful

- 125 ml boiling water

- 20 g beeswax

- 50 g cocoa butter or shea butter

- 100 ml olive oil or sweet almond oil 25 drops essential oil – geranium, lavender, orange and rose are all lovely. If you use cocoa butter, you might like to choose an oil that complements the chocolatey fragrance

TIP:
Go for a sunflower oil and a few drops of rosehip oil if your skin tends towards oily.

MOISTURISER

This is a lovely, gentle moisturiser that you can use for your body, hands or face, if the oils agree with your skin. It is based on a herbal infusion and some simple carrier oils found in most bulk food shops. Look into which herbs and essential oils might provide ingredients that support your skin type. Even better if the herbs are grown in your garden! This moisturiser should last for up to 6 months if kept in the fridge. For a longer shelf life, you may like to look into natural preservative options.

STEP 1

Crush the herbs in your hand and place them in a small jar, cup or coffee plunger.

STEP 2

Pour the boiling water over the herbs to make an infusion. Let this steep for a few hours, then strain.

STEP 3

Place the beeswax, cocoa or shea butter and oil in a saucepan and melt together over a low heat. Stir gently while the wax melts.

STEP 4

Remove from the heat and allow to cool until just warm.

STEP 5

Using a stick blender or whisk, slowly pour in the herbal infusion while blending.

STEP 6

Add your favourite essential oils and mix thoroughly.

STEP 7

Using a spatula, pour the moisturiser blend into clean jars.

VARIATIONS:

Add 20 drops of peppermint oil for a lush, soothing foot moisturiser. Or try some bentonite clay or zinc oxide (1 teaspoon to start, then more if you feel the need), or a rich and protective nappy cream.

PACKAGING

HAIR REMOVAL

There are a range of waste-free or minimal-waste options available for hair removal. Instead of disposable razors or safety blades, Sweeney Todd-style straight razors work well and last a lifetime. Good-quality electric razors can last for a long time, too. Shaving soap can be bought by the bar or made from scratch, or just a well-lathering soap will do. Laser hair removal is a costlier option, or there's the Middle Eastern homemade alternative to waxing: sugaring.

Sugaring involves placing roughly ½ cup sugar with 2 tablespoons of water, 1 tablespoon of lemon juice and a pinch of salt in a saucepan, over medium heat. Add another ½ cup of sugar as the mixture melts. Be careful heating the sugar because it gets very hot! When the mixture has thickened to a paste-like consistency, remove it from the heat, allow it to cool and use it like a wax over your skin. It can be used over and over again until you get the desired result. You can compost the sugar paste (and hair) when you're finished.

Of course, the ultimate waste-free method of hair removal is no removal at all. We're in favour of letting it grow and we're pleased to see a turn away from hair removal by millennials, who are increasingly embracing natural body hair.

MAKE-UP

The cosmetics industry is huge and there are about a million different products for all sorts of situations that can give you a natural or super-glam look. Most of these come packaged in plastic, which is more often than not sent to landfill. There are some businesses making beautiful make-up products in compostable packaging, but you might like to try making something simple at home, using items from your own pantry.

It may be a little tricky to emulate *mega glam* with kitchen products, but it's worth thinking about what's important to you, what you really need in your routine and what you can make for yourself with unpackaged products.

With care, mascara can last longer than the recommended three months. You could try making your own using a mix of waxes and activated charcoal. Look for products such as eyeliner pencils that use natural ingredients – as you sharpen them away, the shavings can be composted. Make your own lip balms and experiment with products that have more than one use, such as lip tints that double as blush. These all help to reduce the amount of packaging you consume and carry in your make-up bag.

MAKE THIS

TIP:
This recipe can be used as a dry shampoo for darker hair – for blonde hair, leave out the cacao. Simply sprinkle it on and brush it through. It will help soak up the natural oils in your hair and keep it looking lustrous – great for camping trips, holidays or days when you don't have time to wash your hair.

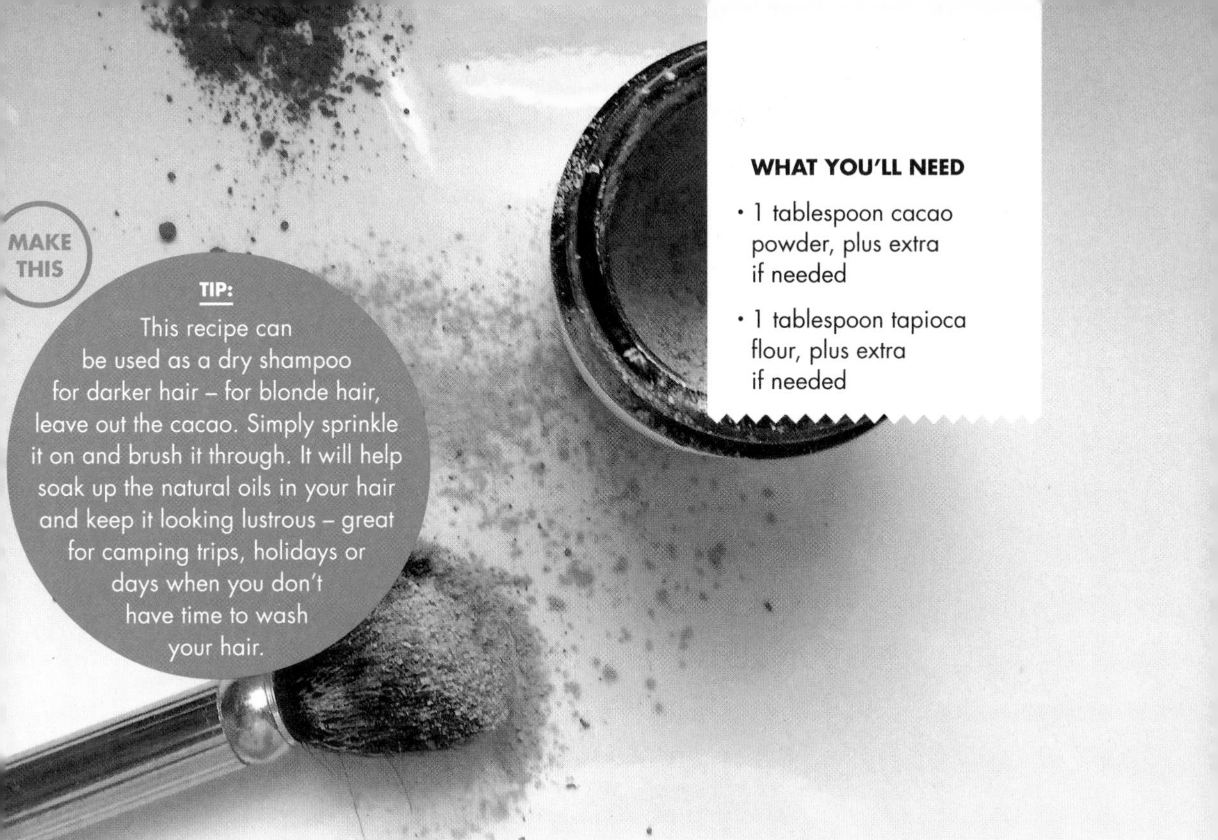

WHAT YOU'LL NEED

- 1 tablespoon cacao powder, plus extra if needed
- 1 tablespoon tapioca flour, plus extra if needed

MAKE-UP POWDER FOUNDATION

This recipe works well as a light powder and it smells delicious! The effect is very soft and light and can work better when applied over a face cream, BB cream, or moisturiser.

STEP 1

Place the ingredients in a clean jar and mix to combine.

STEP 2

Add more cacao or tapioca starch to match your skin colouring.

EYE SHADOW AND BLUSH

Spice up your make-up routine, quite literally. For a dusty eye shadow, try cacao on its own, or go for a smoky effect with a little activated charcoal. Add a little turmeric or paprika for warmer tones, nutmeg for deeper browns. Use dried beetroot powder for pink shades and blush. Have a good look at what you have in your pantry and play with it! A simple selection of natural and compostable make-up brushes could be valuable to have in your kit.

MASCARA

Cake mascaras have been available since the 1900s. They are purported to be easier to keep bacteria-free than tube mascaras, and to keep free from clumping, because you can keep your brush or wand clean between uses. This recipe makes a cake mascara that nourishes your lashes and is gentle on your eyes. It can also be used as an eyeliner and brow filler. It's made using ingredients available at many bulk food shops, and it is compostable.

STEP 1

Place the wax, butter, oil and vegetable glycerine, if using, in a bowl over a saucepan of boiling water. Stir to melt.

STEP 2

Add the powder and clay and stir.

STEP 3

Remove from the heat and stir in the rosemary oil.

STEP 4

Pour into a small clean, shallow, jar or container, and let the mascara cool and harden.

VARIATION:

If you don't have cocoa butter, coconut oil will work, too, but it may harden too much if it gets cold where you live.

HAIR PRODUCTS

People spend lots of money and time on their hair and the products involved in cleaning, shaping, restoring, dyeing and holding it in place can be extensive. We get it. Nobody likes bad hair days. But there are many natural options to explore that may work well for you. For example, some people report wonderful results from not shampooing their hair at all, instead using brushing, water and occasional vinegar or herbal rinses to keep their hair clean and nourished.

If you're not willing to let go of the shampoo just yet, you can buy shampoo bars that are used much like soap, or old shampoo bottles can be reused and refilled at most bulk food shops, which can be wonderfully time saving if you don't have time to make your own.

Look for tools and products that are derived from nature or will last a long time before composting, such as hair brushes made from timber and natural bristle. Henna powder is derived from natural plant extracts and can be found in blocks or powder form in recyclable packaging, and provides a natural, non-toxic colour. Ingredients, such as egg, honey and coconut oil can all provide nourishing masks for your hair. And hair can be held in place with ingredients found in your kitchen cupboard.

WHAT YOU'LL NEED

- 30 g beeswax
- 30 g coconut oil or shea butter
- 2 tablespoons sweet almond oil or olive oil
- 20–30 drops essential oils of your choice
- 1 tin or jar

HAIR WAX

This smells delicious and works just as well as store-bought hair wax.

STEP 1

Put the beeswax and coconut oil in a small bowl and place over a saucepan of boiling water.

STEP 2

When half-melted, add the oil. Melt everything together, stirring occasionally.

STEP 3

Remove the bowl from the heat.

STEP 4

Add essential oils and stir into the mixture. Essential oils are added for fragrance – play with what you like. Rosemary and peppermint can help stimulate scalp hair and add shine, while lime, lemongrass and thyme can help with oily hair. Clary sage, tea tree or eucalyptus can help with dandruff and geranium oil can help strengthen hair. All of them smell amazing!

STEP 5

Carefully pour the mixture into a tin or jar and allow to cool. Store in a cool, dark place. Use as any regular hair product – you may need to warm it up in your hands before applying to your hair.

PACKAGING

WHAT YOU'LL NEED

- 1 ½ tablespoons sugar – you can up the sugar if you find you need more hold

- 10 drops essential oils of your choice – these give your hair a lovely fragrance, help soften the sugar and can help keep away insects, who may find the sugar attractive!

- 2 teaspoons alcohol – vodka is a good choice. This can help soften the sugar and tame frizz (optional)

HAIRSPRAY

Conventional hairspray can be pretty toxic and wasteful if you're using it regularly. It can contain plastics, aerosols and other harmful chemicals. This recipe may not have the ultra-hold of some products on the market, but it can help tame frizz and flyaways, while being gentle on the environment and really cheap to make. Our grandmothers used something similar when they were young.

STEP 1

Place 1 cup of water and the sugar in a saucepan over a medium heat and stir until the sugar is dissolved.

STEP 2

Let cool, then add the essential oils and alcohol (if using).

STEP 3

Pour into a spray bottle and use as you would normally use hairspray.

PACKAGING

PROTECTIVE PRODUCTS FOR THE OUTDOORS

Sunscreens and insect repellents can be important to protect your family from harmful elements and disease. We like to take as natural an approach to these as possible and use clothing and fabric to cover skin and offer protection as much as we can. This is due, in part, to a sensitivity to almost any of these products we've tried over the years and experience with hives and peeling skin due to the harmful chemicals we've come across in the less natural stuff. Yikes!

Fortunately, there are some more natural sunscreens available, a few of which come in compostable or reusable and recyclable packaging. Zinc oxide is the ingredient that will offer UV protection if you're keen to try making your own sunscreen.

MAKE THIS

TIP:
Make sure to check the suitability of your chosen oil for your family, especially if you have children under six years old, or if you are pregnant.

WHAT YOU'LL NEED

- 1 tablespoon apple cider vinegar
- 20–30 drops essential oils – lemongrass, lemon, orange, citronella, tea tree, eucalyptus, rosemary, geranium and lavender all work in any combination. We usually go for lemongrass in the evenings, but be careful during the day because lemongrass can attract bees
- small spray bottle

INSECT REPELLENT

We have some serious mozzie-attractors in our family. This spray has helped keep the bites to a minimum through a few summers, including one where we were the only family at camp to avoid Ross River Fever. We love that this recipe is free from any harsh toxins. It's very similar to our spray-on deodorant recipe, so you can just use that if you don't have time or space for a new bottle. Both bicarb soda and vinegar can help to reduce itching from insect bites, so the spray can help soothe those, too.

STEP 1

Place 1 cup of water, the apple cider vinegar and essential oils in a small spray bottle.

STEP 2

Pop the lid on and shake well before use.

STEP 3

Spray before going outside and re-spray every 2 hours.

PACKAGING

SANITARY PRODUCTS

The average woman will use 11,000 disposable menstrual products in her lifetime, contributing around 120 kg of sanitary waste to landfill. When you consider that disposable sanitary products are made from plastic, conventional cotton treated with pesticides, wood pulp and harmful bleaching agents, you begin to realise the environmental impact the disposable sanitary product industry creates. There is a huge industry in disposable sanitary products. These products are considered a non-essential item in many countries, making them very expensive for half the world's population to use.

Fortunately, there are a range of reusable products available, including absorbent period underwear, menstrual cups, sea sponges and cloth pads. They can be made from a range of different materials to suit your needs and some can last up to 10 years, meaning they more than pay for themselves within the first few months of use. Anecdotally, many cloth and menstrual cup users report a reduction in pain and duration of their period.

When our babies were still in nappies, Lauren realised that the process for cleaning nappies could be similarly applied to reusable cloth pads. So she made the switch to cloth pads and then a menstrual cup and now makes considerable savings each month, while not sending any sanitary waste to landfill. In her stash are some homemade cloth pads made from repurposed fabrics, absorbent bamboo and felted jumpers for extra absorbency. They took an afternoon to make, cost about $1 each and will last for a number of years. At the end of their usefulness, they are completely compostable.

Cloth pads will need to be soaked in cold water before washing, while menstrual cups are sterilised before use each month, then emptied and rinsed with cold water. Rather than flushing or washing all those valuable nutrients away, you may like to consider saving the water from soaking cloth pads and the fluid collected from your cup, to water fruit trees or ornamental plants in your garden. This makes a fabulous, nutrient-dense liquid fertiliser (akin to blood and bone) and can create a nice little connection between you and your garden each month.

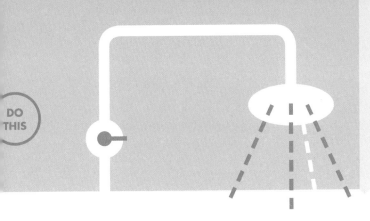

WHAT YOU'LL NEED

- piece of paper and pencil kept in your bathroom
- 1 litre jug
- stopwatch

SHOWER AUDIT

Household water usage is another area where you can reduce the waste you create. Fresh water scarcity is an increasing global concern as the human population increases and water demands increase alongside that. Greywater systems and rainwater collection tanks provide an excellent way to catch and store water for use in your house and garden. But reducing the amount of water you use can make a huge difference. In our house, most of the water seems to be used in the shower – after long days in the garden, hot showers are much appreciated! But shorter, less frequent showers can go a great way to reduce your usage. Understanding your shower usage is the key to reduction.

STEP 1

Keep a tally of each bath or shower, and the length of those showers, for a week.

STEP 2

Work out how much water is consumed per minute by holding the jug under your shower head and using a stopwatch to time how many seconds it takes to fill the jug.

STEP 3

Divide 60 seconds by the number of seconds it took to fill your jug. This gives you your litres-per-minute rate.

STEP 4

How many litres of water does your shower use per minute? How many litres of water did each shower use? How many litres of water did your family use this week?

STEP 5

Try reducing your showers as much as possible for a week. Take shorter showers, or shower less frequently, if you can.

STEP 6

Repeat the audit after a week of reducing your showers and calculate how much water you've saved.

STEP 7

You can save water further by placing a bucket in the shower while you run the water. This can be used in the garden, or for flushing your toilet. You can easily syphon bathwater for your garden beds by running a hose through the bathroom window and placing one end in the bath. Turn the hose on until you see water coming through it, then remove the end of the hose attached to the tap and place it downhill in your garden. The water will draw away from the bath and outside!

PACKAGING

TOILET PAPER

Globally, the paper equivalent of 270,000 trees is either flushed or sent to landfill each day. Of that figure, 10 per cent is in the form of toilet paper. Most brands of toilet paper in the supermarket are wrapped in plastic or plastic-lined paper. Recycled toilet paper offers an improvement, using 50 per cent less energy and 90 per cent less water to create. Its production creates 74 per cent less air pollution and saves 17 trees per tonne. If you're aiming to reduce your toilet paper waste, you may like to try the following:

Use less paper – can you make do with a square or two? Encourage your kids to use less, too.

An even more effective way to reduce your loo-related waste output is to install a composting toilet. This can be a simple bucket and sawdust set-up, or a top-of-the-range composting toilet system. Any method you choose will save around 10,000 litres of water per person per year. It will also help you make the most of a marvellous resource which, when properly composted, can help put nutrients back into the soil. If this is an option you want to explore, make sure you check out council regulations in your area and do some reading on composting humanure.

Choose a bidet! If you're planning a bathroom renovation, or building a home, you may like to consider installing a bidet. Culturally acceptable in many countries, they're one way to eliminate the need for toilet paper completely.

Choose recycled toilet paper, wrapped in paper packaging, if possible.

Avoid the triple-layer, extra-soft paper if you can – it requires more water, more resources and more paper!

DO THIS

WHAT YOU'LL NEED

- Reusable fabric squares – about 5–10 per person in your home. You may like to cut flannel fabric squares or old towels with pinking shears, or hem with a sewing machine. Face washers are an easy, ready-made option.

- Basket or container for clean squares.

- Small container for used squares. A lidded 2 litre yoghurt tub works well.

- Squeeze bottle of water to help you get extra clean (optional).

FAMILY CLOTH

If you're used to washing nappies and cloth pads by now, reusable, washable toilet wipes provide another easy waste-reducing option you may like to investigate. It can help you save money as well as paper and resources.

STEP 1

Use a clean square from your basket or container each time you use the loo.

STEP 2

Place the used square in the lidded bucket.

STEP 3

Wash the full bucket of squares with towels or other washing, or run a separate small load, if you prefer. Water temperatures over 40°C are effective in dealing with most pathogens, while sunlight is an effective bleaching agent.

STEP 4

Replace the clean squares in the basket beside the toilet.

PACKAGING

Waste-free living during illness

— Being sick sucks. And when a whole family gets sick at the same time, those fantastic waste-free habits can easily collapse. When you are ill or incapacitated, it can be more difficult to meet your needs without making waste. There might be a tendency to retreat to the convenience of packaged comfort foods, because, well, you're sick and you want to go easy on yourself. You may not be able to get to a bulk food shop, or prepare waste-free meals from scratch. In these cases, let us be the first to say that *it's okay*. Accept that some additional waste is likely to creep in during difficult times. But having been through a few bouts of illness whilst attempting to live waste free, we can offer a few suggestions for minimising waste through tough times.

- **Be prepared:** Here's where you'll thank yourself for a little meal planning and freezing meals you've cooked in advance. We always try and have a meal or two in the freezer and some broth ready for times like these. If you're in fine health, you'll have extra on hand to share with friends or family who are not so fortunate. We fill the fruit bowl with lemons and make up an extra batch of cordial when sickness is in the house. Planning ahead, drying some herbs and preparing herbal remedies to support your immune system can also help.

- **Seek support:** Work on developing a support network of friends or family who can help when you're out of action. Offer to do the same for them! If they're not on board with waste-free living yet, you might like to suggest they offer food in reusable containers you can return to them when you're feeling better. Or ask your support people to pick up some fresh fruit and veggies to sustain you and your family while you're unwell. We've been very fortunate recipients and happy providers of many care packages over the years and it's in those moments that we are reminded that we're not alone. Much of the convenience food available to us means we can keep pushing through the harder times independently. But it's the times where we support and rely on each other that bring us closer together, making life richer.

- **Choose bulk packaging:** We've found that blister packs of common pain relief medication can be avoided by purchasing those products in bulk containers of 100 or so tablets. Those containers are more likely to have a plausible reuse than blister packs (which are generally not recyclable). It may be worth asking your pharmacist or the company who makes your product of interest whether there are bulk options or less-wasteful alternatives available. Pharmacists can also prepare some medications and provide them in reusable or recyclable packaging, so you can avoid buying the off-the-shelf wastefully packaged products.

- **Stay healthy:** This might seem glaringly obvious, but it is important to remember that we can minimise sickness by eating healthy food and exercising. The less often you get sick, the less requirements for medications. We've found that making the bulk of our food from scratch means that we're eating well and illness is less likely to find us.

PACKAGING

WHAT YOU'LL NEED

- 35 cm x 35 cm square of fabric
- iron
- sewing machine, or needle and thread
- pins

HANDKERCHIEFS

We stopped using single-use tissues a number of years ago, preferring softer, more absorbent and more practical hankies. We're all in a good habit of carrying them in our pockets or handbags. One of the few pieces of worldly advice that Oberon's father handed him was to 'always carry a hanky'! We find them useful for all sorts of things when out and about, aside from blowing noses. Hankies are really easy to make yourself by hand. We prefer to sew ours out of old bed linen, which is usually lovely and soft. Or you can make some out of plain fabric, which you can dye or decorate – they make fabulous gifts.

STEP 1

Place your square of fabric on an ironing board and fold a little bit of the edge over (about 5 mm or smaller, if possible), ironing it flat as you go. Repeat for all four sides of the fabric.

STEP 2

Fold the edge over again and iron flat. This creates a hem that won't fray.

STEP 3

Pin the sides down.

STEP 4

Sew the hems around your handkerchief, removing the pins as you go. A sewing machine will give a more durable hem, but a needle and thread will work, too.

STEP 5

Wash your hanky and it's ready to use! You'll probably want to make a few at a time so you're always prepared.

Your family's first-aid kit

— Once, all our first-aid products – plasters, gauze and bandages – came wrapped in paper. Nowadays it's all wrapped in plastic and often the products themselves are synthetic or plastic-lined. When choosing products for wound care, sterility and ease-of-use are important. There are biodegradable plaster options available and there may even be some growing in your garden! The plant known as wooly lamb's ear has been used for centuries as a wound dressing (it is also known as woundwort), the furry leaves absorb blood, aid clotting and provide antiseptic, anti-inflammatory and antibacterial properties to help the wound heal. Some people have also reported success with making adhesive bandages from kombucha SCOBYs! But if you're feeling less experimental, paper surgical tape, cotton gauze and cotton bandages and, if you can find them, compostable plasters can be worthwhile having on hand for basic first aid and wound care.

Of course, there are times, especially when raising children, where grazes, bumps and bruises are less severe. Rather than going through boxes and boxes of adhesive bandages every time there's a hurt, we recommend helping your child put together their own first-aid kit, with some soft fabrics, face washers and healing salve. A little water for cleaning, a soothing salve for the sting or pain, something colourful to cover and tie around the wound and a kiss go a long way to healing those little bumps and scratches.

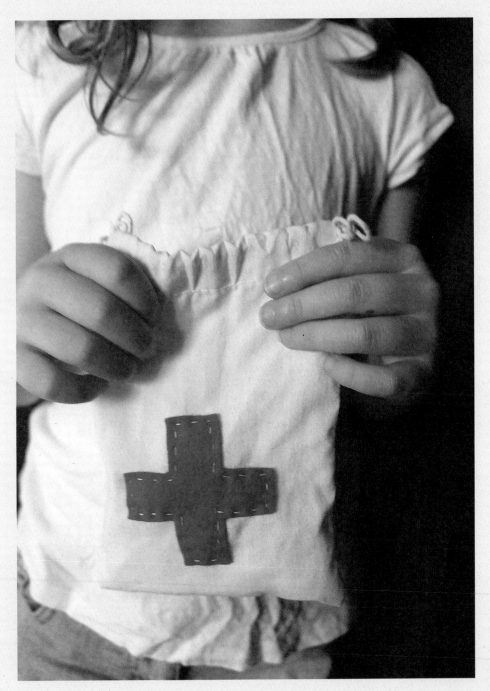

THE MEDICINAL GARDEN

Growing a medicinal garden by your back door can go a long way to providing some natural relief for those times when you need some gentle immune strengthening or first aid. Plants that we can use for self-healing can provide a valuable way to integrate our own needs with the garden surrounding us. We care for the garden and, in turn, the garden provides healthful remedies for us. Consider plants for first aid and general illnesses, such as coughs, colds and allergies, and keep them near to your back door, like the kitchen witches and wise women of old!

Here are some herbs you might like to consider growing and their basic uses. Some can be made into a herbal infusion or tincture, sipped in tea, or made into a compress or herbal salve. These preparations are meant to support and work alongside conventional medical treatments, so run them by your doctor, naturopath or herbalist if you're unsure, particularly if using for infants and children, or pregnant or breastfeeding women.

- **Aloe vera** – burns, pimples, cuts and scratches, sunburn, indigestion

- **Dandelion** – warts, constipation, liver complaints, eczema, respiratory conditions, water retention

- **Calendula** – burns, scalds, conjunctivitis, stomach pain, rashes, cuts, grazes, eczema, cradle cap, warts, stings

- **Feverfew** – headaches, migraines, arthritis, period pain

- **Chamomile** – anxiety, nervous tension, gum inflammation headaches, insomnia, stomach upsets, conjunctivitis

- **Comfrey** – cuts, sprains, bruises, bone or tissue damage, coughs, gastric ulcers, burns – avoid internally if pregnant, or for infants

Echinacea – skin conditions, immune-boosting, infection

Garlic – colds, flu, coughs, ear infections, respiratory conditions, fever, high blood pressure, diarrhoea, insect bites

Ginger – nausea, stomach cramps, chills, colds, poor circulation, toothache, coughs, indigestion

Wooly lamb's ear – wound care, fever, diarrhoea, sore throat, conjunctivitis, bee stings

Lemon balm – colds, flu, fever, headaches, stomach upsets, indigestion, insomnia, nervousness, nervous tension

Lavender – burns, headaches, stings, bruises, coughs, colds, anxiety, nervous tension

Pigface – burns, cuts, stings, ant bites, pimples

Peppermint – indigestion, nausea, colds

Yarrow – fever, wound care, nosebleeds, bruising, period pain, toothache, colds

Raspberry leaf – diarrhoea, uterine conditions, anaemia, sore throat, mouth ulcers

Sage – sore throat, colds, mouth ulcers, indigestion, nervous exhaustion, lung infections, hot flushes – avoid if you're pregnant or breastfeeding

Plantain – insect bites, eczema, splinters, stings, pimples, bruises, cuts, allergies, fevers, bleeding, diarrhoea, cystitis, coughs

Thyme – coughs, respiratory conditions, sore throat, colds, indigestion, diarrhoea, muscle and rheumatic pain

OPTIONAL

Add a sliver of ginger or a crushed clove of garlic for extra kick and healing power. If you like, you can swallow the garlic clove whole and wash it down with the tea.

WHAT YOU'LL NEED

- a few sage leaves
- teacup or mug
- 1 lemon
- boiling water
- 1 teaspoon honey

LEMON, SAGE AND HONEY TEA

This is a classic soothing herbal recipe and it's our go-to when we feel a sore throat or a cold coming on (alongside chicken soup!). Sage is highly antibacterial – our GP swears by it for coughs, colds and sore throats and often encourages patients to swing by her house for a handful on their way home. Fortunately, we have a healthy sage bush and a lemon tree growing in the backyard, so we're set. This recipe makes one cup.

STEP 1

Crush the sage leaves in your hand and put them in a cup or mug.

STEP 2

Juice the lemon and pour the juice over the sage leaves. You can pop half of the lemon rind in to steep, too, if you like. The oils in the lemon rind have antibacterial qualities.

STEP 3

Pour the boiling water over the sage and lemon juice and leave to steep for about 5 minutes. Remove the lemon rind.

STEP 4

Stir in the honey. You can remove the sage leaves if you like, or just leave them to steep longer in the cup and drink around them (we normally do).

OTHER IMMUNE-BOOSTERS

Family life can be so busy, and it's really easy to start feeling run down when you're missing out on sleep or not eating as well as you'd like. We try boosting our mineral intake by taking warm baths with Epsom salts or magnesium flakes, or sprinkling dried herbs and seaweed on meals. We keep a few immune-boosting recipes up our sleeves for when we're feeling extra run-down, particularly for the cold and flu season. Tonics and tinctures made from foods in your kitchen, or ingredients that can be foraged in your neighbourhood, can bring a wonderful immune-system boost to pick you up when you're feeling poorly, or to lessen the severity of symptoms.

TIP
We like to forage for fresh berries and make a syrup in late summer, so we're ready for the start of the cold and flu season.

WHAT YOU'LL NEED

- fresh elderberries
- 1–2 lemons
- raw sugar or honey
- sterilised bottles

ELDERBERRY SYRUP

Black elderberry has long been used as a healing medicine in traditional cultures, and has demonstrated effectiveness against influenza, relieving symptoms and reducing the duration of illness. It stimulates the immune system, is vitamin- and antioxidant-rich, and antiviral. It's perfect to take when you feel a niggling sore throat coming on.

STEP 1

Wash and de-stem the elderberries. The berries fall off quickly when you comb the stems with a fork.

STEP 2

Place the berries in a large saucepan with twice the amount of water.

STEP 3

Add the lemon zest and juice.

STEP 4

Bring to a simmer and cook for 20–30 minutes, or until the liquid has reduced by about half.

STEP 5

Strain the liquid and measure it before pouring it back into the pan.

STEP 6

Add an equal amount of sugar or honey to the pot, then stir to dissolve and mix well.

STEP 7

Pour the syrup into sterilised bottles (see page 49) and refrigerate. Take a tablespoon of syrup when needed, or mix it into some water like a cordial.

PACKAGING

WHAT YOU'LL NEED

- fresh elderberries (enough to almost fill your jar)
- vodka (enough to cover the berries in your jar)
- 1 glass jar
- 1 sterilised glass bottle with a dropper

ELDERBERRY TINCTURE

We like to keep some elderberries aside to make an extract, or fresh plant tincture, which will store for up to two years, and can keep us in good health if the syrup runs out. Adults can take 20–30 drops, up to three times daily, in water or under the tongue. Check with a doctor or naturopath if you're uncertain, particularly if you are pregnant, breastfeeding or have an autoimmune condition.

STEP 1

Clean and de-stem the elderberries, as described opposite.

STEP 2

Place the berries in the jar, leaving about 2 cm at the top.

STEP 3

Cover the berries with vodka and screw the lid on the jar.

STEP 4

Store in a cool, dark place for 6–8 weeks.

STEP 5

Strain and pour into a sterilised glass bottle with a dropper.

STEP 6

Keep stored away from light, and use as required.

WHAT YOU'LL NEED

• 4–5 cumquats

• honey, to taste

CUMQUAT TEA

Cumquats have been used in traditional Chinese medicine for centuries. They are super high in vitamin C, and can relieve symptoms of a cough and sore throat. This drink can be enjoyed hot or cold, and makes a nice change from traditional lemon and honey.

STEP 1

Pour a mug of water into a saucepan and bring to the boil.

STEP 2

Remove from the heat and add the cumquats, squeezing them and breaking the skins a little as you add them. Most of the sweetness and vitamin C is in the peel.

STEP 3

Steep for a few minutes, then strain into your mug.

STEP 4

Stir in honey, to taste.

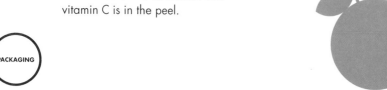

MAKE THIS

WHAT YOU'LL NEED

- 1 large glass jar
- 1 small handful each of rosemary, sage, thyme, mint and lavender
- grated zest of 1 lemon
- 4–5 garlic cloves
- apple cider vinegar – preferably organic

OPTIONAL EXTRAS:

- 5 cloves
- 1 cinnamon stick
- 1 tablespoon grated ginger
- 1 tablespoon grated fresh turmeric

GARDEN SCAVENGER'S VINEGAR

People have been using vinegar, herbs and other common foods as healing medicine since antiquity. Hippocrates is purported to have been a fan of a blend of honey and vinegar (called oxymel). Legend also has it that a vinegar and herb concoction, known as Four Thieves Vinegar, spared the lives of four grave robbers in medieval France from bubonic plague! Due to the antibacterial and antiviral properties of the ingredients, and their ability to deter pests, such as fleas (carriers of bubonic plague), there may be some truth to the legend.

This is our home garden version of Four Thieves Vinegar, using ingredients we grow ourselves (and some we keep in the kitchen). This recipe can be used as an immune-system booster, for the treatment and prevention of coughs, colds and mild fevers, as a digestive aid, a salad dressing, hair rinse, hand wash, deodorant, disinfectant for house cleaning, as mosquito, flea and tick repellent, and as a refreshing skin cleanser and toner. There are probably a bunch of other uses we haven't thought of yet! You might like to investigate the properties of herbs available to you and make up your own family's special blend, arming yourselves with a basket and seeing what you can find around your own (or a friend's) garden. It's lots of fun for kids to make, and you may find they enjoy using a preparation they've had a hand in making themselves.

PACKAGING

STEP 1

Take the clean glass jar and add the herbs, lemon zest, garlic and any optional extras until the ingredients are lightly packed to about 2 cm below the rim of the jar.

STEP 2

Pour the apple cider vinegar into the jar, covering the ingredients and filling the jar to the top.

STEP 3

Screw the lid on, shake the jar, then store away from direct sunlight for 6 weeks, shaking it from time to time.

STEP 4

Strain the liquid and pour it into a clean bottle or jar for use. It should store well for 2 years. You may like to add honey if you're using it as an immune-booster, and sip as needed. Alternatively, dilute one-part liquid to one-part water for skin, hair and insect treatments. Add the liquid to olive oil for a salad dressing.

IN SUMMARY

- Over-consumption, particularly of single-use packaged products, is causing harm to oceans and other environments. Fortunately, the wastefulness of single-use packaging is often avoidable.

- Try to make a conscious decision to refuse to consume wasteful things and reduce consumption of unavoidable items.

- Look for shops where you can buy food and products that can be taken away in your own bags and containers. Embrace reusable packaging that will remain useful for a long time.

- By making some of your own personal care products, you can save money, avoid packaging and you will know much more about what ingredients go into the stuff you use.

- Much of what we send for recycling is not actually recycled. In general, kerbside recycling is not part of waste-free living. Look for ways to avoid the items that you previously sent to the recycling bin.

'Buy less,
choose well,
make it last.'
– Vivienne Westwood

chapter four

AROUND THE HOUSE

Keeping a waste-free home

Now we turn our attention to the bigger things around the house. We talk about the decision-making process behind choosing new things for our homes, our pets, our children and ourselves, and how to clean and care for things so they last longer.

Living without waste involves thinking and acting outside what constitutes normal for most people. But that's not necessarily a bad thing. We reckon if enough people switch to waste-free living, then it might shift the goalposts around acceptable levels of consumption and waste. It is our aspiration that one day (the sooner the better), waste-free living will become boringly normal to most people. With waste-free living normalised, those who produce copious amounts of waste would be an exception, rather than the rule. But, to move towards a less wasteful world, we need to understand more about the waste associated with 'stuff' and look for less-harmful alternatives.

One of the best ways to live with less waste is to be willing to refuse to purchase or consume some things in the first place. Do you *really* need that thing? Some items may not have a waste-free alternative – if so, you will need to decide whether abstaining from the purchase is a compromise you're willing to make. And when you can't refuse an item, how do you go about choosing the least wasteful one?

Let's explore waste-free living in more practical depth. We've covered food waste and packaging waste in earlier chapters, and so here we tackle some of the other stuff that tends to fill our homes, such as clothing, appliances and electrical goods. We also address the waste that comes with children and pets.

The waste-free home

▬ As you spend more time considering the waste created by the things you purchase for your home, you may find that your aesthetic tastes change. You may discover a beauty in owning fewer things. You may find that you come to relish the story behind items that have been collected second hand, acquired as family heirlooms, or made by hand for you. You may feel an affinity for items that will last a long time, can be repaired and you know can be composted at the end of their life. Decluttering towards a more minimal wardrobe or set of belongings can complement the notion of living with less waste and less *stuff you don't need*.

Often, links are made between minimalism and the zero-waste movement. There is a notion that having a sparse house with fewer belongings infers that there is going to be less waste than a house full of stuff. But it certainly isn't a rule that waste-free living means a minimalist lifestyle. If you visit our home, you're likely to find shelves full of books, a kitchen bubbling over with produce and ferments and garden resources by the back door, ready for the next sunny day. Not really minimal, but happy and productive and with everything we need to live an abundant, waste-free life.

Legacy waste

▬ We all accumulate stuff. Some of us more than others. Anyone with a hobby, actually, anyone trying to meet basic needs, will at various times buy, make, inherit, borrow, create and/or otherwise accumulate belongings. Some of our stuff lasts a lifetime or longer, like Great-Grandma's ceramic hand mirror, or lovely old teapots, handed down for generations. But the trend towards things not being built to last, and the trend towards planned obsolescence, means that things break, lose their function and become waste. The waste that results from the stuff you owned before making that decision to go waste free is termed *legacy waste*.

For anyone switching to a waste-free lifestyle, there can be the warm and fuzzy feeling of knowing that you haven't created any new waste in the last week or month or more. But what about all the legacy waste from other stuff that fills your home; belongings from the glory days when ignorance was bliss, when we bought and wasted with reckless abandon?

What about when our nylon clothes fall apart, when the washing machine breaks, when those so-called sturdy plastic storage tubs snap, when the dog chews the elastane out of your slippers, when you find that drawer of old mix tapes that no-one would ever want to hear again? How do we live a waste-free life when we still live in a house containing items from our past that will at some point lose all function and become waste?

AROUND
THE
HOUSE

Ahh, sweet regret. Why did we say yes to the crappy plastic toys that accompany that fast-food takeaway we bought for the kids? Why did we buy that plastic weed mat that seems to attract weeds more than suppress them, only to create a hulking mass of plastic and unwanted plants? Why did we choose the cheaper plastic-handled frying pan rather than the long-lasting cast-iron one? Such is the benefit of hindsight. We can all lose our minds dwelling on past purchases, on our past adventures in wasteful frivolity. Or, we can be practical and do our best to deal with the mess we've made.

We've lived in our home for more than 10 very busy years, raised three children there, cared for a menagerie of animals and tried to be resourceful and generally survive through life, all the while accumulating 'stuff' to help us grow and learn and live. As a sort of final transition, we agreed to collate our legacy waste and dispose of it as best we could – we sold or bartered some items, donated others and retained some items for re-purposing. Some things were so worn and broken, they were only good for landfill.

We'd urge you to take this process on slowly and don't rush to throw out all the items that no longer fit your lifestyle.

We acknowledged the relatively short life span of many items that we previously thought should last a long time. We noted the lack of waste-free options for some items and the wastefulness of buying the cheaper option instead of saving for quality, or avoiding altogether. We acknowledged the impulse garage sale purchases of items that we never really needed. We resolved to take better care of the things that we already owned. That included looking after stuff in the time between finishing with it and finding a new use or home for it. Leaving stuff out in the elements to weather and rot often rendered it useless.

One big benefit in assessing our legacy waste was that our children were part of the decision-making process and became well aware of the consequences of our past mistakes. We hope this means that their legacy will be minimal and conscious choices will be their normal. We talked and ruminated for a while and felt some sadness and regret over the waste that we made before, but felt reaffirmed in our criteria for any new things that came into our home.

There will always be a transition in seeking to live waste free. Transitioning away from legacy waste is an important part of switching to a waste-free lifestyle. It is not necessarily something to feel guilty about, but should strengthen your resolve to *do better* and shop smarter and find those waste-free alternatives. We'd urge you to take this process on slowly and don't rush to throw out all the items that no longer fit your lifestyle. Instead, use the tools and items in your home until they are no longer useful and beg for replacement. Alternatively, find them a loving home somewhere else. After all, there's nothing waste free about suddenly disposing of a large number of useful things, simply for the sake of a new way of life.

Choosing products for your home

Since the 1950s, the average Australian house size has more than doubled. This means there is more space to put stuff; space to feel *obliged* to fill with stuff. Being content with a smaller space can be one way to reduce your demand for possessions, and it's likely to cut your power bill, too! If you do happen to have a house that is chock-full of stuff that you don't need and don't love, then it might be time to re-evaluate the way you accumulate possessions and donate, sell or re-home those items that serve you no use or benefit.

IN OUR HOME

When shopping, rather than asking, 'Do I *want* this thing?', you might ask:

- Do I really *need* this thing?

- How far has it travelled to arrive here?

- How was it made?

- What is it made from?

- Is it long-lasting?

- Can it be mended easily?

- Where does it go when no longer useful?

- Is it compostable?

These are just some of the questions one could ask around the ethics of production.

The more you ask these sorts of questions, the more they can become entrenched in your subconscious mind. Over time, it becomes less of a strain to have to remember every time you go shopping. In essence, we want to find the most environmentally friendly (i.e. low waste, low pollution, low land-degradation, low harm to nature and low harm to humans) options that we can, that are available to us and within our financial means. This decision-making process is going to be different for each household, so take your time to choose carefully and find out what will work best for you.

We think there is still a place for possessing stuff that is wanted, beyond the most basic needs. Waste-free living does not mean imposing a level of frugality on yourself that takes all the fun out of life! For example, we love art, music and books and follow a variety of creative pursuits. These all bring us joy and support our mental health and general happiness. But, as much as possible, we follow these hobbies and activities without accumulating waste. We buy second-hand books and vinyl records that have lasted decades and should last many more with good care. If buying online, we communicate with the seller that we'd prefer compostable packaging for our order. With this approach, you may be able to meet your wants in a low-waste or waste-free way.

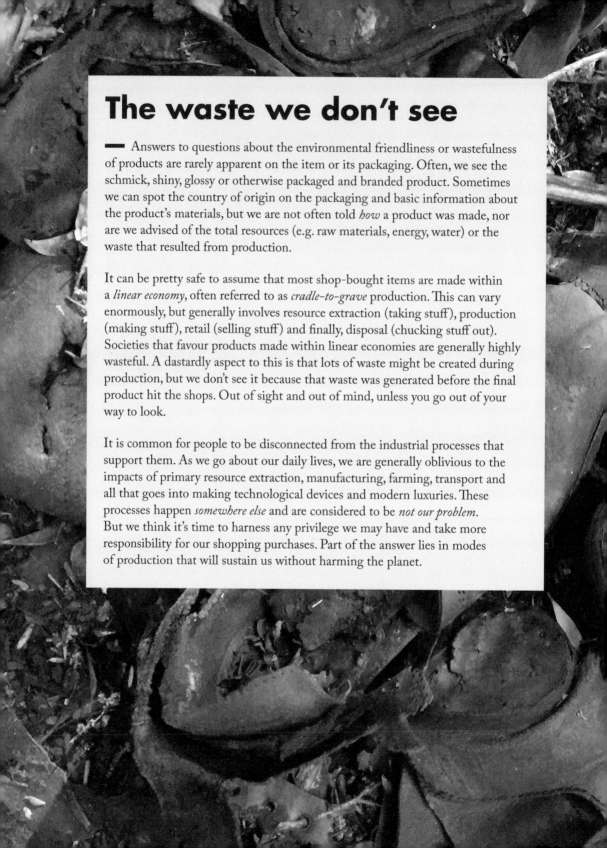

The waste we don't see

— Answers to questions about the environmental friendliness or wastefulness of products are rarely apparent on the item or its packaging. Often, we see the schmick, shiny, glossy or otherwise packaged and branded product. Sometimes we can spot the country of origin on the packaging and basic information about the product's materials, but we are not often told *how* a product was made, nor are we advised of the total resources (e.g. raw materials, energy, water) or the waste that resulted from production.

It can be pretty safe to assume that most shop-bought items are made within a *linear economy*, often referred to as *cradle-to-grave* production. This can vary enormously, but generally involves resource extraction (taking stuff), production (making stuff), retail (selling stuff) and finally, disposal (chucking stuff out). Societies that favour products made within linear economies are generally highly wasteful. A dastardly aspect to this is that lots of waste might be created during production, but we don't see it because that waste was generated before the final product hit the shops. Out of sight and out of mind, unless you go out of your way to look.

It is common for people to be disconnected from the industrial processes that support them. As we go about our daily lives, we are generally oblivious to the impacts of primary resource extraction, manufacturing, farming, transport and all that goes into making technological devices and modern luxuries. These processes happen *somewhere else* and are considered to be *not our problem*. But we think it's time to harness any privilege we may have and take more responsibility for our shopping purchases. Part of the answer lies in modes of production that will sustain us without harming the planet.

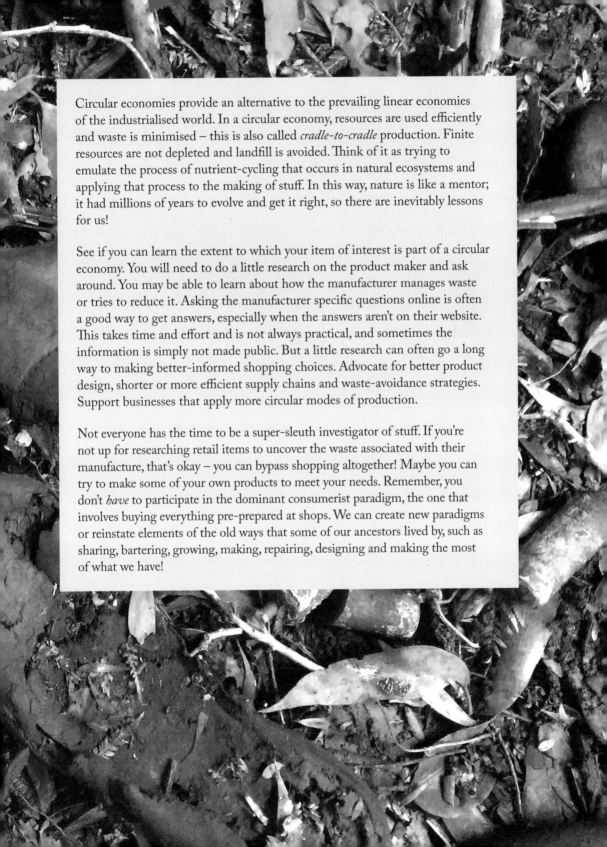

Circular economies provide an alternative to the prevailing linear economies of the industrialised world. In a circular economy, resources are used efficiently and waste is minimised – this is also called *cradle-to-cradle* production. Finite resources are not depleted and landfill is avoided. Think of it as trying to emulate the process of nutrient-cycling that occurs in natural ecosystems and applying that process to the making of stuff. In this way, nature is like a mentor; it had millions of years to evolve and get it right, so there are inevitably lessons for us!

See if you can learn the extent to which your item of interest is part of a circular economy. You will need to do a little research on the product maker and ask around. You may be able to learn about how the manufacturer manages waste or tries to reduce it. Asking the manufacturer specific questions online is often a good way to get answers, especially when the answers aren't on their website. This takes time and effort and is not always practical, and sometimes the information is simply not made public. But a little research can often go a long way to making better-informed shopping choices. Advocate for better product design, shorter or more efficient supply chains and waste-avoidance strategies. Support businesses that apply more circular modes of production.

Not everyone has the time to be a super-sleuth investigator of stuff. If you're not up for researching retail items to uncover the waste associated with their manufacture, that's okay – you can bypass shopping altogether! Maybe you can try to make some of your own products to meet your needs. Remember, you don't *have* to participate in the dominant consumerist paradigm, the one that involves buying everything pre-prepared at shops. We can create new paradigms or reinstate elements of the old ways that some of our ancestors lived by, such as sharing, bartering, growing, making, repairing, designing and making the most of what we have!

MAKE
THIS

BUCKWHEAT HULL PILLOWS

It's recommended that pillows are changed at least every three years to keep you healthy and happy, but as many pillows are made from polyester fibre or foam, that can mean a lot of plastic being sent to landfill. Wool or down are options, although they can be expensive and the ethics of their production can be difficult to navigate. We're lucky to have a sustainably farmed and locally grown plant-based pillow filling near us, so we make our own! Buckwheat hulls have been used for pillows and bolsters in Japan for centuries, and they are often used for yoga props or available to purchase online. If you can find a local supplier of buckwheat, chances are they will have buckwheat hulls available as a by-product, and you might find they're surprisingly inexpensive.

AROUND
THE
HOUSE

Buckwheat hull pillows provide good neck support, and are low-allergy, chemical-free and unscented. The airflow through the hulls keeps them dry and, because they're non-nutritive and the hulls have regular movement, they're not attractive to pests. Buckwheat hull pillows are a little noisier than your average pillow! It's a bit like sleeping on a beanbag, or even a wheat bag/heat pack. They do take a little rearranging and they're a bit firmer than you may be used to, but they're also super comfortable. The hulls are quite light and soft, hold their shape well, and when you get the right position, it's wonderful.

To make your own buckwheat hull pillows, find or make a zip-up pillow protector. Now add a comfortable amount of buckwheat hulls to it. One grain feed–sized bag should be enough to fill two comfy pillows. Zip up your pillow protector, add a pillowcase and you're ready for a good night's sleep. It's that easy! If you'd like even sweeter dreams, scatter dried herbs, such as lavender, rose petals or hops, through your pillow, or place them inside a small handmade sachet before you zip up the pillow protector.

To clean the pillow, unzip the pillow protector and pour out the hulls. Give the protector a wash and if you can find somewhere to spread out the hulls, give them a little sunlight (perhaps on a clean bedsheet or flyscreen away from breezes), which should help to keep the hulls fresh.

Cleaning your home without waste

— Ironically, there can be a huge amount of household waste generated by the products we use to keep our spaces clean. Often the products themselves can be harmful for the environment, polluting waterways and contaminating soil. However, it's really easy to keep your home clean without packaging waste and without the use of harmful chemicals.

Many bulk food shops will sell ready-made, natural cleaning products for your kitchen, bathroom or laundry on tap or in bulk bins, so you can refill your own jars as necessary, or you can make your own cleaners using raw ingredients, also found in bulk.

There are many microfibre products available that eliminate the need for most chemicals, which *could* be a great thing, but unfortunately these release thousands of microfibre plastics into waterways with each use. Look for tools that are compostable at the end of their life, so you can avoid sending plastic to landfill.

YOUR WASTE-FREE CLEANING KIT

Here are some basic household cleaning products we think no home should be without.

- **Bicarb soda** – adds abrasiveness to help remove most tough grime and food. Try one of the cleaning sprays over the page for the bath and shower with a little sprinkle of bicarb for extra abrasion. It removes odours and has antibacterial properties. Sprinkle and soak cookware overnight with water to remove baked-on food. Use it in your dishwasher if you're all out of dishwashing powder.

- **Cloths** – we use old flat nappies or pre-folds for wiping up just about anything. They're great with spills. They replace paper towels for cleaning, are super versatile and last for years. We leave ours in an accessible place so the kids can clean up their own messes quickly.

- **Dish brushes** – we have a few of these for different purposes: bottle brushes for vases and bottles, a small pot scrubber for removing labels from milk bottles, dried food on cookware, or for scrubbing potatoes, and a long-handled dish brush with a replaceable head. Pop the used head in the compost or fire when it's no longer useful.

- **Dish cloth** – ready-made or hand-knitted, these are helpful for cleaning dishes and wiping spills or workbenches.

- **Essential oils** – basil, eucalyptus, peppermint, rosemary, tea tree and citrus oils all have antibacterial properties. They also help remove adhesives and labels from jars. And they help your home smell fresh and lovely.

- **Pegs** – we talk more about washing clothes on page 181, but bamboo or stainless-steel pegs are a must for avoiding the waste from plastic pegs. Plastic pegs only last so long in the rain and sunshine, exploding like plastic confetti under the clothesline when they've had their day. Go for something you can compost, or that will last a lifetime, no matter the weather.

- **Scourer** – scouring pads made from steel wool or natural fibres, such as coconut fibre or luffa, are all compostable. Try growing your own luffa vine for a waste-free cleaning tool.

- **Soap** – good old soap and water is one of the most powerful and versatile cleaners available. You can buy soap flakes, castile soap or liquid soap in bulk. Bars of soap are wonderful in old soap shakers for cleaning the dishes. They use less plastic and leave a 25 per cent smaller carbon footprint than liquid soaps. We find dishwashing detergent useful for making our own cleaning products.

- **Vinegar** – cleans and disinfects surfaces. Sprinkle bicarb in your toilet and add a splash of vinegar, then watch for the fizz – kids love this bit! Add it to surface spray (see over the page). Soften water with vinegar for a final rinse in your washing machine or dishwasher. Use neat as a window or barbecue cleaner and wipe off with newspaper for a streak-free finish.

WHAT YOU'LL NEED

- 1 cup vinegar
- 1 teaspoon dishwashing liquid
- 15–20 drops essential oil – eucalyptus, lavender, rosemary, basil or tea tree oil
- spray bottle

SURFACE SPRAY

We've been making this simple multi-purpose spray from things found in our kitchen for years. We use it to clean kitchen benches and shelves, wipe the dinner table and clean windows and bathroom surfaces. Use this surface spray for the toilet seat, lid and outside of the toilet, or use with a sprinkle of bicarb and a natural scourer for removing soap scum. The vinegar and essential oils act as natural disinfectants.

STEP 1

Place all the ingredients in a spray bottle (reuse an old one if you have one on hand).

STEP 2

Shake until well mixed, then use to clean surfacesaround the home.

FLOOR CLEANER

Place about 1 tablespoon of dishwashing detergent or soap in a bucket with a good splash of vinegar, hot water and some eucalyptus or rosemary oil. Mop the floors while the water is hot so it will dry quickly. The vinegar and soap will help clean and disinfect, while the oil will disinfect and leave your home smelling beautifully fragrant.

WHAT YOU'LL NEED

• peel from at least 1 orange

• 1 glass jar

• vinegar

• spray bottle

ORANGE CLEANER

This is another simple and effective surface spray with natural antibacterial properties. The fragrance is lovely and it makes good use of food waste.

STEP 1

Place the peel in a jar and fill the jar with vinegar.

STEP 2

Screw the lid on and leave it out of direct sunlight at room temperature for about 2 weeks, shaking every couple of days. The liquid will turn orange in colour and have a beautiful orange scent. It will also adopt some of the antibacterial, antifungal and cleaning properties of the orange peel, alongside those in the vinegar.

STEP 3

Strain into a spray bottle and use as any regular multi-purpose spray.

AROUND
THE
HOUSE

DISHWASHER POWDER

Dishwashers are one of those appliances whose usefulness will depend on where and how you're living. They can save water (depending on the model you choose) and they can save you time, although there is waste in their manufacture and transport, and they can wear out your dishes faster than washing by hand. We found a dishwasher incredibly helpful when we had small children who we spent long days and sleepless nights caring for. Unfortunately, we discovered that many dishwashers these days are not made to last much longer than early childhood does, and ours corroded away, requiring more cash to fix than the cost of a new machine after just five years. Fortunately, now our children are a little older, we have volunteers at the ready and hot soapy water and clean tea towels to do the job just as well, and a little faster than our poor old (young!) dishwasher.

If you prefer to use a dishwasher, many bulk food shops carry dishwasher powder you can buy in your own containers. But here's a recipe for dishwasher powder (or tablets) that worked for us, and we've shared with family members who happily use it. It may save you a little money and it's super quick to throw together.

STEP 1

Place all the ingredients in a bowl or food processor and mix until well combined.

STEP 2

Store in an airtight container.

STEP 3

Use 1 tablespoon of powder for a normal wash, or 2 tablespoons for heavy dirt. This may vary depending on how hard your water is and the size of the machine, so experiment a little to find what works best.

STEP 4

To get super-sparkly dishes and glassware, add vinegar to the rinse dispenser.

VARIATION: DISHWASHER TABLETS

To make dishwasher tablets, add ¾ cup lemon juice and omit the citric acid. Pack the mix firmly into ice-cube trays (check the ice-cube size will fit your dishwasher first!), and leave to dry before popping out the tablets to dry completely overnight. Keep in an airtight jar. This recipe makes about 24 tablets.

Clothing

— Clothing retail and production systems have changed dramatically in the last 20 or so years, leading to huge volumes of clothing waste, both in Australia and elsewhere. Lauren witnessed a huge shift in the way the fashion industry operated, while working as a textile designer during the early 2000s. Department stores moved towards selling items in bulk and budget packs, creating more garments at cheaper prices. They also catered to our love of the latest trends and up-to-the-minute style by shifting from two seasonal ranges per year to new ranges released monthly, or even every fortnight.

The demand for new products and higher turnover increased dramatically, leading to higher profits for the department stores and an industry that values quantity over quality. As demand increased, manufacturing moved offshore to countries with poorer machinery and declining fabric and fibre quality. More clothes are being produced now than ever before (approximately 62 million tonnes were produced worldwide in 2017), with millions of tonnes going to landfill each year. In Australia, approximately 6,000 kg of clothing is sent to landfill every 10 minutes. Some clothes can be bought so cheaply that they are considered disposable!

Clothing presents a huge resource problem, with roughly two-thirds of all new clothes being made from synthetic fibres derived from non-renewable coal, oil or gas. Consider also that it takes thousands of litres of water to grow enough cotton to produce just a single pair of jeans, and that cotton consumption is responsible for 2.6 per cent of global water use. Also, up to one-fifth of global industrial water pollution comes from textile dyeing and treatment. Such frightening statistics highlight the need for a more mindful and ethical approach to clothing ourselves.

UNDERSTANDING FABRIC BETTER

To help you keep a more ethical wardrobe – one that produces less waste and requires fewer resources – we've drawn up a simple guide to various common fabrics (see Appendix page 311). Note that the impacts of a particular garment and its component fabrics will vary from place to place, so it's worth researching your chosen clothing brands and materials, if possible.

WARDROBE AUDIT

Have a look inside your wardrobe. What does it look like? Is it bursting with lots
of clothing? What fibres are your clothes made of? Are any looking a little ragged?
Think about how many pieces of clothing you really need, where they've come from
and whether any need to be replaced. Is there anything you can mend or repurpose
in there? Try making a list of any items you may need to replace in the next couple of
seasons and start researching low-impact, ethically produced and sustainable options.
You might like to start saving if those items are a little more expensive than what
you'd normally pay for clothing and footwear.

TIPS FOR CLOTHES SHOPPING, CARE AND LONGEVITY:

- Look for second-hand clothing made from natural fibres.

- Look for quality production – turn over the garment and check the quality of the stitching. How does the fabric feel in your hand? Rub a little bit of the fabric to see if it starts to pill – if yes, then the fibres are immature and the garment is unlikely to wear well.

- Watch for synthetic blends with your natural fibres. Synthetics, such as elastane, can break down and cause the garment to go out of shape, reducing longevity.

- Choose classic styles that will last.

- Think about how many pieces of clothing you really need – don't be afraid to wear the same outfit more than twice!

- Wash your clothes less frequently (only when dirty or smelly), be sure to follow the garment's washing instructions and use gentle soaps in favour of harsh chemicals. Cold water is less expensive and energy intense, and is often sufficient to get your clothes clean.

- Mend clothes and get shoes re-soled at the cobbler. Look for styles that can easily be mended to extend the life of your shoes.

DITCH YOUR DRYER

Clothes dryers can be a convenient way to dry your clothes quickly, especially in winter. But they're energy and resource intensive, with the average household drying 400 loads of washing per year. The energy used to run the average household clothes dryer creates about 1 tonne in carbon emissions. It would take 46 mature trees per year to take up that carbon. Hanging your washing on the clothesline can save you around $150 per year in energy bills. A simple use of passive and renewable energy (wind and sun), line drying is gentler on your clothes, helping to lengthen their life while making them fresher and brighter, thanks to the sun's bleaching effects on fabric. There's nothing quite like fresh sheets dried in the sunshine!

THE DIRT ON DRY-CLEANING

If you've ever had a piece of clothing dry-cleaned, you'll have seen the rows of clothes individually wrapped in single-use plastic bags when you go to collect your garment – it's enough to make any aspiring zero-waster's toes curl. Whilst you can request to have your clothes presented without the plastic bag, there are other wasteful and toxic aspects to dry-cleaning that warrant discussion.

In the process of dry-cleaning, garments are spot-treated with solvents or water (for water-soluble stains) before being submerged in perchloroethylene, a likely human carcinogen (known to cause cancer in other animals). This chemical has been linked to depression of the central nervous system, damage to the liver and kidneys, impaired memory, confusion, dizziness, headaches, drowsiness and eye, respiratory and skin irritations. Perchloroethylene can also be found broken down into toxins that contaminate groundwater and air, plus it is toxic to aquatic life, causing long-term adverse effects to aquatic environments.

FORTUNATELY, THERE ARE ALTERNATIVES AND THEY'RE LIKELY TO SAVE YOU SOME MONEY, TOO!

- **Brushing** – Use a clothes brush regularly to remove surface oils.

- **Hand washing** – Jumpers and garments without lining (even some with lining) can handle a gentle hand wash. Natural fibres, such as cotton, wool, linen, hemp, rayon and washable silks, should all cope just fine. Make sure to use cold or lukewarm water, gently squeeze the water out (do not wring), then reshape your garment and dry it flat. A little steam iron after the process will help return it to the right shape. This may not work for traditional silks or garments with embroidered details, so you may wish to try a different option for those.

- **Steaming** – Try the steam setting on your iron, a garment steamer or hanging your garment in a steamy bathroom while you take a shower. A little spray of lavender-infused water should help bring some freshness to your garment, too.

- **Vodka** – Try putting some vodka in a spray bottle, or dabbing it onto an area of the garment (e.g. underarms) with a soft cloth, then leave it overnight to air-dry. This is possibly the most successful way to remove odours from garments. Any vodka will do, but grab a good-sized bottle that you can reuse when it's empty.

- **'Green' dry-cleaners** – There may be a dry-cleaner near you who avoids toxic chemicals and excess waste. If you're really pushed for options, they may be worth researching further.

- **Read the labels** – You may find it best to eliminate 'dry-clean only' garments from your wardrobe and stick to natural fibres you can clean by hand at home.

AROUND
THE
HOUSE

MAKE YOUR OWN CLOTHES

Learning to sew or knit can add a whole other dimension to your wardrobe.
By slowing down the process of bringing clothing into your home, you can be more
mindful of the materials and resources that go into creating it. Look for quality fabrics
and fibres, think about what styles will last and get making! If you're not skilled at
making your own clothing yet, join a local beginner's workshop, or seek out a mentor
who can help you. Country Women's Associations and similar guilds are often keen
to help beginners. Failing that, there are all manner of helpful beginner's resources
available at your local library and online.

MENDING AND CARE OF BELONGINGS

We live in a disposable society, where reduced quality and mass-production means things cease to be useful quickly. Often we feel we have no option but to dispose of things, straight to landfill. Sometimes things can be repaired, particularly if you choose good quality to begin with. There's value in slowing down and mending our clothes and repairing household items.

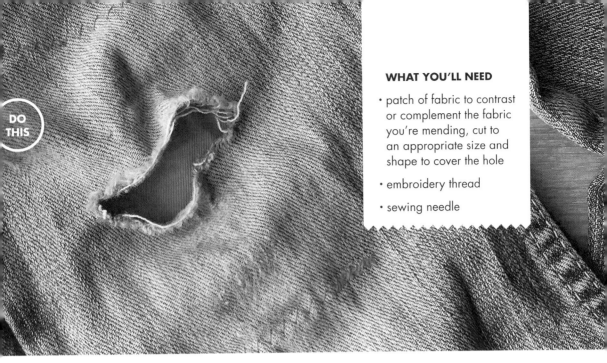

WHAT YOU'LL NEED

• patch of fabric to contrast or complement the fabric you're mending, cut to an appropriate size and shape to cover the hole

• embroidery thread

• sewing needle

VISIBLE MENDING

We can try to hide mending efforts and retain the original form of garments and soft furnishings, but the holes and patches tell a story. There's a certain wabi-sabi, imperfect beauty in a favourite jumper or pillow patched up and stronger than before, ready to be used for many years to come. Visible mending is a method of adding colour or pattern to a loved item, making it individual, creative and truly yours. Try using bright-coloured threads and patches and have fun repairing holes and tears next time you sit down to mend something. Looking to the traditional Japanese mending and stitching methods of *boro* and *sashiko*, you can find lots of inspiration for mending clothing and soft furnishings.

STEP 1

Place the fabric patch behind or over the hole or tear.

STEP 2

Thread a length of embroidery thread through the needle (you can tie a knot in the end if you like), then pass the needle through the fabric using a simple running stitch.

STEP 3

Repeat next to your first line of sewing and keep repeating until the area around the hole has been covered.

VARIATIONS:

You may find the fabric is now stronger and more reinforced than before, and ready for many more years of wear. There are all manner of *sashiko* stitches you could try as you experiment and get more creative with mending your favourite garments and soft furnishings.

Winter boots
(when mending isn't an option)

Lauren had a favourite pair of boots that she wore every day through about eight winters. When they wore out, she mended them as best she could, but eventually it was time to take them to a professional cobbler. Next came the learning curve … the cobbler could only do so much for those old boots. Little plastic patches and glue here and there and a large amount of money to give them just one more winter. These particular boots, although made from mostly natural materials, had been designed using the kind of technology and materials that only allow them one life. So Lauren decided to spend a little more money on a new pair of boots and to make sure her next shoes were simple, with a shape and sole that would be infinitely replaceable for as long as the remainder of the shoes lasted. They'll leave behind less plastic when their days are really through, too. The lesson learned here is that simplicity of design and quality of materials are key. When choosing clothing, footwear and homewares, look for a simple design that can easily be mended and preferably composted at the end of its days.

AROUND
THE
HOUSE

Upcycling

When an item is beyond repair for its intended purpose, finding another use for it before disposal is a great idea. Here are some examples of what you can do with things you might have around the house, once they've finished their intended use. See if you can think of more.

IN OUR HOME

Make sure that whatever you upcycle creates something that is useful, beautiful and long-lasting, so you can avoid sending that once-broken item to landfill for many more years to come. We'd encourage you to upcycle only those waste items and products that you really can't avoid, rather than collecting and consuming a product for the main purpose of upcycling.

- **Shoes and boots** – Planters for small plants and succulents.

- **Socks** – Cut up to make arm warmers, hair ties, or plant ties.

- **Clothing** – Cut up for use in clothing or home projects, such as quilts and soft furnishings, or around the garden, as household rags, or to make stuffing for cushions.

- **Woollen jumpers** – Felt in the washing machine and use for crafting, or to make new, warm clothing and accessories.

- **Sheets and bedding** – Cut up to make rag rugs, twine, clothing or quilts.

- **Pots and pans** – Make musical instruments, a mud kitchen, bird bath or pot plants.

- **Appliances** – Give them to the kids to pull apart and explore, turn into planters, or recycle the components as best you can.

- **Glass bottles and jars** – Make lanterns, terrariums or vases.

- **Bath tubs** – Make a worm farm, garden bed, outdoor bath or duck pond.

- **Tyres** – Make a tyre swing.

- **Broken crockery** – Use for drainage in the bottom of pot plants, or for mosaic art projects.

Appliances and electronic waste

— We live in a culture of convenience and planned obsolescence, where items are designed to have a short life span. This is highly evident when it comes to new mobile devices, gaming consoles, cameras, drones and other gadgetry being released each year and marketed as *must-have* items. New electronic gadgets can be tempting, but they contribute to a vast quantity of waste.

Electronic waste (also called *e-waste*) can come from computers, televisions, appliances, mobile phones, batteries and other electronic devices. Almost all of the approximately 4 million computers and 3 million televisions bought in Australia every year will end up in landfill. When sent to landfill, harmful chemicals, such as mercury, arsenic and lead, which commonly occur in some of these items, can leach into the environment.

So, what can be done to reduce or better manage e-waste? Firstly, check your local waste-management facility to see what electrical goods and appliances are accepted for recycling (this varies greatly between areas). You might like to see if you can buy the item second hand, or borrow it if only needed for a short time; or you may find non-electronic alternatives (e.g. switching from an electric toothbrush to a bamboo one). You may also like to look into options for electronic devices that have replaceable parts to avoid having to discard the entire device when it breaks.

WHEN SELECTING NEW ELECTRONIC ITEMS, IT'S IMPORTANT TO CONSIDER THE FOLLOWING:

- **Durability** – Look for long-lasting, quality objects.

- **Repairability** – Can parts be replaced or fixed?

- **Toxicity** – Does the item contain toxic or hazardous chemical or components and can they be safely disposed of at the end of their use?

- **Efficiency** – How much energy does the item consume in operation?

- **Other ethics** – Are there excessive carbon miles associated with the item and are the makers of the item treated fairly and ethically?

WHAT YOU'LL NEED

• Access to the electricity meter and electrical power points in your home.

DO THIS

ELECTRICITY AUDIT

If your electricity is derived from fossil fuel–based sources, such as coal or gas plants, then you're going to have strong reasons to try not to use more than you have to. Every time you switch on a light or leave a phone charger plugged in unnecessarily, you're going to be expending fossil fuels and contributing to the massive atmospheric pollution that can come from power generation.

Understanding your electrical usage can give insight on how to reduce energy waste. It can save you good money, too. Going through this process helped us to reduce our energy use by 60 per cent in just two weeks!

What is the difference in electricity consumed between the two time periods? How much can you save in a day? The difference between the two time periods multiplied by 365 will provide an estimate of the amount of electricity that you might be able to save in a year with relatively little effort or change to your present lifestyle. You could also aim to save even more if you consider things like switching from a fridge to a deep freezer, having switch-off evenings, showering less often, or by insulating your home so that less energy is required to heat and cool it.

STEP 1

Look at how electricity reaches your home and how your power is generated. Is it coal? Solar? Hydroelectricity?

STEP 2

Note down the current total output on your electricity meter. Usage is usually measured in kilowatt hours (kWh), which is the amount of energy converted if work is done at an average rate of 1,000 watts for one hour.

STEP 3

After 24 hours, note down the total output again.

STEP 4

Make note of the difference between the two recordings.

STEP 5

Now, take a little tour of your house, switching off any power points that are not in use or do not have to be switched on (you'd probably leave the fridge on!).

STEP 6

After another 24 hours, record the electricity usage output again and calculate the difference in kWh since the last recording.

AROUND THE HOUSE

When the fridge breaks

Occasionally, we are faced with an appliance breaking down and the dilemma of what to do about it in a way that results in minimal waste. We'd owned our fridge for about 14 years before it decided to, well, stop working. We felt pretty anxious when that happened – what were we going to do? Say, 'Look, here's my small jar of waste for the year … oh, besides the fridge.'

We considered the idea of building and using a cool-storage cupboard instead of a fridge, but given our requirement to keep meat, for ourselves and our pets, and a week's milk and cheese cold (our milk is only available to purchase in reusable glass bottles at the weekly market), we felt that a cool-storage cupboard would not be sufficient. We did discuss that we might be in a better position to subsist without a fridge once the pets have passed on and the kids have left home!

We weighed up the various factors in buying a new appliance – longevity, repairability, efficiency and the quality of the design and build. The trick was to find the size that would best meet our family's present and near-future needs. We decided to purchase the equivalent model to our existing fridge – very solid build with no flimsy plastic parts that would easily break. With care, it should last our family another 10–15 years. Whilst we found some fridge models with a higher efficiency rating, those fridges had a weaker build and we expected they would not last nearly as long as the model we settled on.

We considered upcycling our old fridge, but then we learned that the shop we were buying our new fridge from had a program for collecting broken fridges for scrap-metal recycling. We removed the glass shelves and plastic-coated metal baskets and the shell of the old fridge was taken for recycling. Also, the old shelves could fit the new fridge if any shelves happened to break in the new one, or we could find another use for them. We understood that not every part of the fridge could be recycled, but the bulk of it would. We found this to be an acceptable compromise.

The new fridge came in a big cardboard box – perfect for a cubby for the children to enjoy and then to be returned to the earth as part of sheet mulching. The fridge had sticky tape holding down the doors and holding some of the interior parts – no option but landfill for that. The bottom of the new fridge had one square of polystyrene – we asked around but there was nowhere to recycle this locally, so it was used as beanbag filler.

Children and babies

—— Discussing the moral dilemma around bringing children into the world, despite the oft-wasteful nature of humans, could constitute a whole book in itself. Human overpopulation is certainly something any waste-conscious human should consider. But, if you do decide to raise a child (or your own mini-squad), there are plenty of ways to keep their waste production and ecological footprint to a minimum. The waste-reduction actions that are considered practical and acceptable will be different for each household, so take what works for you and incorporate what you can into your home life, while meeting everyone's needs in the best way you can.

BABY ESSENTIALS

During pregnancy, you will probably be met with all sorts of options for maternity wear, products to make you more comfortable and sample bags of new products to try. There will be plastic and stretchy fabric and elastic waistbands. There will be lots of decisions to make. So how do you prepare your home and space for your baby? What do you actually need? And, what are the best waste-free alternatives?

For all the helpful contraptions and devices marketed for convenience to new parents, the needs of most babies are quite simple: food, warmth, to be held and to have somewhere to sleep. Oh, and a way to deal with outputs, of which there can be surprisingly many for such a tiny package! As usual, when we look at the options that are closest to nature, we are often met with those which also result in the least waste.

FOOD

The most waste-free and close-to-nature first source of food for human babies is human breast milk. Requirements around making breastfeeding comfortable for mothers in the beginning might include a comfortable maternity bra, or a singlet and some breast pads. Fortunately, there are a huge variety of reusable and washable breast pads available for purchase, or they're easy enough to make by hand. Natural fibres, such as wool, hemp, bamboo and organic cotton, are all wonderful material options to investigate for their warmth, softness, absorbency and antibacterial properties. You may find a comfy pillow comes in handy, too, and although there are a number of purpose-built cushions on the market, the period of time for which they are useful is so small that a regular pillow will often suffice.

AROUND
THE
HOUSE

If breastfeeding is not a viable option, or you've explored avenues of support and have decided to pursue alternatives, you might consider donor milk, milk banks and milk sharing. Donor milk is supported by the World Health Organization and UNICEF as the first alternative for infant feeding where breastfeeding is not available. The use of donor milk is associated with a lower incidence of gut disorders and infections in infants during hospitals stays after birth.

Breast milk can be screened and donated for babies to access from birth, and in some cases parents can receive donated milk from donors well into their child's development. Donor breast milk is an obvious choice because it is perfectly designed for human babies. It is natural, freely available and can be a relatively low-waste option, utilising soft plastic bags, which can usually be recycled. If this is something you'd like to pursue, look into options in your local area.

Formula alternatives are next in your line of options if breast milk is unavailable to you. Homemade formula is possible, but will require a good amount of research and is generally not recommended for very young babies. Commercial brands of formula are also an option, but you will need to consider what you would like to do with your empty tins, whether it be recycling or upcycling (homemade stilts, anyone?).

Feeding aids, such as glass bottles and natural rubber teats, can provide lower-waste, or less harmful options (than plastic) for feeding breast milk, donor milk or formula to your baby. Breast pumps can be hired from your local chemist or breastfeeding association, or can be purchased new. If you choose to buy products that are long-lasting, be sure to pass them on to someone near you who might need them once you've finished with them.

Once it's time for your baby to begin eating solid food, you may notice all manner of contraptions and appliances on the market designed to make feeding time easier. Baby food is often sold in single-use jars and pouches. If you're looking to minimise waste, making your own food is the most reliable alternative, so explore ways to make food in small portions, or freeze larger dishes in small servings, avoiding waste and saving time. Bowls, plates and sippy cups are usually not essential items, but if you do decide to purchase some utensils for feeding your baby, look for options that are long-lasting, or will have use beyond the baby and toddler years.

You might also like to explore baby-led weaning, which does not require the use of special equipment or utensils, or much preparation of food separate to that of the family. Baby-led weaning often focuses on family mealtimes, with baby sampling food from their parents' plate as babies have done for generations.

> Breast milk can be screened and donated for babies to access from birth, and in some cases, parents can receive donated milk from donors well into their child's development.

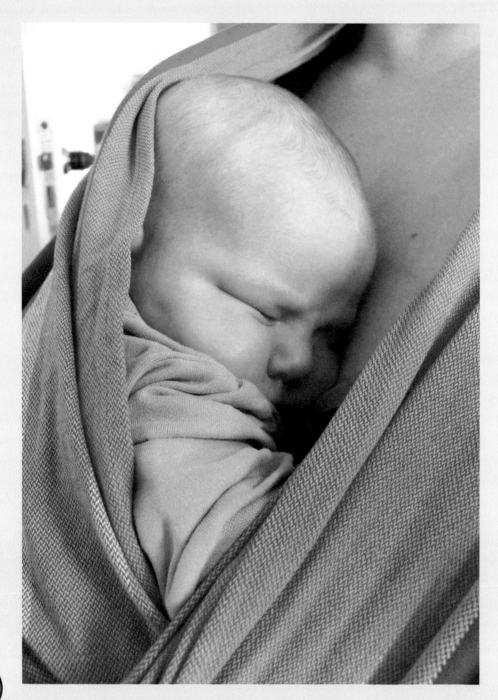

CLOTHING, BEDS, CARRIERS AND MORE ...

We've found that a good approach to choosing baby-related accessories is to apply the same thought process that we apply to our own things. We look for products that will last. We look for products that will serve a purpose well – even better if they serve more than one function. We look for second-hand products first and, particularly if buying new, we keep in mind what we will do with them when they are no longer functional.

It's quite easy to come across good-quality second-hand baby goods. Those baby years really are so short and often the baby will outgrow the products well before those items stop functioning. Making use of second-hand goods can also be a great way to test out what works best for you, because every parent and baby will be different. If you're lucky, friends and family may be more than willing to pass on what they no longer need and you may find you can pass them on again when you're finished.

Do look to your community and see what can be shared.

In our community of friends, there are several pieces of clothing that can be traced through many babies and it's so wonderful seeing them re-emerge on a new little one as the years have passed. Do look to your community and see what can be shared. Perhaps you can pitch in with friends or family to buy products together, with an understanding that they will be shared when there's a need. See if there's a local baby-wearing group that offers slings to try before you buy, or to borrow for a period of time.

Alternatively, you might consider making use of hire companies that hire out baby goods, including clothing and other equipment (e.g. strollers and high chairs). Opportunity shops and second-hand buy-and-sell groups are also fantastic places to find baby goods. Make sure to check for safety standards and recall numbers so your little one will be transported or held safely. Make sure to care for each item well so they will last for any future babies, or for you to pass them on when you're finished. Above all, though, do stop and think before choosing to bring each item or product into your home. Explore the alternatives and what they might offer. Will you need a cot or bassinette, or will you share your own bed with your baby? Will you need to buy a car seat or can you hire one, or will you use public transport or a bike instead? Will you need a pram or pusher, or will a good carrier or wrap work better for you? Will you need a highchair, or is your baby going to be more comfortable on your lap? Without opening another can of worms, you might also like to think about whether you'll be comfortable with that pink, frilly baby blanket if any future children are sons and if not, why not? There can be waste involved in upholding gender stereotypes, and birth (or even earlier, if gender-reveal parties are your thing) can be just the beginning of that. How you choose to parent your children can directly affect the amount of waste they create.

NAPPIES AND WIPES

There are a range of options available to parents when it comes to one of the major tasks of those early childhood years: dealing with ablutions. It can be surprising at first to see just how much waste those tiny bodies create! Your decision to use cloth nappies, disposable nappies or no nappies at all will be a personal one and will depend on your circumstances, so it's worth looking into all options and working out what is best for you.

- **Disposable nappies** – These nappies make up a huge proportion of weekly landfill waste for many families. In Australia, 95 per cent of all nappy users rely on disposables. That makes roughly 5.6 million nappies per day, or 2 billion nappies per year. Each child using disposable nappies produces 700 kg of waste that goes to landfill each year. On average, disposable nappies will cost you $3,500–$4,500 per child. By law, they require you to scoop any solid waste into the toilet before bagging (another potential cost) and binning. Disposable nappies may take up to 500 years to decompose in landfill. Nappies must be sent to landfill, as just one nappy placed in a recycling bin will contaminate a whole truck load of recycling and require it all to be sent to landfill.

There are many disposable nappies available on the market and among them are a range of 'eco' nappies which claim to use biodegradable or compostable materials. To our understanding, there is only one brand of certified compostable nappies available in Australia, which requires commercial composting and an agreement with your council, or a designated pick-up service.

Compostable nappies are also resource-intensive. Most biodegradable nappies still use a portion of plastics, with the fluffy inner forming the majority of biodegradable material. In the anaerobic environment of landfill (as described on page 30), these do not break down. Similarly, disposable wipes and liners create additional waste in landfill. If you're trying to minimise your family's waste, there is little to recommend in disposable nappies.

- **Nappy wash service** – If you're looking for the convenience of a nappy you can remove and bin, but without sending the waste to landfill, then a nappy wash service may be for you. Nappy services can provide a wonderful support during those early newborn days, or busy periods of family life. For roughly the cost of a week's supply of disposables, you are provided with a bin and a weekly supply of cloth nappies, which are removed at the end of each week for laundering, leaving fresh nappies in their place. Companies providing this service usually use environmentally friendly detergents and some even recycle the fabric at the end of each nappy's life. The hidden waste in this product is likely to be in the transportation of nappies to your door.

- **Cloth nappies** – Gone are the days of terry flat nappies lined up on the clothesline, although these were a wonderful option for quick-drying, long-lasting and versatile nappies for generations. Modern cloth nappies have a similar form and function to a disposable, with absorbent natural fibres, such as organic cotton, hemp and bamboo, available to keep your little one feeling comfortable and dry. They don't require soaking overnight or harsh chemicals. Instead, cloth nappy users can adopt a dry pail method, as described on page 200.

  Cloth nappies use 2.3 times less water, less energy and a smaller area of land for raw materials than disposable nappies. They also create more than 20 times less solid waste than disposable nappies and generally result in toilet independence at an earlier age. Cloth nappies cost on average $1,000 per child, although this cost can vary. Given the potential financial outlay, many councils, businesses and local community groups offer nappy libraries where you can trial different styles before making a purchase. Nappies can also be found for purchase second hand, with many of them lasting well for a number of babies, if treated with care. Wipes are easy to make and care for alongside cloth nappies, reducing costs considerably. You may like to make your own from old towels or face washers, or repurpose bought soft fabrics.

- **Elimination communication** – The only true waste-free alternative, elimination communication requires a relationship to be developed between parents and child, in which cues are looked for to determine whether a baby needs to poo or wee. With a little commitment and time spent observing their baby, parents will notice particular expressions and hold their little one over a bowl or toilet to catch each poo or wee. This process can be used with great success much of the time and can lead to early toilet independence and a close communication bond between parent and child.

- **Cloth wipes** – Disposable baby wipes didn't exist until the 1990s, and it wasn't long before they were considered a parenting essential. We've found simple face washers or fabric squares make wipes that are just as convenient and even more effective than disposable wipes. They can be washed along with nappies quite easily. They also come without the chemicals that can affect delicate baby skin and they're far less wasteful. Some families prefer to make pre-dampened wipes with a solution containing ingredients such as water, oils and herbal teas. We kept wipes near the bathroom tap for easy access and dampened them with warm water on the way to the change table, or used a water bottle to wet the wipe. No waste at all and when our babies no longer wore nappies, the wipes became our family cloth system for the toilet (see page 143)!

AROUND THE HOUSE

A tale of two babies
(what worked for us)

We have three children, and between the first and third baby there were some major changes in how we parented, and also what products were available on the market. For baby number one, we pretty much decked out the whole nursery in new products. Beautiful, simple and functional products. We had a bassinette, cot, change table, feeding chair, terry flat and disposable nappies, the appropriate number of clothes (all brand new except for a few heirloom pieces), maternity clothing and bras, disposable breast pads, bottles and pumps (just in case), a baby bath, toys, books, bunny rugs, nappy bag, giant pram and more. There was a whole room ready and waiting for this tiny person. We had everything. We were ready.

And when the time came, as determined by the hospital, she was born with the aid of synthetic hormones, her placenta discarded as medical waste and we began the whole entire process of discovering how to care for a tiny human, encountering all manner of plastics and disposable convenience products along the way. Her waste output had begun at birth. We got the hang of breastfeeding, with some difficulty (and the aid of a hired breast pump) in the beginning, but fortunately without incident after that time. We were given a nappy wash service for three months and then began exploring the world of cloth nappies, which led us on a whole new path of discovery about waste and natural products and alternatives.

Our third child was born in our lounge room, in a hired pool filled with water that was later siphoned onto the rose bushes in our garden. Her placenta now feeds a healthy mulberry tree. She breastfed at birth (thankfully, with great ease). She shared our bed, so the feeding chair became the reading chair and the cot found a new home elsewhere. We were given a pile of pre-loved cloth nappies, so she never wanted for those. We carried her in a simple wrap, which doubled as a picnic blanket or place to rest in the grass while her sisters played. She sat on her mother's knee at mealtimes and happily sampled simple foods while we ate.

The pram and pusher found new homes when we realised they were gathering dust. The only piece of equipment we actually utilised was the car seat, which was still in good shape from the baby who came first. And her clothes were all passed on from her sisters, or from friends and family who wanted to give her something of her own. So far, she has cost very little and has created very minimal waste. And it's our hope that she will continue as such for the rest of her days.

The difference in parenting situations between our first and third child was, for us, huge. The change was representative of the path we walked as parents, learning and questioning the alternatives as we discovered what worked and what didn't work for us. What works for you might be different again, but we feel it's important that everyone asks and learns and hopefully, unlike us, you'll explore those things in the beginning. Or if not in the beginning, then like us, you'll be kind to yourselves and move on gently in a way that feels right for you, your baby and the world they will inherit.

WASH NAPPIES USING THE DRY PAIL METHOD

This is the simplest nappy washing system we know and takes very little time once you have the hang of it.

STEP 1

Remove the nappy and scrape or rinse off any solid waste into the toilet (remember you should be doing this for disposables anyway). This can be done with a special hose attachment that connects to your toilet, a bucket with a small amount of water in it that you use to flush down the toilet, or a spatula.

STEP 2

Place the nappy in a bucket with a lid. Rinse the nappy to dilute urine if you like. You may like to add a few drops of lavender or rosemary oil to the bucket for freshness.

STEP 3

When your nappy bucket is full (usually every second day), pre-wash the nappies on a cold or warm cycle.

STEP 4

Wash the nappies on a warm or heavy-duty cold cycle using regular detergent. Any temperature up to 60°C is fine, with temperatures over 40°C effective in dealing with most germs. Higher than 60°C may lead to the faster deterioration of the nappies' fabric and structure.

STEP 5

Hang on the washing line to dry. Sunlight will help bleach any staining.

STEP 6

It is possible to wash nappies with your clothes and regular laundry. You will know best which nappies you feel comfortable doing this with. It might be just some, none or all. It's recommended that you reserve a designated wash for nappies worn during a tummy bug outbreak and use a warm setting of around 60°C or just below.

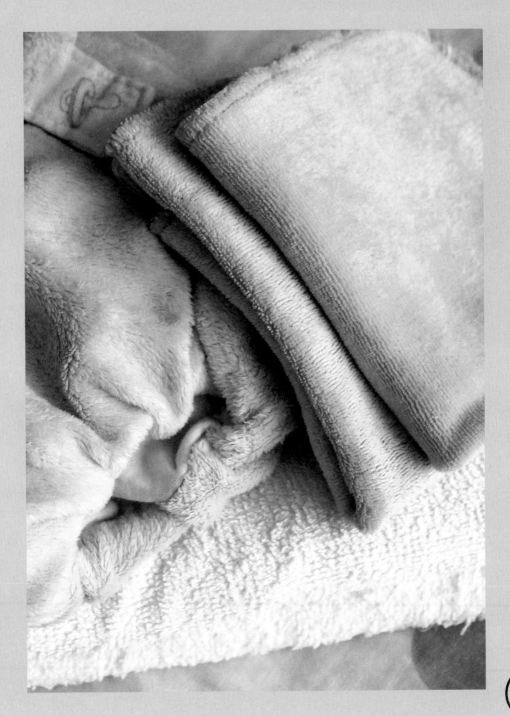

TOYS

It's likely that along the way, your little one will accrue a pile of their own belongings, especially toys. It's really tempting to fill their lives with one of everything. Sometimes it can get a little out of hand and you can end up with a range of toys that sit unplayed with. We reckon there are some simple questions worth asking before welcoming new toys into your home and it's similar to the thought process behind other things you choose to bring into your lives.

Will your child like the toy? This might seem a silly thing to ask, but are you choosing it because you like it, or does it really match the interests of your child? It can be easy to choose a toy you love the look of, think your child *should* have or love for nostalgic reasons, but what if your child doesn't share your interest/taste?

How can the toy be used? Very specific toys that can only fill a singular play purpose can be limiting and your child may lose interest in them sooner. Toys that are open-ended can inspire play over a range of years and offer more versatility.

How long will the toy be useful for? Some toys are built to last, while others satisfy an interest for a very short time. If your toy falls into the latter category, think about a plan for what happens next.

What will happen to the toy when you've finished with it? Can you hand it on to friends or family? Can you pop it away for small visitors to your home? Can you re-sell it? Can you pass it onto a local playgroup or shelter? Is it compostable?

What is the toy made from? Some toys made from hard plastics and natural materials can be very durable and last for generations. Others can break within minutes. Plastic toys make up 90 per cent of the toy market and most of those toys cannot be reused or recycled at the end of their life. It's worth looking at the construction of any toy and checking it for quality and longevity.

Consider whether your child is likely to mouth the toy and whether or not there are any potential toxins present. Battery-operated toys can run the risk of breaking sooner and creating more waste. Plus, they may require specialised batteries that are short-lived and not easily recycled. Toys made from durable natural materials can be easier to repair and dispose of naturally by composting when their time of usefulness has finished.

Can you source the toy second hand? A great way to reduce waste is to buy good-quality products second hand. Look for those classic toys you love at op shops, garage sales and local buy-and-sell groups, or ask your friends or family before hitting the shops to buy something new. You can often find toys in excellent condition and give them a loving new home. Our kids are masters at saving up pocket money to source their favourite toys second hand. They have a particular interest in a certain type of vintage toy that will hold value for resale once they have finished with it. And it provides hours upon hours of imaginative play and storytelling fun for them.

Can you borrow the toy? If your child wants a particularly wasteful toy, then you might like to visit a toy library, suggest they borrow a friend's, share one with a sibling (reducing the waste that could be produced) or offer alternatives. Explain to your child why you don't recommend that particular wasteful item, in a way that might be meaningful to them.

Since our shift to waste-free living, our children seem to have developed their own waste filter when considering toys – our youngest daughter will observe when toys are too plasticky, or if there is a toy with some plastic packaging she will quite cunningly offer us suggestions as to how she will reuse the packaging! Of course, this leads to more conversation and questioning together, putting her front and centre in the decision-making process and helping her understand personal responsibility. Thinking about waste is not a burden for our children; it's just become subconsciously embedded into their psyche, because it is part of their normal.

HELPING KIDS CARE FOR THEIR BELONGINGS

Caring for belongings appropriately can be a valuable lesson for children to learn. By modelling care for your own belongings, you can show your children how to care for theirs. You may find they really enjoy the responsibility of doing meaningful work alongside you. Explain to your child how caring for their belongings means they can last longer. Tell them the story of how they came to own certain toys and why they were chosen for them. Or help them to save up and buy their own.

In our experience, a playroom full of every toy under the sun can be a lot to take in, and can lead to toys being treated with less care. Try rotating some baskets of toys or a small collection of playthings each week, keeping the toys fresh and interesting. Place your children's belongings in an area that's easy for them to access and put away when they've finished with them. We're big fans of baskets and shelves where everything is visible and easy to peruse, easy to place on the ground for play and easy to clean up when finished with.

Show your child how to bathe their dolls, polish wooden toys and surfaces, wipe down plastic toys, wash winter woollens, sharpen pencils, use the washing machine, polish boots, mend tears in fabric, sew buttons … involving your children in these slow and simple acts of care (even if they don't do them very well at first) can help pass on these important lifelong skills. It can also encourage them to care for and value the belongings they own. This can, in turn, extend the life of those belongings and make them available for others to enjoy in the future.

Waste-free pets

▬ People clearly love having pets and have done so throughout history. The majority of pet owners view their animals as being part of the family. In Australia, approximately 62 per cent of households own a pet – domestic dogs and cats are the most common pets (with 4.8 and 2.8 million dogs and cats, respectively, recorded in 2016). And the desire for pet ownership seems to be increasing, as the dog population rose by 600,000 between 2013 and 2016. Australians spend more than $12.2 billion on pet products and services each year. So we are talking about a massive industry and a whole lot of mouths to feed.

Most people feed their dog or cat pre-prepared and processed pet food, and the majority of pet accessories available are made from synthetic and plastic materials. The environmental impacts of owning a pet are often not immediately apparent, but with a considered approach, you can keep the impact of owning a pet to a minimum.

It's well worth taking the time to decide what sort of pet is right for you, and taking the waste that comes with owning a pet into account. Would you like to buy a pet from a breeder or give a loving home to a pet that has been abandoned? Do you want your pet to provide food, such as eggs, for your family, or fertiliser for your garden? Will keeping your pet create excess waste to send to landfill? Is a large pet going to create more waste than you can feasibly deal with on your patch of land? Will your pet require food that needs to travel from afar, or come in plastic or non-recyclable packaging? If so, how do you plan to deal with this?

AROUND
THE
HOUSE

DOGS

Ah dogs, the ultimate waste-disposal units. Always willing to lend a hand to clean the plates after a meal and fantastically useful for keeping the floor tidy after toddler dinners – who needs a robotic vacuum cleaner? Dogs can also generate a bit of waste, particularly in the puppy phase, if you're not careful. Be sure to offer fresh bones and toys made from compostable materials and keep your slippers safely away to avoid any mishaps!

There's also the waste created through dog poo and how it is dealt with. It's important that you clean up after your dog when out in public, to prevent disease and unfortunate (and stinky) accidents for others. Many public parks provide plastic dog poo bags for collecting waste and sending it to landfill, but there are compostable options to consider, too. There are home compostable plastic bags you can buy, but we prefer to reuse paper bags and bring them (and their contents) home to compost in our worm farm (see page 212).

CATS

Cats provide excellent company and help prevent mice and rats from nibbling away at food stores, creating waste. But they also love to prey on local wildlife, especially birds. Birds are important for biodiversity and can help pollinate, fertilise and keep garden pests to a minimum, so if you decide to own a cat, do keep in mind ways to protect your local wildlife from your beloved pet (this includes dogs, too). Most pet cats in Australia eat food that comes in small cans or plastic packaging. This does not have to be the case though, with some cats eating a raw meat or homemade diet with great success. See page 214 for our favourite pet food recipe.

Cats can create litter, which will need to be disposed of carefully. Cats are the main carriers of the parasite that can lead to toxoplasmosis infection, which is potentially dangerous for pregnant women and not great for humans in general. Parasite eggs (oocysts) are found in cat poo. Toxoplasmosis can also harm sea life, affecting mammals, birds and other creatures globally. Sewerage treatment doesn't kill the parasite's eggs, suggesting that your toilet is not a suitable place to dispose of your cat's poo. A compostable bag or newspaper to landfill is another option, but in an anaerobic landfill environment, all that kitty litter will be there forever.

Another option is a purpose-built worm farm. Compost from your worm farm can be buried around fruit trees and ornamentals, keeping your family (and the environment) relatively safe from this toxin. If you discover you have too much litter once the poo has been removed, it can make useful mulch around plants in out-of-the-way spots in your garden. Choose a natural clay or paper litter so it will break down in your garden.

WHAT YOU'LL NEED

- spray bottle
- apple cider vinegar

FLEA TREATMENTS

Fleas are, unfortunately, something most pet owners will have to deal with at some point. Commercial flea treatments usually come in vast quantities of non-recyclable plastic and can be quite toxic, requiring disposal in landfill. Here are a few treatment options to help your four-legged friend avoid those dreaded fleas, along with ticks and other nasties. These remedies are all quite gentle and can be used for cats, dogs and rabbits, but do tread carefully when treating pets, especially when using any essential oils, and watch them for any discomfort. Consult an aromatherapist if you're unsure.

VINEGAR FLEA SPRAY

Note that this is the same recipe as our bicarb-free deodorant spray!

STEP 1

Half-fill the spray bottle with apple cider vinegar.

STEP 2

Fill the remainder of the bottle with water.

STEP 3

Shake to combine.

STEP 4

Apply daily, or as needed, avoiding the eyes and respiratory areas.

LAVENDER OIL
FLEA TREATMENT

Dilute lavender essential oil in 10 ml of olive oil and drop or massage a little at the back of your dog or rabbit's head and base of the tail. Avoid lavender for cats and use rosemary oil instead. Neem oil is also effective for cats, and a little dropped on their collar can act as a flea repellent. Make a similar flea collar for dogs, using lavender.

GARDEN SCAVENGER'S
VINEGAR

This is also effective as a flea treatment – see page 158 for our recipe.

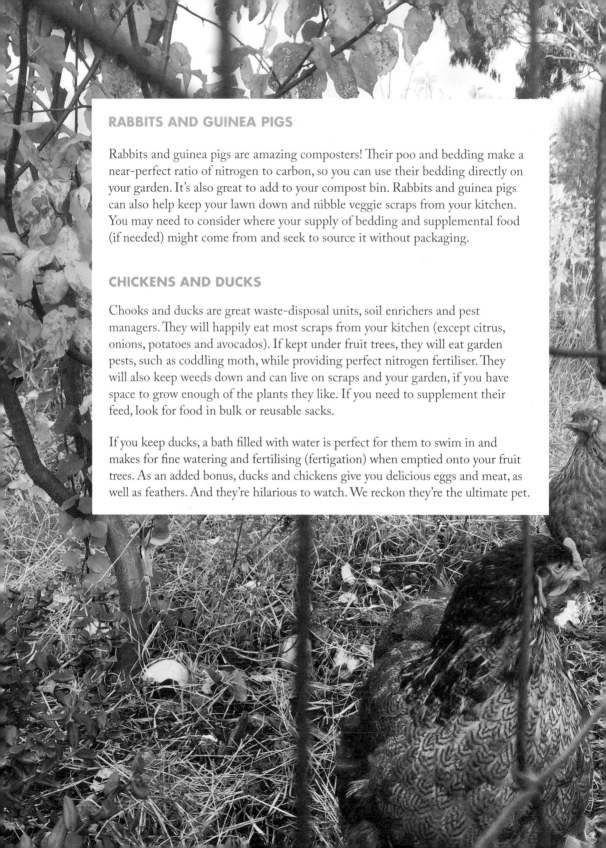

RABBITS AND GUINEA PIGS

Rabbits and guinea pigs are amazing composters! Their poo and bedding make a near-perfect ratio of nitrogen to carbon, so you can use their bedding directly on your garden. It's also great to add to your compost bin. Rabbits and guinea pigs can also help keep your lawn down and nibble veggie scraps from your kitchen. You may need to consider where your supply of bedding and supplemental food (if needed) might come from and seek to source it without packaging.

CHICKENS AND DUCKS

Chooks and ducks are great waste-disposal units, soil enrichers and pest managers. They will happily eat most scraps from your kitchen (except citrus, onions, potatoes and avocados). If kept under fruit trees, they will eat garden pests, such as coddling moth, while providing perfect nitrogen fertiliser. They will also keep weeds down and can live on scraps and your garden, if you have space to grow enough of the plants they like. If you need to supplement their feed, look for food in bulk or reusable sacks.

If you keep ducks, a bath filled with water is perfect for them to swim in and makes for fine watering and fertilising (fertigation) when emptied onto your fruit trees. As an added bonus, ducks and chickens give you delicious eggs and meat, as well as feathers. And they're hilarious to watch. We reckon they're the ultimate pet.

FISH

Fish can be wonderful and useful pets. A humble goldfish will provide fertilised water for your garden or keep bugs to a minimum in a backyard pond. Fish in an aquaponics system will provide fertiliser for plants and food for your family! One difficult part of keeping fish can be maintaining a balanced ecosystem for them to live in. Nitrogen and pH levels need to be kept in check, occasionally requiring the use of cleaners and conditioning agents. Food for fish generally needs to be fed from an external source and often comes in plastic, so do look into the best source of food for your fish if you intend to keep them in a low-waste way.

WORMS

We reckon no household should be without some earthworms! Whether they're composting your pet poo or food waste, or living in your compost bin or veggie patch, they're great to have around. Even the smallest apartment home should be able to keep a small worm farm to dispose of food scraps and provide lush compost for balcony or indoor plants, or a friend's garden.

BIRDS

Pet budgies and parrots can provide wonderful company and nitrogen-rich poo to add to your compost. They'll happily eat garden weeds, such as chickweed, dandelion and milk thistle – do check the weed is right for your bird first, though! Some pet stores offer bird food in bulk or paper packaging, so they can be a relatively low-waste pet. If you're looking to keep a small bird, however, we highly recommend quails. Like a mini-version of chickens, they can provide you with eggs or meat, provide great garden fertiliser and work particularly well for small backyards.

AROUND
THE
HOUSE

WHAT YOU'LL NEED

- A container to keep the worms in. Try an old bath, bin or barrel, styrofoam boxes, old car tyres, a purpose-built box or a kit from your local nursery.

- A piece of mesh to cover any holes and keep the worms in. Fly screen or shade cloth are ideal.

- Some bedding material. Try mushroom compost, garden soil, coconut fibre or garden compost, or lightly dampened shredded paper (this is ideal if you want to compost pet poo).

- Worms! You'll need about 1,000 worms specifically bred for farming. Look for tiger worms or red or blue wrigglers. Common garden worms are great for soil improvement, but not so effective in a worm farm.

- Worm food. For composting pet poo, *don't feed them other food* along with the poo as they'll just eat the food and ignore the poo (who wouldn't!). If you want a regular worm farm for your veggie scraps instead of poo, make sure to stay away from citrus and onions. Worms love soft food scraps, hair clippings, crushed egg shells, vacuum cleaner dust, coffee grounds, tea bags, sawdust, soaked cardboard and shredded paper.

- Dampened newspaper and hessian or similar to cover the worms.

A PET-POO WORM FARM

It is possible to use the waste pets create as a resource in your garden. You can convert their poo to compost in a dedicated worm farm and use the compost to feed ornamental plants and fruit trees (we'd keep it away from veggies and edible herbs, so as to avoid any immediate toxins).

STEP 1

If you're creating a layered box system to collect worm tea, you'll need something watertight for your bottom layer. In a bath, you might choose to place a bucket under the drain hole. If you're using a styrofoam box, place a watertight one on the bottom. Grab the box or container that will house the worms and make sure there are holes in the bottom for drainage. Place it on your watertight, tea-collecting bottom layer, if you have one.

STEP 2

Place the mesh over the holes. If you're using a bath, cover the plughole.

STEP 3

Place the worm bedding material in the box or container.

STEP 4

Add the worms to the middle of the box. If you're using a bath, place them at one end.

STEP 5

Add some poo for the worms to eat. Use the worm farm when you're cleaning up your pet's litter tray or dog poo in conjunction with carbon matter, such as shredded paper or recycled paper kitty litter. Try to keep a good balance between the carbon- and nitrogen-based matter in your worm farm, as we did when making compost (see page 32). If you're using a bath, just feed the worms up the end where the worms were placed.

STEP 6

Place a doubled-up sheet of dampened newspaper on top of the worm farm to retain moisture and keep the worms comfy. Then pop a cover on the worm farm – a layer of hessian or the lid your kit came with will work.

STEP 7

In a few weeks you'll be able to collect worm tea to feed your garden! Stick to ornamentals and fruit trees if your worms are eating pet poo.

STEP 8

As the worm farm fills up, you'll be able to place another box or layer on top and fill it with bedding and food for the worms to migrate to. If you're using a bath, start feeding the worms at the other end of the bath and they'll move along to their new feeding place.

STEP 9

Harvest the beautifully broken-down compost from the previous nesting and feeding box and use it on the garden. Happy farming!

TIPS:

Make sure not to overfeed your worms. Start with a small amount of food and watch to see how quickly they can break it down. Keep an eye on them as you add more.

Don't feed pet poo to your worms if you've recently wormed your pets – worming medication will kill your worm farm!

AROUND THE HOUSE

WHAT YOU'LL NEED

- 1 kg wallaby or kangaroo mince, or organ meats
- 2 cups oats, rice or quinoa, or even leftover cooked grains
- 1 head of broccoli (including the stalk)
- 1 head of cauliflower
- 3 carrots
- 3 potatoes, or 1 large sweet potato
- 6–8 eggs

OPTIONAL EXTRAS:

- 1 teaspoon ground cinnamon (for fresh breath)
- 1 tablespoon ground eggshells (for extra calcium)

- 1 teaspoon ground turmeric (to prevent inflammation and promote good health)
- 1 handful of parsley (for extra minerals and fresh breath)
- 1 tablespoon olive oil or similar (especially if you're using a low-fat meat such as wallaby)
- 1 fish oil capsule added to the meal when serving (for extra nourishment and silky fur)
- 1 raw egg served with the meal a couple of times per week (for extra nourishment)

PET FOOD

There are a range of options for feeding your pet a zero-waste diet, from raw meat diets to home-cooked food. Cats are carnivores, so generally do best on a raw meat diet, including small bones, fish and organ meats, although they can tolerate some vegetables and even certain grains (such as rice) in small amounts. They also like a little raw egg and fresh greens. Some cooked foods can also be tolerated.

Dogs have omnivorous tendencies and can cope with a broad range of foods, so do well with raw meats and bones, vegetables, some grains, eggs, greens and leftovers. Some butchers make their own raw pet food, or you can buy raw bones and meats and make your own. We've found a combination of cooked food and raw bones works well for our pets, but check with your vet first if you're unsure if it's right for yours. It's also important to transition pets towards a different eating approach slowly so their digestive system can adjust.

This is our base recipe for pet food which we alter depending on what we have in the fridge and what's seasonal. We use wallaby mince because it's a local, ethically sourced wild meat and our animals prefer it. But most other meats will be fine.

STEP 1

Place all the ingredients in a large slow cooker. Add water until everything is just covered.

STEP 2

Cover and cook in the slow cooker for 6–8 hours. If you don't have a slow cooker, place the ingredients in a large stockpot on the stove, bring to the boil, then turn down the heat and simmer for 2 hours, or until the vegetables are soft, stirring occasionally.

STEP 3

The mixture should have boiled down by now and become a delicious (to pets) mushy mess. Break up any large chunks and mix it a bit with a potato masher.

STEP 4

Cool and place in jars or containers to freeze, saving some aside to introduce to your pet when ready.

IN SUMMARY

- Waste-free living extends well beyond the kitchen. When purchasing clothes, toys, electrical appliances or other household items, consider the full life of the item and what its end of life might be.

- Find items that have qualities that extend their life, such as durability and repairability. Quality items may cost more, but they should last longer, which will end up being cheaper and less wasteful in the long term.

- There may be large amounts of energy consumed and waste produced before something reaches the shop shelves. We don't often see what goes on during production, and this makes it hard to know if we are making ethical choices. Consider buying second hand in order to minimise the dependence on new and inherently wasteful products.

'Live in each season as it passes;
breathe the air, drink the drink,
taste the fruit, and resign yourself
to the influence of these.'
– Henry David Thoreau

chapter five

CELEBRATE & VENTURE OUTSIDE

Gather without waste

Following the seasons and keeping in touch with nature can help us make minimal impact, while still having lots of fun! Here we look at waste-free gatherings and celebrations with family and friends, exploring nature, travelling, going out to eat, and what to take with us to avoid making waste in the world outside the home.

During times of celebration, it can be easy to forget those waste-free ways and give in to the urge to splurge – to celebrate and show loved ones how much we love them by indulging on decorations, excess food and gifts. We might feel like it's okay to let ourselves off the hook, just this one time. However, waste volumes increase dramatically during the major celebrations, especially around Christmas, due to millions of unwanted gifts, discarded packaging and wrapping, and mountains of wasted food. But it's actually not that hard to celebrate without waste and to do it in a way that still feels fun and a bit indulgent. It might mean creating some new traditions, slowing down a little and simplifying. But, in our experience, that makes those celebratory times seem all the more special.

By planning ahead and being a little resourceful when you celebrate, you can avoid creating a heap of waste. You'll be treading a little lighter on the earth, too, which is cause for celebration in itself.

Seasonal celebrations and new traditions

Following nature's cues provides a logical way to keep waste to a minimum and this also applies to times of celebration. In the southern hemisphere, we tend to celebrate the biggest festivals at seasonally inappropriate times so the meaning and origins of certain traditions can get a bit lost. For example, celebrating Halloween and carving pumpkins during spring when all around us are blossoms and berries, or celebrating with Easter eggs and spring chicks during autumn as we're harvesting pumpkins and apples!

It makes much more sense to celebrate Yule traditions of eggnog, fire and warming foods when daylight hours have dwindled, it's cold outside and you need something to brighten the days. Traditional Yule during summer? Not so much. It just doesn't make sense and feels totally disconnected from nature. So, along with the regular festivals, we like to take a leaf out of our ancestors' books and celebrate the seasons as they happen.

Creating new traditions is something our family loves to do. A little ritual and seasonal nourishment helps mark what's going on around us and puts a little rhythm in our days. We figure you can never celebrate too often. Every celebration is an opportunity to learn new things, start new traditions and have lots of fun. Each time we celebrate, we revisit themes, keeping some traditions and finding new ones. It's a great way to define a family culture and tradition that works for you and to find waste-free alternatives along the way.

If celebrating festivals during traditional calendar times, or at culturally significant times, is something your family prefers to do, look to nature for ideas for food and decorations to minimise waste. The best Christmas and birthday celebrations we've had are the ones where we've taken advantage of the abundance of berries, garden veggies and seafood available to us locally. Plum pudding and dried fruit mince pies make no sense at all when cherries or mangoes are dripping off the trees, which is why fruit-topped pavlova is such a southern hemisphere festive favourite. Have a look at what's available around you, or if there's something traditional that you really yearn for out-of-season, do some forward planning to source and preserve it when it's seasonally available, so you'll have it in time for your celebration. Looking forward to your favourite foods makes celebrating with them even more special, particularly if you've collected and preserved them yourself.

Decorating for celebrations

━━ There tends to be a common urge to go all out when decorating for celebrations and to pay little regard to how those decorations will be put to use or disposed of later. Plastic tablecloths, tinsel, balloons and confetti can all seem like wonderful ideas at the time, but their environmental impact can be devastating and long-lasting, while their period of usefulness can be short-lived.

Balloons are cheerful and colourful, perfect for birthdays or almost any occasion, and balloon releases have been known to occur at weddings, funerals, footy grand finals and community events. Lauren remembers one National Tree Day, standing on the school sports oval at eight years old, holding a green balloon with a little paper packet of seeds tied to the string. Watching the balloon float across the neighbourhood, she wondered what might happen to the balloon and those little seeds. It seemed such a roundabout way to plant a tree! In 2014, the CSIRO found that balloons (most of which are made from a latex- or foil-type polymer) are among the primary sources of Australian marine debris. That accounts for a whole lot of wasteful celebrating. The impact to marine wildlife is shocking, with seabirds and mammals, turtles and fish heavily affected when they attempt to digest balloons, mistaking them for food. Seals are particularly attracted to green plastics, so here's hoping Lauren's tree day balloon didn't make it to the local bay that seals frequent.

Other waste associated with celebrations, such as glow sticks, have been known to turn up in the belly of seabirds, too, so those one-off moments of celebration really can have a lasting harmful impact. So, what are some options? As usual, our cues come from mother nature, the ultimate decorator.

Flowers and foliage collected from your garden or neighbourhood make beautiful seasonal decorations with minimal effort. Fill jars and vases with lush greenery in the spring, or dried flowers and foliage for a winter celebration. Look at what's going on around you outside and bring those seasonal observations into your decorating scheme. Compost them when you're done. Or you could grow indoor plants to bring a little greenery to an indoor winter celebration and then keep those plants around for the long-term. To make the most of natural decorations, you might even like to consider celebrating outdoors or in a garden. We saved a lot of money, effort and waste by holding our own wedding in a conservatory amongst potted flowers and foliage. Our guests were impressed with the floral decorations and overall feel, while all we needed to do was show up!

Ornaments and decorations for celebrations can be made by hand from all sorts of compostable materials. Woollen pom-poms make wonderful baubles and Christmas

CELEBRATE
& VENTURE
OUTSIDE

crackers can be made from old toilet paper rolls and recycled paper you've decorated yourself (see page 224). Bunting can be made from old bed sheets or paper. Hand-crafted newspaper party hats can be as elaborate, colourful and wild as your imagination! If you don't have time to make your own, make sure to look for ready-made decorations and party favours made from reusable or compostable materials.

At Christmas time, choose a Christmas tree that will last for generations growing in a pot, or go for a drive and harvest a weed tree. One of our favourite Christmas traditions is to visit public land and harvest a young pine tree that might have escaped into native bush. Pine trees often escape from plantations and grow on public land nearby. Check local regulations and make sure you're not trespassing on private land and only harvest weeds on public land if it's safe to do so. After Christmas, you might like to compost the tree, try your hand at *hügelkultur* (a method of raised-bed composting using woody debris and other organic matter, to emulate decomposition on the floor of a forest), or save it to burn in the winter, like a traditional Yule log.

Ditch the disposables

━ One major source of waste that is created when people gather to celebrate comes from disposable plates and party ware. It makes sense that we want the host to celebrate with us and not spend the whole party and hours afterwards in the kitchen cleaning up. Sure, single-use plastic crockery and cups can save on cleaning, but the amount of waste generated by just one party can be overwhelming. Plus, it can be lovely to spoil your guests with the real thing – food on *real* plates and drinks in *real* glasses. Use the good china and silverware.

Use real cutlery and cloth napkins and a real tablecloth. Make an occasion of it! Ditch straws, or find reusable ones instead of single-use straws, if you need them at all. Budget options might include plates and old glasses or jars collected at op shops to drink out of, or napkins stitched out of vintage bedsheets.

If you party regularly, you might like to set aside a box of your collected party ware for those special occasions, or collect a shared party stash with friends that you take around from party to party. If you're really on a budget, or not keen on heaps of washing up, consider asking friends to bring their own reusable crockery and cutlery. You could create washing-up stations to encourage guests to share the cleaning load with you, so you have more time to spend with them. You may find they're more excited about spending time with you than the quality of your decor, and guests will be happy to eat off a real plate rather than a disposable one. Celebrate the times you come together with the people you love and take the time to wash up and laugh together after the celebrating is done!

WHAT YOU'LL NEED

- tissue paper, crepe paper, plain paper or newspaper, at least 60 cm in length

- sheets of A4 paper – reuse something colourful, or decorate your own

- paper tape

- toilet paper rolls

- Christmas cracker snaps – some craft shops sell these loose, or you can buy in bulk and share them, or have them on hand for years to come. You can always leave these out and shout 'BANG!' at each other, which is also hilarious if everyone's on board

- trinkets – choose useful things, such as packets of seeds, small tubs of homemade lip balm, pencils and sharpeners, tiny cookie cutters, honey dippers, little nail brushes, wooden spinning tops, wooden yo-yos, keyrings or soaps

- string, yarn or ribbon

CHRISTMAS CRACKERS

Lauren realised early on that the trinkets in Christmas crackers or bonbons were pretty junky, and the paper packaging and waste involved in this Christmas tradition was through the roof. So she's been making crackers for the family Christmas meal since she was 12 years old. Making your own is a great way ensure your trinkets are useful, the hats fit the right heads and the jokes are good (or so bad, they're good!).

STEP 1

Think up some hilarious jokes and write or print them out on small pieces of paper.

STEP 2

Cut strips of tissue, crepe, plain paper or newspaper, measuring approximately 60 cm x 15 cm.

STEP 3

Cut an interesting or zigzag shape along one side of each paper strip (fold them up to make this faster). These are your crowns. You can decorate them if you like, leave them plain, or include crayons in your crackers for people to decorate their own. Use the paper tape to join the ends.

STEP 4

Take an A4 piece of paper and place a toilet roll in the centre of it. Make sure the long edge of the toilet roll matches the long side of the paper.

STEP 5

Wrap the paper around and tie one end of the cracker with string. You can place a little tape in the centre of the roll if you need.

STEP 6

Place your joke, hat and trinkets inside the toilet roll, add the snap so it pokes through each end and tie the other end with string.

MAKE
THIS

REUSE YOUR TEALIGHT CANDLE CASES

At some point, before going waste free, we bought a huge box of tealight candles to burn under oil burners and in candle holders on the table at meal times and times of celebration. Then we were left with loads of aluminium cases and wick bases. Rather than buy new reusable glass cups with new wicks, we decided to try and reuse what we had. They're still going strong after a number of reuses.

CELEBRATE
& VENTURE
OUTSIDE

STEP 1

Prepare the wick base. Using a tapestry needle, try to widen the hole where any old wick may be stuck, then remove the wick.

STEP 2

Thread the needle with some new wick and push it through the hole where the old wick was.

STEP 3

Use the pliers to squeeze the hole of the wick base, holding the new wick firmly in place.

STEP 4

Using the scissors, cut the wick long enough so that it sits at least 1 cm above the candle case.

STEP 5

Cut the bottom of the wick so the wick base can sit flat in the case.

STEP 6

Repeat the above steps for as many tealight candles as you want to make.

STEP 7

Place some baking paper or regular paper on a tray and then place the empty tealight cases on it, ready to fill with wax.

STEP 8

Make a double boiler for the beeswax by half-filling a saucepan with water and adding a tin or jar filled with the beeswax. Melt the beeswax in the double boiler or melt it in a jar or glass jug in a microwave.

STEP 9

Using your fingers or tongs, pick up the wick and wick base and lower it into the beeswax.

STEP 10

Place the wick base in the centre of the candle case and straighten the wick again before repeating step 9. This helps the wick stand up straight and secures the wick base to the bottom of the case.

STEP 11

Carefully pour the beeswax into each candle case.

STEP 12

Allow the wax to cool and harden, then store the candles for future use.

MAKE
THIS

WHAT YOU'LL NEED

- 5 or 6 lemons – give them a good scrub and if they're shop-bought, try to make sure they're not waxed

- a few good handfuls of mint – about 60 g or more. Give it a light rinse to remove any bugs

- 1.5 litres boiling water

- muslin cloth or similar

- glass bottles

- 750 g sugar – we like organic raw sugar for cordial, but any sugar you have will be fine

- 2 teaspoons citric acid (optional). Add it as a preservative and for a little extra tartness, if you like. We tend not to

LEMON AND MINT CORDIAL

This cordial is deliciously refreshing and can be added to alcoholic drinks or carbonated water. You can freeze the diluted cordial to make icy poles, or add it to gelatine to make jelly or gummies. You can pasteurise the concentrate in bottles to keep it for up to 1 year. Otherwise it will keep for about six weeks in the fridge. A batch never lasts long enough in our house, but fortunately mint and lemons are available in our neighbourhood for most months of the year, so a new batch is never far away.

CELEBRATE
& VENTURE
OUTSIDE

STEP 1

Remove the zest from the lemons using a grater or lemon zester.

STEP 2

Place the lemon zest and mint (stalks and all) in a large bowl.

STEP 3

Pour the boiling water over the ingredients and cover the bowl with a tea towel, leaving it to infuse overnight.

STEP 4

Place a muslin cloth, lightweight fabric or fine-mesh bag (we use our produce bags!) over a saucepan and pour the mint, lemon zest and liquid through the fabric, like a sieve.

STEP 5

Sterilise some glass bottles to hold your cordial. We usually do this in a stockpot on the stove, making sure the water boils for 10 minutes. You can do it while you prepare the cordial. If you don't expect your cordial to last long, bottles washed in hot, soapy water and rinsed well will do.

STEP 6

Gather up the corners of the fabric or bag and squeeze any liquid from it into the saucepan. Place the squeezed contents of the bag in the compost.

STEP 7

Squeeze the lemons and strain the juice to remove any pulp and seeds. Add this to the pan.

STEP 8

Add the sugar and heat the pan gently, stirring to dissolve the sugar. Add citric acid if you like.

STEP 9

Simmer for 2 minutes.

STEP 10

Using a funnel, pour the hot cordial liquid into your hot, sterilised glass bottles. Pop lids on the bottles, then allow to cool on the kitchen bench before transferring to the fridge.

STEP 11

If you need to preserve your cordial for longer, fill the bottles to about 2.5 cm below the rim, allowing room for the liquid to expand. Screw the lids on lightly. Pasteurise the cordial by placing the bottles in a large stockpot of water, then slowly bring to a simmer (around 90°C) for 20 minutes. Remove the bottles from the water bath and tighten the lids. The pasteurised cordial should last for up to 1 year.

VARIATIONS:

Try using 3 good handfuls of lemon balm leaves, or about 25 heads of elderflower or lilac blossom, with 3 lemons. You can also experiment with other citrus, such as lime or orange.

Party drinks

— Humans have been brewing and fermenting drinks and celebrating together with them since ancient times. Whether you drink beer, wine, mocktails or tea and coffee with friends and family, there's usually something raised in a glass or cup when people gather. The new year is often seen in with hefty load of rattling recycling waiting on the kerb for the recycling truck. But there are lots of ways you can gather and enjoy a drink without waste.

You might like to have a go at home-brewing beer or cider, or making fruit wines, sparkling or otherwise. Home-brewed kombucha, water kefir, ginger beer and lemonade are wonderful fizzy options, too, with some leaning to the less alcoholic side of things. You could gather with friends and hold a brewing party weeks before the celebration as a way of extending festivities. Some wineries will even facilitate gathering and stomping grapes and then bottling your own wine, which is perfect for a wedding celebration, while making the most of people power. Alternatively, some cellars and microbreweries will happily refill your bottles or growlers, which means you can save lots of glass and cans from going to waste.

As for tea and coffee, you might like to consider creating your own tea blend from garden-grown herbs. Coffee roasters and some tea vendors, even bulk food shops, carry loose tea and coffee, so taking along your own jar to be filled is an option. The majority of tea bags are not compostable, as they include a heat-resistant polypropylene to stop them falling apart when dunked. Brew tea in large pots and enjoy the ritual of it. Instead of sachets of sugar, opt for old-fashioned sugar bowls, teaspoons and milk in jugs. Brew your guests a perfect cup of coffee and serve it in real cups or mugs, then enjoy the warmth of time spent together, as well as the drink.

Gifts for partygoers

— So, you've gathered with your friends and had a wonderful time, and you'd like to give them a little something to take home to remember your special occasion. Gifts also make for a smooth transition for guests not keen to leave! It can be overwhelming creating little gifts in large quantities, but it doesn't mean you need to reach for something that is wasteful or less than useful.

WEDDING FAVOURS

The traditional wedding bomboniere, or small bag of sugared almonds in a little synthetic organza bag, can certainly be improved upon. We gave our wedding guests a tree sapling. In places all around the country, there are now several large river red gums growing with the good thoughts and intentions of our wedding guests. We decorated the wrapping paper ourselves, for a handmade feel.

If traditional is what you're after, you might like to consider a bag made from silk organza or other natural fibres, or try one of the following suggestions instead:

- handmade candles
- jars of personalised lollies
- jars of homemade jam
- bottles of cordial or homemade wine

- handmade soaps
- homemade cookies
- potted succulents

- a mix of seeds of your favourite flowers or edible plants. Offer them in a paper packet, or as a seed bomb (see page 232) – they'll think of you when they bloom!

PARTY BAGS

Children's birthday parties are often synonymous with little plastic party bags full of lollies and noise-makers that break in the car on the way home. But they don't need to be! We've held many birthday parties offering take-home loot, often the winnings of a treasure hunt around the garden.

IN OUR HOME

Here are some alternatives to the small plastic bag of lollies, which might last a little longer and create less impact on the planet:

- Seeds to plant in the garden when they get home.
- Small, stitched drawstring bags made from reclaimed fabrics or bought ready made from organic cotton. Fill with lollies, wooden spinning tops, coloured pencils and other useful treasures.
- Beeswax sandwich wraps.
- A pot plant – herbs that they can eat or cook with later are wonderful.

- A friendship bracelet kit to make at home. This is as simple as some instructions, some yarn or embroidery thread and a safety pin.
- Homemade bath bombs – these can be easily made from ingredients found at your local bulk food shop.
- Seed bombs – these make an excellent party activity and a take-home gift to grow later.

WHAT YOU'LL NEED

- some old paper or newspaper. Add some coloured paper, flower petals, natural colouring or fibre if you want to create a decorative effect

- bucket

- sieve or colander

- blender or food processor

- some seeds – choose edible flowers, such as nasturtiums or calendula, herbs, or something meaningful to you

- tray

SEED BOMBS

Make the most of old newspapers and any seeds you've saved to bring diversity to the garden! Seed bombs store for a few months and make wonderful gifts or party favours.

STEP 1

Tear or cut the paper into small pieces and place it in the bucket.

STEP 2

Fill the bucket with enough water to cover the paper, then leave it overnight.

STEP 3

Pour the bucket water through the sieve or colander. You'll be left with a wet pulp.

STEP 4

Place the pulp in the blender or food processor to mash it into smaller particles.

STEP 5

Take handfuls of the pulp and sprinkle some seeds into it – it can get wet and messy so have a few towels on hand.

STEP 6

Squash or roll the pulp and seeds into a tight ball and squeeze out as much water as you can.

STEP 7

Place on a tray in the sun to dry. This might take a few days, so if you're making these with little guests as an activity, cups cut from egg cartons can be useful to dry them in.

STEP 8

Encourage your guests to plant the seed bombs at home, when they are dry. Or they may like to try a spot of guerrilla gardening (sneaky gardening in public spaces) – just make sure your seeds aren't noxious weeds that can harm the local environment!

CELEBRATE & VENTURE OUTSIDE

Celebrating with others

— If you're keen to stick to your waste-free principles, even during times of celebration, you might like to begin by having a conversation with your friends and family. Let them know what you're attempting to do and why. Suggest low-waste or compostable alternatives they might like to consider for gift-giving and meal planning. Be gentle and listen to their concerns or reflections. Lead by example, choosing low-waste alternatives yourself. Be respectful, patient and gracious around the waste brought into your home by loved ones and focus on taking responsibility for yourself. You may be surprised at how much thought friends and family put into giving you low-waste gifts. We've found our friends and family get really creative with it and sometimes make beautiful and thoughtful upcycled and useful gifts.

Resourceful, low-waste gifts

— Birthdays and gift-giving celebrations can easily bring so much excess stuff into our homes. Plastic toys, fads and gimmicks have great impact on the gift-giving day, but often don't bring much joy beyond the first week. Fortunately, there are ways to offer meaningful gifts that create little to no waste.

- **Choose experiences over things** – Gifts that get you out and about experiencing new things can be just as special and enriching as the ones that sit on a shelf at home to be played with. Even better if the gift-giver can experience it with you. A camping trip, massage, a special dinner at a restaurant or perhaps classes for learning a new skill are all great ideas. We've been lucky to receive family season tickets to orchestra performances before, which was a wonderful treat we all enjoyed. You might like to hand-make a special card to explain the gift so the recipient has something to hold on the day – get creative with it!

- **Choose good-quality, useful gifts** – Something practical that can be used over and over again, making the recipient's life easier or more joyful, is a great idea. Perhaps gardening tools, a sewing machine, a hand-knitted scarf or some beeswax wraps? They'll enjoy thinking of you when they use it, play with it or wear it, for years to come.

- **Choose second-hand gifts** – If you're planning to buy something, start with second hand. Spend the time to seek out that super-special vintage gift that you know your recipient will love. Or have something you've loved fixed up and pass it on to your child or loved one. Think heirloom gifts! Our children have all loved receiving treasures from us and the stories that come with them.

- **Choose compostable** – Give some thought to what will happen to the gift once its time of usefulness has been served. Is it easy to repair if it breaks? Avoid battery-operated gifts if you can. Something that can go back to the earth when its useful period has ended is ideal. Give some thought to the packaging your gift comes in and whether it can be reused, composted or recycled.

- **Make it by hand** – Something you've grown, cooked, knitted or sewn with your own hands is wonderful. The love and thought you've put in to create the gift from scratch really shows. Even better if it's something the recipient particularly likes or needs.

- **Use the 'four gift' giving rule** – It's really easy to go overboard giving your loved ones more than they can make use of. You might find it helpful setting some ground rules for how many gifts you choose. The 'four gift' giving rule can be really useful when giving to children, so you remember to not go overboard. It goes like this: *something they want, something they need, something to wear and something to read.* Following a framework like this means you can make sure you're providing your child with useful things, as well as that one thing they may have their heart set on. We often take advantage of gift-giving times to give clothing, shoes, drink bottles and lunch boxes, bed linen and other practical things that our children will enjoy and use well. And a beautiful book to curl up with is a must!

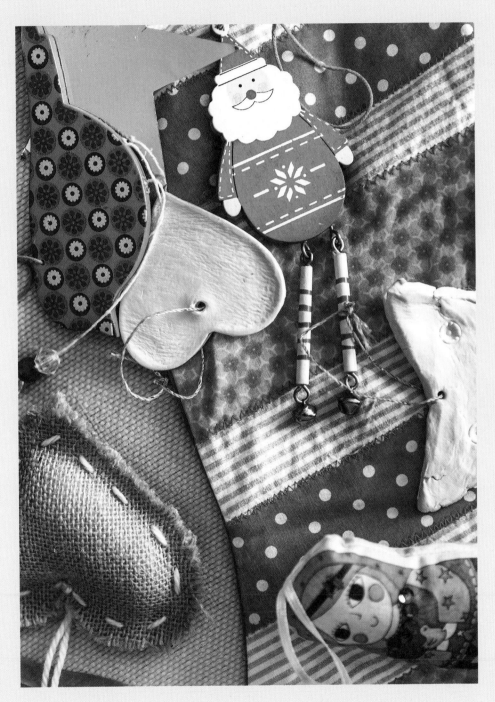

WHAT YOU'LL NEED

- Something old that you can no longer use. Things like teapots and tea cups look beautiful. Colanders, old billies, saucepans, wok lids and tin cans can look wonderful, too.

- A piece of hessian or mesh (this is helpful if your chosen container has lots of holes).

- Some potting mix, or a mixture of garden soil and compost. You can buy potting mix in bulk from landscaping suppliers.

- Plants! Pots full of herbs or succulents make wonderful, easy-care gifts. They're easy to grow from seed or cuttings, so you can make a gift with impact for minimal cost. A colander full of herbs for the kitchen bench or a teapot full of succulents would make a gorgeous gift.

- A drill with a glass, tile and masonry drill bit, or a hammer and nail (optional).

AN UPCYCLED POT PLANT GIFT

One of the great things about plants is that they'll grow in just about anything. This includes things you no longer need, such as old boots and tea pots. Plants also have a habit of making these old, unwanted things look really good, while giving them new life. We reckon they make great, inexpensive gifts, too.

STEP 1

Prepare your planter. If you've chosen a teapot or ceramic cup, you'll need a glass, tile and masonry drill bit to drill a drainage hole in the bottom. If you're using a tin can or billy, have a go at making a drainage hole with a hammer and nail. Things like colanders, wok lids and some utensils might already come with ready-made holes.

STEP 2

Place some hessian or mesh at the bottom of your pot, if you think you'll need it. It's a good idea to line a colander with something to slow drainage a little.

STEP 3

Place the potting mix in your planter.

STEP 4

Plant plants, cuttings or seeds in your pot and give it a water.

STEP 5

Care for your pot plant until it's ready to be given to your lucky recipient.

Low-waste gift wrapping

— When it comes time to present or wrap the gift you're planning to give, there are a few options you might like to consider. You could try making your own wrapping paper from old newspaper, children's artwork, old maps, wallpaper or anything that might go to waste, including old wrapping paper. Drawstring gift bags are another fabulous and easy reusable option.

Another wrapping option is *furoshiki*. These traditional Japanese wrapping cloths are so beautiful and can be a wonderful way to wrap gifts without waste. We've also found them to be quieter and quicker, which is great for late-night, last-minute wrapping sessions! Buy traditional *furoshiki* or make your own using second-hand vintage fabrics, organic cotton or old pillowcases with trims that reflect the recipient's style and favourite colours. Afterwards, collect the fabrics together and keep them in your stash to use next time, or make them part of the gift for the recipient to enjoy and reuse!

WHAT YOU'LL NEED

- fabric pieces – old bed sheets, thrifted fabrics or new organic cotton fabrics work well. These can be a mix of printed or plain fabrics. We find it handy to have some plain white or neutral pieces in our kit for more versatility. Old silk scarves can work well, too, and add a touch of luxury to your collection

- pinking shears or scissors

- sewing machine or needle and thread

- ribbon or twine for decoration

FUROSHIKI GIFT-WRAP KIT

STEP 1

Wash and iron your pieces of fabric and place them on a clean, flat surface.

STEP 2

Measure your fabric into squares in a range of sizes. We find 90 cm x 90 cm and 45 cm x 45 cm work well for most gifts. You might like to cut some longer, rectangular pieces for decorative panels.

STEP 3

Cut and finish your wraps – this will prevent fraying and make them last longer. Pinking shears can work well for edging quick, no-sew wraps. Be sure to cut as straight as possible! If you prefer a sewn edge, fold over each edge, iron it flat, then fold it over again to create a neat hem. Now sew with a straight stitch on your sewing machine, or by hand.

HOW TO USE FUROSHIKI GIFT WRAP

There are many different *furoshiki* folds. Here are the two we use most often:

- Place the wrap on a flat surface, with your gift diagonally in the centre of the wrap. Bring two opposite corners together and tie. Tuck these corners in, or leave them as a decorative feature. Bring the remaining two corners together and tie.

- Place the wrap on a flat surface, with your gift diagonally in the centre of the wrap. Fold opposite corners of the wrap into the centre, laying one over the other and folding in the point of the last corner. Fold the remaining two corners into the centre, folding the points under. Wrap a rectangular panel of decorative fabric around the middle of your parcel. Wrap a piece of ribbon or twine around the parcel and secure with a bow.

CELEBRATE & VENTURE OUTSIDE

Venture outside and tread lightly

— There is a big, beautiful world out there and most of us need (and love) to get out and do stuff in it. But how can we as individuals and families step outside our front door in a way that does not cause environmental harm, or create large quantities of waste? While it's important to look at how your home life impacts the environment and to take responsibility for that, it's equally important to take responsibility for how you interact with the world outside your front gate.

The ways we choose to travel, eat, holiday and connect with our community can all have an impact, but any harmful impact can certainly be minimised. It might mean being more mindful in your preparation before you set out on an adventure, or re-evaluating the activities that bring you joy. We think it all starts with reconnecting with nature and applying lessons from the natural world to other aspects of daily living.

Reconnecting with nature

— We think that one of the root causes of wastefulness in modern society is a disconnection from nature. There is a tendency for people to feel (and often be) apart from nature, rather than a part of it. But when we observe nature and see it as something we are connected to and part of, we can begin to view it differently. Research shows that a connection with nature promotes the adoption of pro-environmental behaviours and the most effective way to form this connection is to get out in it. So, as far as we're concerned, it's absolutely vital for the future of our environment that we experience nature regularly, so we can provide meaningful experiences in nature for our children.

You can bring yourself a little closer to nature very simply, by spending time in your garden or backyard, or (if you don't have a yard) at a local park or reserve. Your children may already spend time interacting with nature, making mud pies, collecting insects and climbing trees – we hope they do! Or you can go on bigger adventures that take you into wilder spaces. In any case, here are some ways to broaden your family's interaction with and observation of nature, by utilising all of the senses and having a little adventure.

DO THIS

WHAT YOU'LL NEED

- Some adventuring gear! Pack a backpack with some snacks and a camera and gear for looking at the world – we're heading outside!

ECOSYSTEM EXPLORER

Observing different ecosystems in nature gives us clues as to how we can keep our own home systems in balance, and helps us connect with nature. It can be as simple as wandering outside your back door, or going on an adventure further afield.

STEP 1

Visit a local ecosystem – a beach, forest, garden, park, pond or compost heap!

STEP 2

Spend some time exploring and playing.

STEP 3

What animals and plants are living there? Is there lots of habitat for a diversity of life?

STEP 4

Take some photos or draw a picture.

STEP 5

Look for evidence of human interaction. Is the area overgrown with an introduced species? Is there rubbish? Are there any built/manmade structures?

STEP 6

Talk about how humans might interact with the environment with minimal impact.

STEP 7

Is there anything you can legally and sustainably harvest or forage, such as flowers, fish, fruit, leaves or firewood? What do you think might happen if you do?

STEP 8

Is there anything we can do to keep the area healthy for the next visitors, e.g. is there litter to pick up? Try and leave it better than, or just as, you found it.

CELEBRATE & VENTURE OUTSIDE

PAGE 242

GO ON A FUNGI WALK

Fungi are the unsung heroes of native ecosystems. They're the ultimate zero-wasters. They help to decompose dead and decaying matter, and many species have mutualistic relationships with plants. However, it is easy to walk through a forest and overlook these often small, but beautiful, organisms. The easiest place to look for larger fungi is in a wet forest or rainforest, although they occur in almost all ecosystems. You may even notice some in your garden. Fungi can usually be found at any time of year, although autumn tends to be the best time for viewing. Children tend to spot fungi easily, as their eyes are usually closer to the ground! Take a camera along and see how many species you can find. Our philosophy is to try not to pick or disturb fungi needlessly, so that the next walkers can see and enjoy them.

DO THIS

HUNT FOR BEACH TREASURE

Our coastlines are a diverse and interesting place, where things can grow and nutrients collect. They can also be where a lot of our waste ends up, both new and old, so you might like to have a beach clean-up as suggested in the Change chapter (see page 281). Otherwise, go for a stroll along a beach and see what treasure you can find there. Children adore treasure hunts and while you're looking, you can check in with the balance and health of this very fragile and important ecosystem. Your treasure might include:

● **Beach glass** – how many different colours can you find? Can you find the rarest of all, red glass?

● **Old pottery** – sometimes old pieces of pottery or china get swept up along our coastlines. It's fun to speculate where it may have come from and how long it may have been at sea for.

● **Driftwood** – lightweight and weathered, this treasure can tell a tale!

Pebbles and stones – can you find any special shapes, colours or textures? They can give you hints about the geology of the area.

Seaweed for eating or composting – check with the local council what their regulations are around harvesting seaweed (some don't mind). Only take what you need!

Seashells – how many different shapes, colours and sizes can you find?

Shore birds – an unusual sort of treasure, but a very important one that's worth spotting and protecting!

EVENING NEIGHBOURHOOD WALK

Our local areas can look completely different at night time, and you may be surprised by the wildlife that is living alongside you most nights if you go for a wander outside your door. Our neighbourhoods can come alive with possums, bats, owls, cats, foxes, insects and so much more.

Urban environments especially can be spaces where certain nocturnal animals thrive, and they can even have a hidden connection to us through the waste we create or the food that we grow. Make sure you're warmly dressed, grab a torch and some friends and go for a wander around your local neighbourhood. Spend some time being very quiet and listen to the sounds all around you and just observe what's going on. How many animals do you see? Is there anything you come across that is unexpected?

While you're outside, flop on the grass, rug up and spend some time looking up at the stars. What do you notice? Do you recognise any constellations? Try drawing lines between stars to invent your own constellations! Consider your place on the planet and in the universe. Remember that you are made of stardust. Tell stories, watch for shooting stars and satellites, look at the moon and enjoy the space and peace of the evening sky.

FORAGING

One of the best ways we know to feel a sense of abundance and satisfaction is to provide food for our family and loved ones. It's even better if that food has been grown ourselves, bartered for, or foraged and provided for free. Foraging is a great way to get an idea of what foods are seasonal, and it's a fun way to get closer to nature while it provides for you. Foraging is an excellent way to reduce food waste in the community, while helping feed your family on a budget. In many suburban and rural areas, there's free food absolutely everywhere, if you know where to look!

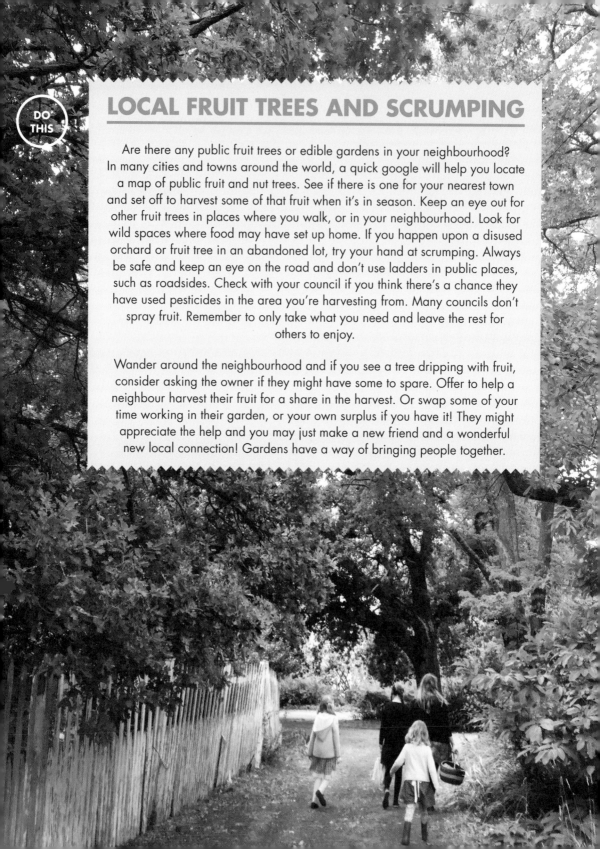

LOCAL FRUIT TREES AND SCRUMPING

DO THIS

Are there any public fruit trees or edible gardens in your neighbourhood? In many cities and towns around the world, a quick google will help you locate a map of public fruit and nut trees. See if there is one for your nearest town and set off to harvest some of that fruit when it's in season. Keep an eye out for other fruit trees in places where you walk, or in your neighbourhood. Look for wild spaces where food may have set up home. If you happen upon a disused orchard or fruit tree in an abandoned lot, try your hand at scrumping. Always be safe and keep an eye on the road and don't use ladders in public places, such as roadsides. Check with your council if you think there's a chance they have used pesticides in the area you're harvesting from. Many councils don't spray fruit. Remember to only take what you need and leave the rest for others to enjoy.

Wander around the neighbourhood and if you see a tree dripping with fruit, consider asking the owner if they might have some to spare. Offer to help a neighbour harvest their fruit for a share in the harvest. Or swap some of your time working in their garden, or your own surplus if you have it! They might appreciate the help and you may just make a new friend and a wonderful new local connection! Gardens have a way of bringing people together.

WHAT YOU'LL NEED

- about 1 kg apples
- 2 cups rosehips
- muslin or old stocking
- sugar – we use organic raw sugar, but rapadura sugar, coconut sugar, fruit juice or honey is fine
- clean jars

WILD APPLE AND ROSEHIP JELLY

STEP 1

Roughly chop the apples, cores, stalks and all.

STEP 2

Pop them in a large stockpot with the rosehips and cover with water.

STEP 3

Bring to the boil and then simmer until the fruit is soft. This will take between 30 minutes and 2 hours depending on the variety and ripeness of your fruit and rosehips.

STEP 4

Place a colander over a bowl and cover with some muslin or an old stocking.

STEP 5

Strain the fruit – leave it overnight if necessary. Try not to squeeze the fruit as the jelly will be clearer if it drains naturally.

STEP 6

Measure the amount of strained liquid and add half the amount of sugar along with it to a saucepan. For example, for 4 cups of juice, add 2 cups of sugar. Most recipes will suggest you use an equal amount of sugar, but we find it just too sweet – this will also depend on what sweetener you choose. There is enough pectin in the fruit to set the jelly anyway.

STEP 7

Simmer the juice and sugar until it becomes jelly. Scoop off any foam that forms on the surface.

STEP 8

Place some clean jars in a stockpot of water on the stove and boil for a around 10 minutes.

STEP 9

Place a saucer in the freezer. Test the consistency of the jelly every now and then by dropping some onto the saucer. When the liquid thickens and holds its shape a little when you run a finger through it, the jelly is ready. Have your jars ready, then ladle or pour the jelly into the jars and pop the lids on to seal.

CELEBRATE & VENTURE OUTSIDE

DO THIS

EDIBLE WEED WALK

Weeds are almost everywhere and many of them are safe to eat and more nutritious than some vegetables we put on our tables! Keep your eyes peeled for nutritious and useful weeds in your garden and neighbourhood. Make sure you're absolutely certain of what they are and that you collect from areas that have not been sprayed. Some of our favourite common weeds you might also find delicious and useful include:

Cleavers – also known as sticky weed. Great nutritious boost for green smoothies and blended soups.

Blackberry – perfect picking for jams or crumbles.

Chickweed – try it in pesto, salads, green smoothies, frittatas and stir-fries.

Dandelion – use leaves for salads and stir-fries, flowers for omelettes, salads or decoration and roots roasted and ground for a coffee substitute!

Fat hen – steamed, stir-fried or used as a spinach substitute (it's delicious and often more nutritious!).

Fennel – often found along roadsides and train lines, fennel gives an aniseed flavour to soups, salads and chicken or fish dishes. Harvest the seeds for tea.

Nettle – super nutritious and fantastic when blended, dried or cooked to remove the sting. Try it in soups, pesto, spanakopita or tea.

Mallow – harvest young leaves for salads and wherever you might usually use spinach. Harvest young seed heads for a protein, fat and carbohydrate boost.

Nasturtium – enjoy the leaves or flowers in salads.

Wild brassicas – use young leaves in soups and stir-fries.

Plantain – try young leaves in green smoothies, soups, salads and stir-fries.

See if you can throw together a meal with the food you've collected. Maybe try your hand at fishing, or see what you can swap from your own garden with a neighbour, to put together a meal that has cost you nothing but time and a little adventure!

Sow thistle/milk thistle – use young leaves and flowers in salads and cook leaves as you would cook spinach, only an even more nutritious version!

WHAT YOU'LL NEED

- large watertight container or bucket
- muslin cloth or handkerchief
- sieve
- tray or shallow, wide container, or a wide saucepan
- wooden spoon

HARVEST YOUR OWN SEA SALT

If you have access to clean, unpolluted seawater, you might like to try this and make a pot of your very own salt! A happy keepsake from a family holiday or summer at the beach, or just a practical way to access a useful resource without waste. One litre of seawater should yield about 1–2 tablespoons of salt.

CELEBRATE
& VENTURE
OUTSIDE

STEP 1

Scoop up some seawater in your container and transport it home.

STEP 2

Put the muslin cloth or handkerchief inside the sieve.

STEP 3

Hold the sieve over the tray and pour the water through. This should sift out sand or debris.

STEP 4

Make sure you have water no more than 2 cm deep in your tray.

STEP 5

If you live somewhere where the sun is hot and constant, leave the container out in the sun for the water to evaporate and leave you with salt.

STEP 6

If the sun isn't so hot near you, place the water in a saucepan on the stove and bring the water to a steady boil.

STEP 7

Keep an eye on the pan as the water level drops, then watch closely as you reach the last centimetre as things will start happening faster now!

STEP 8

A film of salt will appear at the surface of the water and the water will become cloudy.

STEP 9

Push the salt around the bottom of the pan with a wooden spoon and gradually turn the heat down.

STEP 10

You'll be left with a slightly soggy pile of salt crystals. Scrape these into a bowl to dry somewhere warm. Salt crystals spread more thinly will dry much quicker.

TREAT YO'SELF!

Living waste-free can mean adopting new activities as part of your week, such as shopping at the market, or spending time gardening or preserving. Life can become very full! But it's important to take time out to have fun and pamper yourself a bit. A little splurge, or slowing down, can make tricky weeks easier and remind you to focus on the good things. Self-care is so important. Here are some of our favourite waste-free, simple and fun things to do:

- Book in for a massage

- Make your own chocolates or sweet treats

- Have a picnic dinner outside

- Feast on a seasonal fruit platter

- Invite friends over for an impromptu gathering

- Order your favourite takeaway food or go out for a meal

- Pamper yourself with homemade skincare products made from food in your kitchen

- Take a bath with some Epsom salts, herbs and rose petals, with some beeswax candles nearby

- Go op shopping! Remember to look for things you find beautiful or useful, long-lasting and preferably compostable at the end of their life

- Go and see live music

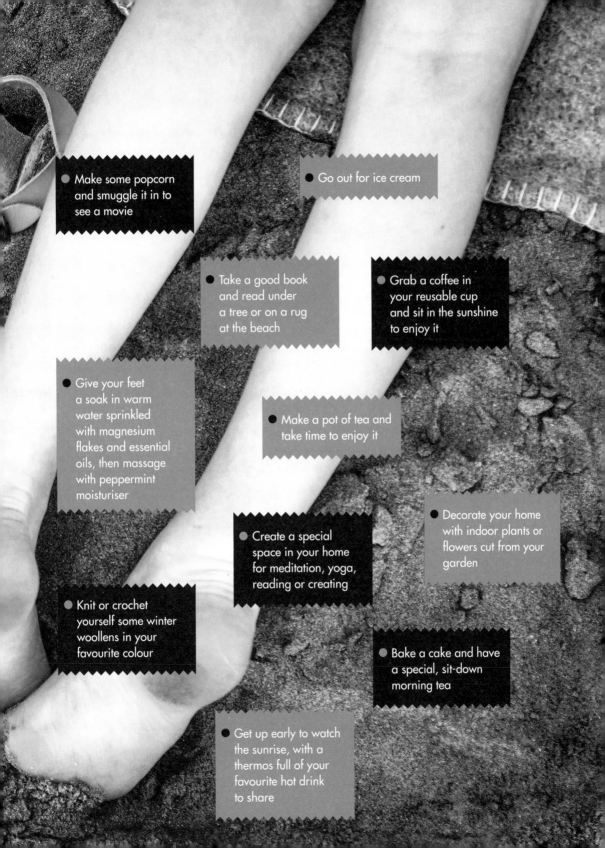

- Make some popcorn and smuggle it in to see a movie

- Go out for ice cream

- Take a good book and read under a tree or on a rug at the beach

- Grab a coffee in your reusable cup and sit in the sunshine to enjoy it

- Give your feet a soak in warm water sprinkled with magnesium flakes and essential oils, then massage with peppermint moisturiser

- Make a pot of tea and take time to enjoy it

- Create a special space in your home for meditation, yoga, reading or creating

- Decorate your home with indoor plants or flowers cut from your garden

- Knit or crochet yourself some winter woollens in your favourite colour

- Bake a cake and have a special, sit-down morning tea

- Get up early to watch the sunrise, with a thermos full of your favourite hot drink to share

LEARN ABOUT LOCAL BUSH FOODS

We can learn lots about our environment and our place in it by learning about the foods that are naturally occurring there. Spend some time finding out about the edible and medicinal plants and foods that are indigenous to your area. Think about the seasonality of food plants. Are berries, fruits, tubers, grubs or game meat available at specific times of the year? Botanical gardens in most major cities will dedicate an area to indigenous plants and their uses. See if you can find out about the medicinal uses of indigenous plants, too.

One of our favourite local bush foods is pigface (*Carpobrotus* sp.) – it's edible, found along most coastlines and works well to treat ant and bee stings, which is very handy when out and about! The entire plant is useful and edible. Leaves can be used in salads and wherever you might enjoy juicy and salty hints of flavour. It's also great for burns and pimples, and the fruit makes a sweet and salty snack and the wonderful jam opposite.

PIGFACE JAM

This jam is an interesting dark colour, but the flavour is amazing! Pigface fruit tastes sweet and salty, with hints of strawberry and guava. This jam is all of that but sweeter – delicious on sourdough with a little butter. This recipe makes 1–2 jars of jam.

STEP 1

Peel the pigface fruit pulp. The red, fleshy skin peels away from the inside ball of pulp quite easily. Save about 2 cups of pulp and pop the skin in the compost or use it for salads or salty snacking.

STEP 2

Place the pulp in a saucepan with the sugar and 3 cups of water.

STEP 3

Cut the lemon in half, squeeze it a bit and throw it in, peel and all.

STEP 4

Bring to the boil while sterilising your jars (see page 49 for how to do this).

STEP 5

Simmer and test the jam until it has thickened to a suitable jammy consistency – it can be really stretchy, which is quite unlike any jam we've ever seen before!

STEP 6

Strain the jam if you like (we don't), then ladle into the sterilised jars and store in the pantry for up to a year.

CELEBRATE & VENTURE OUTSIDE

Out to eat

— Moving towards waste-free living doesn't mean you can never go out and enjoy yourself in the world again. In fact, it's quite the opposite! We all have evenings where we don't feel like cooking a family meal, or we're really craving a favourite food or feel like splashing out a little. While there are some restaurants and types of food that you may choose to no longer support or consume, with a little conversation, you may find restaurants that are willing to make changes to accommodate a waste-free way of living.

CAFES AND RESTAURANTS

If you're out and about and need to eat and haven't brought food from home with you, sitting down to eat at a restaurant is the easiest way to reduce single-use packaging waste. Most good restaurants and cafes will go out of their way to make you comfortable, so you can usually feel confident in expressing your desire to keep waste to a minimum and have that respected. Take some time to get to know your favourite restaurants and their waste practices. Some are going to great efforts to compost food waste and keep their packaging waste to a minimum, so if you can, give these sorts of establishments your support.

> Take some time to get to know your favourite restaurants and their waste practices.

When you eat in at a restaurant or cafe, the main types of waste you will likely be confronted with include straws, napkins and single-use condiment dispensers (such as soy sauce bottles). Straws tend to sneak up on you when you're out and about, so you have to be on your toes and say 'no straws please'! In Australia, we go through 10 million plastic straws per day, and globally that figure is 1 billion – that's a whole lot of single-use plastic. Reusable drinking straws are an option, or you can just use your lips!

Paper napkins are often placed down on the table, according to health and safety standards, to provide a barrier between the table and your cutlery. You can bring your own napkins from home, or if you do end up with a paper napkin, take it home with you for reuse or composting. If sauces and condiments are presented to you in single-use sachets, try asking if sauces can be dispensed into a small bowl or cup from bulk containers in the kitchen (many cafes and restaurants will happily do this).

If there happens to be no reusable crockery and cutlery options at the cafe you've chosen (this is happening more and more) and you've forgotten your kit from home, then see if you can take responsibility for any single-use packaging you acquire. Consider whether you can compost or reuse these at home, or if left at the food outlet consider whether they are likely to be composted or recycled.

CELEBRATE
& VENTURE
OUTSIDE

TAKING IT AWAY

If you can't eat in, there are a few ways you can eat takeaway food in an environmentally conscious and sensitive way. Some single-use takeaway packaging options are made with home compostable materials, such as paper, card and other plant-based packaging. Single-use takeaway packaging made from petroleum-based plastics and certain bioplastics are likely to end up in landfill, and a lot is littered. So choosing what you eat and how it's presented to you is important.

Traditionally, meals like pizza and fish and chips come in compostable paper packaging (they're often our night-off go-to). You may like to discuss with other restaurants if they are willing to place their food in your own reusable containers,

so you can enjoy their cooking at home. Our parents remember taking a lidded saucepan to the local Chinese takeaway to have it filled and then easily reheating it at home. Such a simple and easy solution that many of us have forgotten!

A reusable container in an appropriate size should pose no problem for most takeaway restaurant or cafe owners. Many have already embraced reusable coffee cups, thanks to public pressure and the revelation that nearly 1 billion disposable coffee cups end up in landfill in Australia each year, the majority of which are not recycled. Generally there is no health and safety law against using your own reusable container, however a business can reserve the right to refuse your containers and that should be respected. Remember, it's always important that your reusable containers are clean and appropriate for the food or drink you're buying.

WASTE-FREE OUTINGS KIT

Leaving the house and our usual home habits can be where our waste-free intentions fall by the wayside. Here are some ideas for tools for eating and drinking that you might like to keep in a bag or in the car, or to help you plan ahead before stepping outside your front door:

● thermos

● reusable coffee cup

● reusable straws

● reusable chopsticks

enamel plates/cups

lunchbox or container

drink bottle

cloth napkin

reusable cutlery

Getting there

— The world is a far more connected place for humans than it used to be. In the good old days (we're talking pre-nineteenth century), few people ventured far from their home turf, except for intrepid explorers, merchants, pilgrims and military folk. But since the advent of trains, planes and automobiles, and especially since the advent of affordable aviation, millions of people have been scooting around the world with reckless abandon.

Long-distance travel has become the norm, rather than the exception. The vast majority of long-distance travel by humans is by oil-fuelled cars and planes, which contribute large quantities of greenhouse gas emissions. Globally, the tourism sector is responsible for approximately 5 per cent of global carbon dioxide emissions and 75 per cent of this comes from transport (car, rail and planes).

We often rely on cars and motorised vehicles for short-distance travel and this, too, contributes considerable greenhouse gas emissions. Petrol-fuelled cars may require up to 10 km driving distance before they warm up and operate at their most efficient. Rather than falling back on the convenience of the car, consider what shops and services you can get to with just the power of your feet. Remember, your body is a renewable resource! Use your own body's energy to help you get around by walking or cycling.

Walking helps to keep us healthy and allows us to interact more directly with our neighbourhood. We recognise that walking expends energy, which means needing to replenish ourselves with food. So, as long as the carbon footprint (or other impacts) relating to your food is relatively low, walking will be a better choice for you and the environment.

The mode of transport that works best in your situation will depend on your local public transport service, topography (too hilly?), safety concerns (waiting in dark, dodgy train stations and bus stops alone are not fun), weather, time of day, fitness level and personal preference. We sometimes find that if Oberon is late for work and in a rush, we might drive our car to the bakery to pick up bread, when ideally we would walk or ride a bike. This reminds us that we can be less wasteful if we try to be a little more organised, especially around food, and to remember that it's okay to slow down.

If you are in the position of choosing a car to buy, consider the fuel efficiency of the vehicle. A compact two-wheel drive car may emit only half of the fuel-related greenhouse gas emissions as a four-wheel drive of the same model. Cars are often promoted for power and space features, but these may come with poorer fuel efficiency. The efficiency and lifetime carbon footprint of cars varies enormously, so be sure to do your research first.

In general, travelling by train or bus will contribute far fewer carbon dioxide emissions per person than driving a car. However, some new electric cars fuelled by renewable energy can emit far less greenhouse gas than the average petrol-fuelled vehicle. Support those modes of transport that cause least environmental harm.

Air travel

— It may go without saying, but we think it is worth considering the need to travel. Of course, only you can determine whether a plane flight or long car drive is necessary, whether it is for work, pleasure of for other personal reasons. We think it is worth keeping in mind that sometimes alternatives to travel exist; for example, with new technologies, such as video conferencing, some work meetings can be conducted without numerous people having to travel long distances. It helps to ask yourself: can I do what I need to do with fewer trips, or by travelling somewhere closer to home? Air travel can be a wasteful process, so let's talk about ways to reduce that waste.

Australian airline travel contributes approximately 3 per cent of Australia's carbon dioxide emissions. When planes fly in the upper troposphere and lower stratosphere, the gas emissions (e.g. carbon dioxide and nitrous oxide) have multiplying impacts on the earth's climate to the extent that the impact of a plane is approximately double its carbon dioxide emissions. So, we're already off to a pretty wasteful and polluting start, even before the snacks are served.

Once the plane gets to cruising speed, the cabin crew roll their meal carts down the aisle and dish out snacks. On longer domestic flights, you might get a more substantial meal. Usually, there is also an in-flight food menu available. Packaging waste is inevitable – by way of confectionery wrappers, plastic coffee stirrers, plastic wrap, plastic milk pods, headphones wrappers and other assorted single-use waste. Ugh. On a single long-haul flight, there can be 500 kg of waste produced! In 2017–18, there were approximately 60 million passengers carried on domestic flights in Australia. So, what appears as small amounts of waste to the individual can add up to quite the waste monster when multiplied by tens of millions per year.

Some airlines are making efforts to reduce waste production and to improve their own waste management, such as by offering headsets without plastic wrapping, reducing plastic packaging for other on-board amenities, increasing the recycled content of plastic cups and installing more recycling bins in airports. Hopefully, these and other initiatives will see big reductions in waste in the airline industry. That said, we can do much to reduce our own waste produced when we fly (see page 269).

Holidays

▬ Holidaying tends to come with its own set of waste issues – think of all those tiny sachets of jam and vegemite, single-serve plastic shampoo and conditioner bottles, plastic cutlery, takeaway food, packaged snacks, bottled water … and that's after you've travelled the long distance to get there. Just because you expect to see some waste whilst on holidays does not mean you have to accept excessive waste. With a little forward planning and preparation, you can enjoy a waste-free holiday without taking all the fun out of it.

HERE ARE IDEAS FOR MINIMISING WASTE ON HOLIDAYS:

- Explore travel destinations closer to home, to avoid the fuel consumption brought about by travelling long distances.

- Look into transport methods, such as train, boat, bike, bus and carpooling to reach your destination.

- Choose accommodation options where you can self-cater and bring food along with you, or find low-waste food suppliers nearby.

- You may find items that are free to take in hotel rooms or other holiday locations. But you know, you don't have to take them just because they are being offered! If you know that you're going somewhere that offers free sample-size offerings of toiletries and so on, you might like to come prepared with your own products from home, in a reusable container.

- If you're staying somewhere that happens to offer a self-serve buffet-style breakfast, then look for the options that do not involve excess packaging or single-use plastics. Note that laid-out spreads of bread and cheese and cereals in self-serve canisters may have been decanted from regular store packaging.

- Take along your waste-free outings kit so you're prepared for eating out.

- Look for a local market or greengrocer and buy fresh food snacks, such as fruit and veggies, that naturally come without packaging.

- Check if there are composting and recycling facilities where you're staying and make the most of them, or if it's feasible, come prepared with your own container to collect them for composting when you get home.

CELEBRATE & VENTURE OUTSIDE

TIPS FOR WASTE-FREE FLYING

• Take your own snacks in your own home-bought container. If you are in a rush to get to the airport, take your empty container and ask a food vendor at the airport to put food into it (we recommend something non-leaky like a nice bit of lemon tart).

Choose foods that don't require utensils, as you're unlikely to be permitted to take your own on the plane. Check your airline's restrictions with regards to this.

• Carry your own reusable drink bottle. Free water can be found at the airport in the bathrooms or water fountain stations.

• Carry your own fabric napkin or serviette, for those turbulence spills.

• Say 'no thanks' to wasteful airline food. You have the power of choice.

• Utilise on-board recycling facilities, if available. Otherwise, keep your waste with you until you find a suitable recycling location for it afterwards.

• Keep food scraps for composting later, but only if you're allowed to bring those food items into your destination location – check local quarantine laws.

• You may want to carry on a lightweight bag or container for storing food scraps.

• Take your own headphones, because really, why does anyone need those free in-flight ones?

• Take your own reusable cup for your warm drink of choice. You may like to check beforehand whether these will be accepted by your airline. However, most cafes in airports should accept them.

• Carry lighter luggage, because a reduced load will mean less fuel required and fewer greenhouse gas emissions.

• Offer solutions to your airline – you may want to let them know that you would like them to reduce their food and packaging waste and provide in-flight recycling or composting facilities.

• Support airlines that are accountable for the waste they produce and that demonstrate significant positive actions to reduce waste.

• Carbon offsetting is a widely promoted action that is intended to address the greenhouse gas emissions produced by flying. This involves paying money for someone to plant enough trees or undertake clean-energy projects that offset the emissions from your flight. However, there are criticisms of this approach; for example, that offsetting somehow absolves people of their wasteful or environmentally harmful actions and effectively allows people to pay for their complacency around waste. We recommend that people give priority to their own behaviours and try to reduce waste through their actions.

Events and festivals

— A commonly observed phenomenon occurs when people congregate in large groups, especially in celebration. Large areas are quickly strewn with waste. Depending on the event, you're likely to find drink bottles and cans, food packaging, cutlery and napkins and other assorted waste littering the ground and overflowing from bins. New Year's Eve celebrations, sporting events, markets and music festivals are notorious culprits of this phenomenon.

Fortunately, some event managers are leading the way in striving to run waste-free events. Some have introduced systems for collecting organic waste for composting, improved signage for recycling and other waste types, switching to reusable cups and crockery (e.g. using a deposit-return system) and using renewable energy to power machines and equipment. Our favourite local music festival is the Panama Music Festival in northern Tasmania, hosting approximately 1,000 campers for a few days and usually ending up with only a small bag of rubbish for the whole event!

The Panama organisers process compostable and recyclable materials on site, provide reusable cup and crockery options, use solar power, grow some of their own food and brew cider on site in returnable bottles, and encourage attendees to take their own waste home with them. Also local to us in Tasmania, the Museum of Old and New Art (MONA) runs a market during the summer months, where all food comes on returnable and washable enamel crockery. Bins are easily accessible and very specific, clearly marking where landfill, recyclables and compostable waste need to go. The result is a very low-waste event, with minimal impact on market grounds and the environment.

Irrespective of the event, there are things you can do to reduce your own impact at events. As usual, take your reusables kit. For music festivals, don't forget to take your reusable earplugs, too! Avoid giveaways if you're not going to make solid use of them. Consider carpooling to travel to and from the event.

SCHOOL FAIRS

School fairs can provide a great opportunity to engage with children and the local community on waste issues. Many school fairs are run to raise funds for the school or a particular cause, but reducing waste is not normally a primary consideration. We've been to fairs that sell or donate balloons, have goody bags full of and made from plastic and have lots of food stalls with single-use plastic cups and plates, or plastic- wrapped food. A few ways to try to minimise waste at school fairs include:

- Reduce (accidental) waste to landfill by creating clear signage on strategically placed recycling/composting bins around the event.

- Provide reusable (ceramic) crockery and cups for food and drink and set up a wash station to clean these on site.

- Run low-waste (plastic-free) stalls that encourage reusing and sharing items among the community. School fairs are a great place for clothes swaps, second-hand books and toys, and plant or produce stalls.

- Foster a waste-free culture within the school community. If reducing waste is set as a clear aim for the event, then more people will likely participate and identify waste-free solutions relevant to their role in the fair.

- Hold workshops on how to reduce waste, or make useful waste-free items.

- Fundraise with useful products made by the students, such as beeswax wraps or produce bags.

- Offer reusable cloth bags instead of plastic bags at stalls.

- Encourage rides and activities that use people power, rather than relying on generators. Climbing walls, the coconut-shy and wheelbarrow rides are sure winners at our local Steiner school fairs.

- Create a compost heap on site to deal with compostable waste after the event, or arrange for it to be commercially composted.

- If possible, place cake-stall food under cloches, or behind a cabinet display, and transfer to containers brought from home or paper bags. This will help to avoid plastic wrap.

- Encourage the reuse of jars for homemade preserves to sell.

- Make crafts and toys to sell using natural fibres and compostable materials.

- You may also consider making waste (or the lack of it) a particular focus for your school event. We have participated in a number of zero-waste festivals at schools, and these can be a fantastic way to engage teachers, students, family and the broader community around positive solutions to reduce waste at school and elsewhere. These could be timed to coincide with the end of a curriculum that focuses on waste in the classroom.

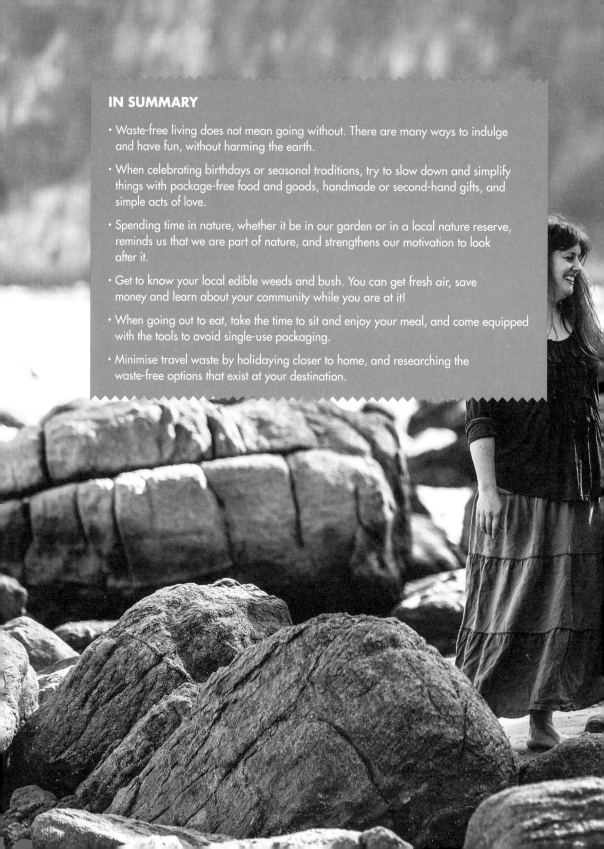

IN SUMMARY

- Waste-free living does not mean going without. There are many ways to indulge and have fun, without harming the earth.

- When celebrating birthdays or seasonal traditions, try to slow down and simplify things with package-free food and goods, handmade or second-hand gifts, and simple acts of love.

- Spending time in nature, whether it be in our garden or in a local nature reserve, reminds us that we are part of nature, and strengthens our motivation to look after it.

- Get to know your local edible weeds and bush. You can get fresh air, save money and learn about your community while you are at it!

- When going out to eat, take the time to sit and enjoy your meal, and come equipped with the tools to avoid single-use packaging.

- Minimise travel waste by holidaying closer to home, and researching the waste-free options that exist at your destination.

'Never doubt that a small group of thoughtful, committed citizens can change the world. Indeed it is the only thing that ever has.'
– Margaret Mead

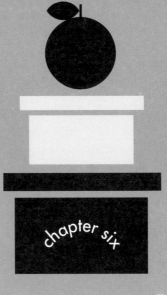

chapter six

CHANGE

Foster a waste-free community

Moving beyond our own homes, we look at how each of us can help make positive change in our communities. Beginning with making connections with the people around us, we move on to alternative economies, reducing work and school waste, communicating with others and inspiring the people around us to take action.

Waste has infiltrated almost every part of modern life and created mountains of problems, both literally and figuratively. These waste problems can often feel so much bigger than our ability to try to solve them. It can be especially disheartening when we take the effort to reduce our own waste, but continue to see the wastefulness of others. So, how can you bring about broader positive change, beyond your own home?

Firstly, remind yourself that the actions that you take as an individual can enact broader positive change. You can speak and act with your wallet, you can shop consciously or abstain from certain products, brands and retailers. By reducing your own waste, you can inspire others to think about their waste and prompt them to reduce some of it. As an example, after many months of not putting our own kerbside bins out on bin night, some of our neighbours noticed and asked if we could help them to reduce their own household waste. The influence of your actions will vary, depending on circumstances. But every positive action is a step in the right direction.

Connecting with your community

— Community can be considered to be the sum total of the connections that you have with people in your local area. We'd extend that to include those in your online sphere of contacts, too. Strengthening your involvement with a local community can make waste-free living easier. And it can be reassuring to have people around you who support the way you live and who are supportive in times of need. Goodness knows, we all have those tough times.

We know that it can be tricky to find your people. You know, the ones who get you, the ones who don't judge your lifestyle choices even though they may not understand them all.

We know that it can be tricky to find your people. You know, the ones who get you, the ones who don't judge your lifestyle choices even though they may not understand them all. But finding community can be a real challenge, wherever you live. Our own challenges in finding community arose in part from moving away from childhood family and friends and trying to find like-minded folk at a time in our lives when we are focused on raising children and paying bills. Connecting with strangers certainly requires a willingness to put oneself out there and to be open-hearted to others.

Acting and living locally can help minimise waste because there is generally less driving involved, emitting fewer greenhouse gases. If you have a long, daily commute to work, school or the shops, then apart from being exhausting and expensive, it can be highly polluting from all the fuel used. One solution might be finding someone in your neighbourhood to carpool with. Another might be establishing a shopping co-op. You may or may not be able to change those commutes, but we recommend looking for areas in your life where you can bring what you do closer to home.

When interacting with your community, there will inevitably be some groups and activities that lend themselves to being less wasteful, which are built around an ethic of care for the environment.

HAVE A LOOK FOR SOME OF THESE GROUPS, OR IF YOU HAVE A STEELY CONSTITUTION, YOU MIGHT WANT TO INITIATE YOUR OWN

- Join a local gardening group. Share seeds, produce and plants and learn about what grows well in your area to help create a garden that meets more of your own food needs.

- Rent a community garden plot. Grow food whilst chatting to people from your neighbourhood, learning from each other as you go.

- Join a Landcare, Coastcare or other environmental protection group. These can provide a good opportunity to learn about some of the threats to your local environment and to share ideas about addressing those threats. These groups might undertake litter clean-ups on beaches, riverbanks or in forests. There may also be opportunities to acquire grants to address waste or other issues that your area faces.

- Join a bushwalking or naturalist group and spend time in nature while observing ecosystems.

- Join a craft group. Learn to knit, crochet, spin, weave, sew or mend, and do it alongside people who can share their skill and experience, whilst forming connections and having fun. You can learn skills to become more self-reliant and together you may like to initiate a project that benefits the broader community.

- If you have the energy and time, you may want to form an action group with some friendly locals to address a local cause. This might be as simple as litter clean-ups, or a lobby group to push your council to improve waste management.

HOST A WASTE-FREE PICNIC

Sharing a meal is a wonderful way to spark discussion. Reach out to friends
or extended family, and if you feel inspired to network with locals who are trying
to reduce their waste, you might like to put a call-out on community noticeboards
or social media groups. Host a picnic and aim to bring food from home, using only
reusable containers, cups and picnic-ware. Grab a thermos and a hamper and
have a gorgeous day in the sunshine!

CHANGE

BEACH CLEAN-UP

Reducing waste in our own homes is wonderful, but you may find you're even more aware of the waste around you now, especially in natural areas. The oceans are one of our most at-risk areas from pollution and rubbish, with much of the plastics we discard ending up there and harming sea life. Grab a large bag (reuse one if you can!) and some sturdy gloves and help clean up your local beach or nature reserve. You may like to get in touch with your local Landcare or 'Friends of ...' group and see if they have any clean-up events happening near you. Or invite some friends along and make a day of it!

CHANGE

Bartering and borrowing

— Before industrialised societies developed in the eighteenth century, many people lived in villages where needs were met collectively. Locals were inclined to support each other by way of bartering for goods and services because there was no other viable way of surviving, given the technology at the time. Food was for the most part grown locally and household supplies were made locally by specialists. Co-dependence between neighbours in a village strengthened resilience and reduced demand for each house to have one of everything.

On page 56, we mentioned the World War II effort to localise food production to backyards and neighbourhoods, with neighbours often banding together to share ownership of pigs and livestock to supplement meat rations, swapping home-grown goods and reusing food waste in households and local businesses. Shopping locally was the only option. In the UK, if space for growing food was scarce, people could take out allotments on public land (much like community gardens) and grow food for their families there. It was understood that food grown locally saved fuel and resources, to strengthen the nation's chances of winning the war and to help people keep themselves fed.

In stark contrast, these days, many people live in suburbs where each home operates like its own habitable island surrounded by a metaphorical, treacherous sea. In any typical home you might find at least one of every conceivable item that one could need to get through daily life. But with that siloed approach comes plenty of unnecessary waste. For example, a single suburban street might be expected to have dozens of lawnmowers, when one or two would suffice for the amount of lawn there is to mow. How many ladders, sewing machines, irons, shovels, pasta-makers and cars do we really need in our own home, when so many of these items already exist nearby? In some ways, the resourceful and less-wasteful ways of village life have become lost. We've created our own fortresses, losing sight of the consequences to the natural world. Bartering and borrowing is no longer the norm.

It is common for people to feel too proud to borrow from others, or like they've somehow failed by not having demonstrated the means to provide that item for themselves. Maybe we have been conditioned to measure success by some sort of stoic, household independence and by the accumulation of belongings? As a result, we have accrued more stuff than we actually need to thrive.

At the other end of the spectrum, we can consider modern examples of a sharing culture. Communal societies or intentional communities (e.g. Findhorn Ecovillage in Scotland) became popular in the 1960s. These are usually a cluster of houses built in a shared space, often with a shared common house with a kitchen and dining room, where neighbours are encouraged to share items, such as tools and lawnmowers. Urban streets are rarely designed with a culture of sharing in mind, but we can introduce those concepts to reduce waste and save money.

CHANGE

ENGAGE YOUR COMMUNITY

Being available to barter for goods, or to lend items to neighbours and friends in need, can help to strengthen connections within our community. In permaculture thinking there is an ethic of sharing called 'Fair share of the surplus', which suggests that when we produce or consume above and beyond what we need to sustain ourselves, we share the excess. Sharing is a practice that by its very nature results in less waste.

Here are some actions you can take to foster a culture of sharing:

- If there is an appliance or tool that you need, but which you're not likely to use very often, ask neighbours or friends if you can borrow theirs. Conversely, offer to lend out your own tools or appliances to friends in need.

- Utilise your local book library, tool library, toy library and hire places. If these don't exist, put a call out to work with others on setting one up in your community!

- Participate in your local online bartering groups.

- Establish an online group or network in your local community that facilitates a culture of donating services or goods and helping each other without expectation of reciprocity.

- Start a book exchange. Set up a space for books to be taken, read, swapped or returned by members of your local community.

- Offer surplus fresh produce to your neighbours.

- Hold a mending workshop in your community and trade skills to fix broken items that can be mended.

- Host or participate in a cook-up with friends that ends with each participant taking home a number of meals for the family to share.

- Join or maybe start a local community exchange program. These provide an online space to buy, sell, swap, share, barter or gift your goods, skills or services.

- Join your local permaculture association and participate in a 'permablitz', where people gather to help revitalise or improve a household's garden, whilst learning from each other and sharing good food!

Waste at work

— These days, workplaces can include pretty much any location: home, office, field, car, hospital and so on. Work waste can include the same sorts of waste created at home, such as food, paper and plastic waste, but there may be waste types that are particular to the job, e.g. clinical, chemical, construction or office waste. There may also be a difference in the level of control that we have, or think we have, to manage or reduce waste. At work, people's attitudes towards waste may tend to be lax. Consider who is responsible for producing waste at your work and whose job it may be to try to reduce it.

In Australia, more than 20 million tonnes of waste were generated from offices, factories and institutions in 2014/15, and approximately 7 million tonnes of this went to landfill. This is substantially more than the waste made from municipal and local government sources, with approximately 13 million tonnes generated and 6.5 million tonnes to landfill. Consider that another 20 million tonnes of waste were generated by the construction and demolition industry (7 million tonnes to landfill), to which regular householders contribute. The scale of waste issues in workplaces is conceivably the topic of a whole other book, so we'll just dip our toe in the water here. There is a lot to reduce!

> In Australia, more than 20 million tonnes of waste were generated from offices, factories and institutions in 2014/15, and approximately 7 million tonnes of this went to landfill.

In general, reducing waste at work saves money for the employer and can reduce damage to the environment and to us. This alone should provide motivation to try to reduce waste, but many people work for others and either do not directly suffer the financial burden of wasteful work practices, or do not see the impacts of waste that is produced. If you try to bring about a waste-reduction initiative in your workplace but it is met with scepticism or resistance, you could approach it by framing your proposal in terms of financial savings or other benefits. Your employer may also be receptive to waste-reduction arguments couched in terms of improving the physical or mental health of colleagues or the environment.

Working from home is becoming increasingly acceptable to some employers and can save energy and reduce waste, especially because there is no need to commute by car, bus or other means, thereby saving fuel and money. There is no need to pack a lunch, or feel compelled to buy lunch out and create any waste that might occur with takeaway food.

Additional heating or cooling energy demands might be low if the rest of the family are at home, learning, working and playing. And it's lovely working nearby the ones you love most. Working from home won't work for everyone, but if you can operate effectively from home, ask your employer if you can avoid the commute and some of the distractions of the office. As offices are one of the most common workplaces, here are some ways to help reduce typical streams of office waste from entering landfill.

CHANGE

- Collect food scraps from the tea room in a lidded reusable bucket and empty it at one or more employees' home compost bins.

- Make your desk a bin-free zone! Remove your own desk-side bin and share rubbish bins amongst multiple colleagues, rather than one plastic-lined bag bin for each person. Oberon found that removing his own desk-side bin served to remind him to remain accountable for waste and so he brings food scraps home for composting.

- Consider minimising paper waste/use by switching to a paperless office. Your digital footprint is not without waste. For example, it takes massive amounts of energy to power the server space that holds all the internet's information within massive data centres. Some data centres are powered using renewable energy (e.g. solar and wind energy), but many are not. All of those photos and files that you keep in the cloud (i.e. those files that you do not need or use) may be considered to be a form of digital waste.

- Recycle waste paper, cardboard, glass, metal and plastic.

- Consider recycling programs for recycling printer cartridges, batteries and light bulbs. Some printer cartridges can be refilled rather than replaced.

- Look for reverse-garbage programs near you, which offer office and industrial waste products for reuse by artists and schools.

- Explore local options for recycling or repurposing e-waste, such as old computers, printers and mobile devices).

- When replacing furniture and still-functioning office supplies, consider charities that will be able to re-home those items.

- Take your lunch to work in your own reusable container, or if you're planning to eat out, bring your own cutlery kit (knife, fork, spoon, chopsticks, napkin, metal straw – or whichever of these you use!).

- Use a reusable cup for your daily coffee or tea and/or see if you can get a coffee machine at work that does not rely on single-use coffee pods. Drink from a ceramic cup.

- Review your system for leasing and replacing computers – can computers be repaired instead of replaced? Replace only when needed rather than because of a date stamp. Consider using reconditioned computers instead of buying new.

- Explore options when organising catered business meetings. Source a caterer who can provide food with minimal packaging waste.

- Carpool to work to reduce carbon emissions. Consider options in relation to business car travel – can some meetings be conducted via phone or Skype instead of travelling a long way?

- Use ethical, compostable stationery and avoid plastic-bound folders and notebooks.

Small-business waste

Alongside Oberon's work outside of the home, we are small retail business owners, and one of the aims of our business is to keep postage and packaging waste to a minimum. This means that we look at what we have on hand when it comes to postage and make use of everything we receive. Referring to the five Rs (see page 19), we seek to reduce and reuse where possible, which sometimes means reusing plastic satchels we've received (turning them inside out), that still have some life left in them and asking that our customers recycle them. It's not as preferable as compostable packaging, but it's a good reuse for an existing waste stream. The beautiful products that we send off inside these satchels are wrapped in compostable, recycled brown paper, or sometimes reused bubble wrap.

Sometimes we reuse boxes or, as a last resort, we use new satchels, with each parcel considered with care as it leaves us. Our postage is carbon offset, making it carbon neutral, whilst helping to grow Tassie forests. Any other soft plastic we receive is recycled, cardboard is used in our garden and our only source of landfill waste is packing tape. We haven't quite filled a small household bin with business-related waste in the past year. Our business is located in our home, keeping heating and electricity costs to a minimum, while accessing solar energy on the roof. These are some small ways that retail businesses, both bricks and mortar and online, can make a difference to how we send and receive products.

CHANGE

Reducing school waste

━ Educating children about waste is important, otherwise it can be perceived by them as boring and irrelevant. In our experience, children are often receptive to waste issues, especially when they see and understand some of the impacts of harmful plastic packaging on the marine environment. We've given talks at primary and high schools about our waste-free lifestyle, and children ask so many great questions and have great ideas about how to reduce their own waste. With a little encouragement, children can problem-solve their own waste reduction, setting them on a trajectory to live as waste-free adults.

We remember when we had to pick up rubbish at recess as kids. There were chip packets and flavoured milk cartons with those mini plastic straws, plastic wrap from sandwiches, icy-pole sticks and probably tons of lost scrunchies and shrinky dinks. To us, waste was just a consequence of a good time in the playground – and it wasn't a particular concern. We removed litter because teachers told us to, but we didn't necessarily consider that the litter was harmful in any way. It was just communicated to us that it was unsightly and, thus, should be binned and sent 'away'. We've seen school bins that are overflowing with icy-pole wrappers, pie packets and yoghurt tubs. Some things never seem to change.

HERE ARE A FEW KEY WAYS TO HELP REDUCE THE WASTE PRODUCED WITHIN THE SCHOOL SYSTEM:

- **School supplies** – When it comes to sourcing school supplies, look for low-waste options for those items that are not specifically compulsory. A sturdy canvas school bag can be composted at the end of its life, whereas the more common nylon-based ones cannot. Seek second-hand options for compulsory school uniform items and re-home clothing to other families once your child outgrows them. You can contact your child's teacher and start a conversation with them about how they manage classroom waste. So many of the tools used in class are made from plastic – markers, Blu-Tack, glue, plastic stationery, art and craft materials and laminated posters. Although laminating can be very pleasing to the eye and can help paper products last longer, give some thought to the reams of plastic that go into decking out classrooms each year and where all that plastic will end up! In most cases, there are compostable options for notebooks, stationery and other supplies, such as wooden sharpeners, rulers and pencils and paper notebooks without plastic covers and without metal spiral binding. These options may not be front and centre in the minds of all teachers. Try having a chat with them before booklist time comes around.

CHANGE

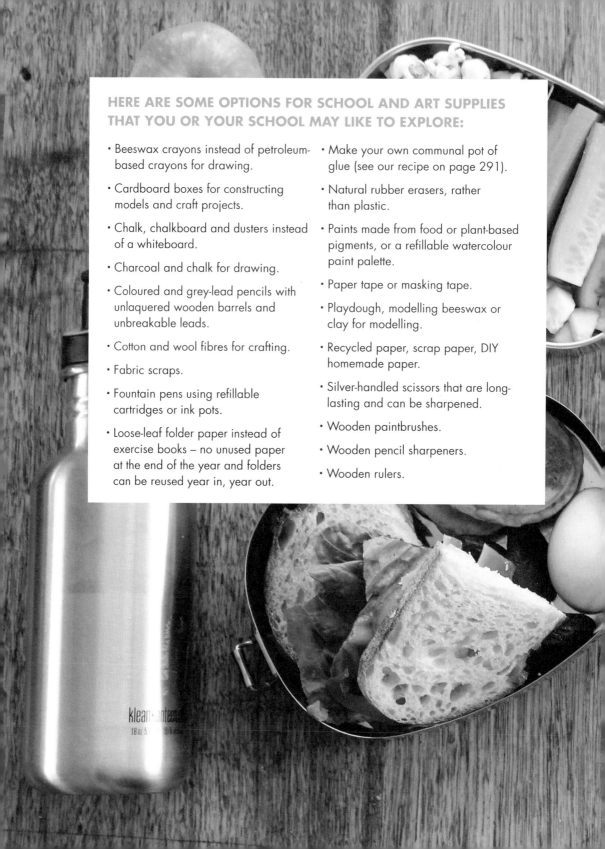

HERE ARE SOME OPTIONS FOR SCHOOL AND ART SUPPLIES THAT YOU OR YOUR SCHOOL MAY LIKE TO EXPLORE:

- Beeswax crayons instead of petroleum-based crayons for drawing.
- Cardboard boxes for constructing models and craft projects.
- Chalk, chalkboard and dusters instead of a whiteboard.
- Charcoal and chalk for drawing.
- Coloured and grey-lead pencils with unlaquered wooden barrels and unbreakable leads.
- Cotton and wool fibres for crafting.
- Fabric scraps.
- Fountain pens using refillable cartridges or ink pots.
- Loose-leaf folder paper instead of exercise books – no unused paper at the end of the year and folders can be reused year in, year out.
- Make your own communal pot of glue (see our recipe on page 291).
- Natural rubber erasers, rather than plastic.
- Paints made from food or plant-based pigments, or a refillable watercolour paint palette.
- Paper tape or masking tape.
- Playdough, modelling beeswax or clay for modelling.
- Recycled paper, scrap paper, DIY homemade paper.
- Silver-handled scissors that are long-lasting and can be sharpened.
- Wooden paintbrushes.
- Wooden pencil sharpeners.
- Wooden rulers.

- **Waste management at school** – Find out how your school manages its waste – do they offer recycling facilities? If so, what materials are accepted? Can the canteen reduce the number of packaged items on the menu? Does your school have functioning compost bins?

It is becoming more common for schools to have their own kitchen garden, with a worm farm or other compost bays. The school's garden can be a great focal point for discussing waste in other areas of the school or your child's life. It can also be where learning about waste, composting and making food from scratch begins. This knowledge can then travel home with children and have broader reach outside of school, into the local community.

Schools can be great advocates for social change, and waste is an accessible topic where they can have practical and positive impact.

- **School fads and consumerism** – One of the biggest factors influencing a child's desire to get stuff comes from other children who have stuff. Cast your minds back to your childhood and the playground talk and the peer pressure that came with it. Stuff that is in fashion will mostly stem from advertising and the media's influence, and this gets children thinking they need certain gadgets to be accepted. Experimenting with different styles and popular fads can be a normal part of growing up and finding your identity. Fads come and go and it can be difficult to compete with those influences. Try discussing the waste involved in creating and disposing of the things they want. Imagine future historians looking back at our time and scratching their heads about fidget spinners – talk to them about that! Look for compostable and homemade alternatives together. Help your children take responsibility for the waste they create and give them space to make their own decisions about what they feel is important.

- **Learn outside of school** – Another approach to reducing the waste that happens at school is to educate your child outside the traditional school system. In much the same way that working from home is becoming a popular option for forward-thinking workplaces, home education is becoming increasingly popular. We have found it to be an excellent way to reduce the waste involved in equipment, uniforms, lunches and travel.

Home educating also makes forming a family culture around waste somewhat easier, with family connections and interests strengthened by time spent together, working and learning in partnership. It means that you can follow lines of enquiry and explore them in your own family's time, leading to greater whole-family learning. Home education does not mean learning in isolation, with home-school groups and co-ops forming to bring together families with similar or different approaches. These can also be places where families can encourage change, share ideas and talk about issues, such as waste reduction. If you're in a position to spend time facilitating your child's education, we highly recommend it!

WHAT YOU'LL NEED

- 350 ml tepid water
- 65 g plain flour or gluten-free flour
- 100 g sugar
- 1 tablespoon vinegar
- 3 teaspoons bicarb soda
- 1 glass jar

CRAFT GLUE

You may like to have a go at making your own glue for art and craft projects at home or at school. Here's a simple craft glue recipe using ingredients found in the kitchen. It makes a surprisingly strong adhesive for paper, yarn, fabric and wood.

STEP 1

Pour the tepid water into a large saucepan and place over medium heat.

STEP 2

Add the flour and whisk well to combine and avoid any lumps.

STEP 3

When the mixture is hot, add the sugar and whisk well until the sugar has dissolved.

STEP 4

Stir in the vinegar. Keep whisking!

STEP 5

Add the bicarb and whisk quickly. You'll notice the bicarb react with the vinegar, making the mixture fluff up a bit.

STEP 6

Whisk together as the mixture thickens slightly, then remove the pan from the heat.

STEP 7

Pour into a glass jar and seal.

STEP 8

Store the glue in the fridge when you're not using it. It should last up to 6 months.

CHANGE

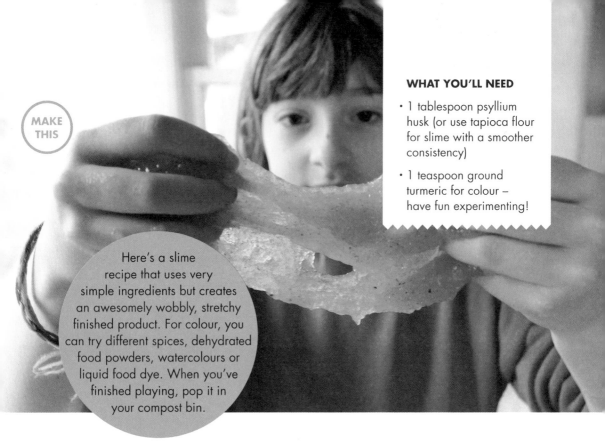

MAKE THIS

WHAT YOU'LL NEED

- 1 tablespoon psyllium husk (or use tapioca flour for slime with a smoother consistency)

- 1 teaspoon ground turmeric for colour – have fun experimenting!

Here's a slime recipe that uses very simple ingredients but creates an awesomely wobbly, stretchy finished product. For colour, you can try different spices, dehydrated food powders, watercolours or liquid food dye. When you've finished playing, pop it in your compost bin.

PSYLLI SLIME

Sensory play is so important for kids. Playdough has always been a waste-free hit in our home and playing with slime is something our kids love just as much. Lots of commercially bought slimes and recipes for homemade slime contain glue and other chemicals that are difficult to source waste free. This has led to lots of creativity in our kitchen.

STEP 1

Place the psyllium husk in a bowl.

STEP 2

Pour in 1 cup of water and stir a little to wet the psyllium. Set aside for 5 minutes.

STEP 3

Add the turmeric or other colouring and stir until the colour is evenly dispersed.

STEP 4

Heat in a microwave for 5 minutes, or heat in a saucepan on the stove, until the mixture boils and starts to bubble up.

STEP 5

Remove from the heat (or pause the microwave for a moment) and then restart, or reheat until the liquid thickens.

STEP 6

Remove the mixture from the heat again and allow it to cool. You can try adding a couple of drops of essential oil to the mixture whilst it cools. Put the bowl in the fridge until it's cool all the way through. Then play!

CHANGE

PAGE
292

WHAT YOU'LL NEED

- 2 cups plain flour
- ½ cup salt
- 3 tablespoons olive oil
- 2 tablespoons apple cider vinegar
- 1 cup boiling water, plus extra if needed
- your choice of colouring – beetroot powder, cacao, turmeric, nettle or spinach powder all work well to create a natural colour. Add small increments until you get the desired colour
- 5 drops essential oil of your choice for additional sensory play (optional)

MAKE THIS

PLAYDOUGH

Playdough is an all-time family favourite for all ages, but it's especially great for young children. Our kids like to make patterns in playdough, or use it to make people, animals, food and play scenes. We make this recipe with ingredients found at our bulk food shop. It will keep in a jar in the fridge for a number of months.

STEP 1

Place the flour, salt, olive oil and vinegar in a bowl.

STEP 2

Add 1 cup of boiling water.

STEP 3

Stir until well combined and dough-like. Add more water, if needed.

STEP 4

Knead through the colourings and/or essential oil.

STEP 5

Play! Then store in a glass jar in the fridge for next time.

CHANGE

Clinical waste

— In the grand scheme of things, clinical waste, which includes medical, dental and pharmaceutical waste, might be reasonably considered a lower priority than other aspects of our lives where plastic can be more easily reduced. The treatments for many types of illness and disease only come in plastic, and not necessarily the easily recycled kind. Sometimes plastic and packaging waste will be unavoidable.

Plastic acts to keep surgical instruments sterile and hospital items are commonly single-use, or only used a couple of times, to maintain hygiene standards. There is hospital waste associated with surgical dressings and instruments, gloves, curtains and other packaging. Most waste from hospitals (called biomedical waste) is treated as hazardous and is usually trucked away, treated and incinerated. Some medical supplies are sterilised in an autoclave after use and may be reused, although this is becoming less common and even stainless-steel implements are commonly treated as single-use items.

The treatments for many types of illness and disease only come in plastic, and not necessarily the easily recycled kind.

Another source of waste in hospitals comes from food and drink packaging. If you're scheduled for a procedure, find out beforehand whether you can bring food and drink from home in your own containers, otherwise there may be no waste-free options provided by the hospital.

Certainly, if you're sick or living with disability, then the priority should be your health and accessibility, rather than valiantly trying to avoid every bit of plastic packaging you come across. At times like this, waste ceases to be your personal responsibility and becomes the responsibility of the broader community. As patients or as general citizens, it is difficult to influence the items used or the packaging produced in hospitals or other clinical contexts. It is also difficult to distinguish between the waste that is medically justified from the packaging or other waste that is generated simply to keep costs lower.

If you do identify clinical waste streams, then you may like to address them when you're not ill or sick, or you may have friends or family help to push for changes and better design. Engaging with professionals in the medical industry who may be receptive to discussing waste issues can be a good way to identify areas where waste could legitimately be reduced.

CHANGE

Talking about waste with others

— A significant reduction of kerbside waste by a single household is a huge achievement – worthy of many a high-five. But it is certainly not the norm. The norm is for a household to produce, on average, two tonnes of kerbside waste per year. The norm is to expect spotless, well-shaped fruit and vegetables all year round. Many expect to acquire the latest gadgets and meet this week's fashion trends. It is normal to expect convenience, sterility and material reward served in plastic bags and to possess all desires immediately.

Following this, it is normal to discard those items we no longer want, even if they are still functional, without consequence or accountability for the impacts of those choices. So, how do we bridge the gap between the waste-free household and the normal two tonnes per year of household waste? How do we normalise waste-free living? It all starts with a conversation. It's pretty much a fact of life that people around you are going to make waste. This can bring up a whole range of feelings and reactions. They might feel awkward, apologetic and self-aware about creating unnecessary waste in front of you. You might at some point have lived like this, too, and so understand their more wasteful actions. It might be disheartening and you might feel sad or even angry, depending on the person and the context. It can be challenging to know when it is the right time to speak up (if at all) and when to offer waste-free solutions, if they exist. In our experience, people can carry different feelings around their waste, ranging from blatant disregard or downright indifference, through to guilt and a desire to make a positive change.

> How do we normalise waste-free living? It all starts with a conversation.

HERE ARE SOME THINGS TO CONSIDER WHEN TALKING TO OTHERS ABOUT WASTE AND WAYS TO REDUCE IT:

PAPA DON'T PREACH!

Not everyone within your circle of friends or family will necessarily be on board with your attempts to reduce waste. Some may even oppose it. If you share space with people who aren't all up for waste-free living, we do not recommend that you preach waste-reduction ideas to them, as you are likely to meet resistance or resentment and you may even become alienated. Remind yourself that everyone is (at least partly) the sum of their own experience and so they may not see the world as you do. You may find more traction if you raise waste issues in a sensitive manner and provide gentle solutions.

LEAD BY EXAMPLE

If you do your best to reduce or avoid waste and utilise waste-free alternatives when shopping, then people around you will inevitably be influenced by your actions. Some might be motivated to change their ways. They may be more likely to change if they learn about waste-free solutions, especially where they can foresee savings in money or time.

The way that you shop can influence many people around you. For example, if you shop using cloth bags, there is a strong chance that your choice to use those bags will be noticed by other customers, the checkout attendant and friends who visit your home – or online, if you happen to share your stories via social media. People will start to see it as normal practice to bring one's own bags and this can influence change in others. When asked 'why are you doing that?' (or similar) in relation to your cloth shopping bags, reusable containers, or even when you're refusing items, such as plastic bags or straws, use those opportunities to explain why you think reducing waste is important.

LISTEN TO ALTERNATIVE VIEWS

Waste issues need to be talked about. Talking leads to shared learning and this can lead to action. But not everyone will see waste issues the way you do. Everyone comes with their own knowledge, their own perceptions and their own experiences. And the sorts of waste specifics you discuss will vary depending on whether you're talking to a loved one, child, friend, or a work colleague, shopkeeper or politician.

In all cases, try to hear out those differing viewpoints (whether you can come to respect them or not is another matter). Other people may have different needs to you (as far as certain products go), or they may have different abilities (or may be less-abled). And as far as waste reduction goes, there are many approaches to it; yours may not work for others, just as other people's may not work for you.

EXPLAIN YOURSELF

Not everyone is going to immediately understand why you want that food item in your home-brought bag or container. Waste is not necessarily at the forefront of their minds. Explain why you prefer to keep food waste separate to use in the garden. Explain why you prefer to buy food in your own containers, if it comes up. If you're trying to enact a 'new' process in a shop, then it can help to initiate things by explaining why you want to do what you want to do; for example, 'I'm trying to avoid using any plastic and so I'd really love if you could use those tongs to put that bread straight into my bag.' We've found that a brief explanation of the why can really make the difference for some people, and it gives them food for thought.

PROBLEM-SOLVE TOGETHER

There will be times when you have the best intentions to avoid waste, but for whatever reason, the step that relies on working with others creates some waste. It might be while shopping, having guests over, doing something at work or organising a function, for example. Talking about what you're trying to do, and inviting others to help find solutions with you, can be a great way to facilitate the change you want to see. We find that once people understand the concept of waste-free living and start thinking of options, they enjoy the challenge of discovering more!

YOU DO YOU

Expecting others to live by your standards may be unrealistic and unreasonable. Every individual's situation is going to be different. Take responsibility for yourself and the waste you create. Do the best you can with the knowledge you have. Reassure those around you that you are taking responsibility for your own, or your family's, waste and enjoy time with others without judgement.

Remember, change happens incrementally and sometimes generationally, but please do not underestimate your own positive influence!

STUMBLING BLOCKS

Every now and then as you work towards
reducing your waste, you may hit a stumbling
block. Perhaps you can't access a package-free
option for a certain product you rely on, or a
family member is really resistant to change
for a particular reason. There are often creative
ways around these problems and there are
usually alternatives. You may be met with
the choice to reduce or eliminate the product
altogether until a suitable option becomes
available to you – we did this with cheese
until we found a local package-free option.

Sometimes there is no suitable option
available to you, but you still require
access to a certain product and so you
will need to continue to bring it into
your home. We'd ask you to accept
your limitations and focus on living as
gently on the earth as you possibly can.
At other times, you may be willing to
reframe things and refuse those items
that you previously felt dependent upon.
This is going to look different for every
household and every individual.

But keep asking, questioning
and pushing for the changes
you want. Ask others to help
you problem-solve. Magical
things can happen when the
burden is not tackled alone,
but shared.

CHANGE

Men – it's time to step up!

━ It may seem a peculiar thing, but we've observed that the overwhelming majority of people who actively participate in pursuing a waste-free lifestyle are women. The majority of people who buy this book and put new habits into practice will be women. Often women will ask how to live waste free when their partner will not get on board, despite the wealth of research and information they have shared with them. Women carry much of the burden of the mental load of the household. In general, men just don't seem to be motivated to step up and take responsibility for much of the waste they produce. There are exceptions, of course (including the male co-author of this book and a few other notable zero-wasters), but it does beg the question of why? The gender bias around waste-free living makes this very much a feminist issue.

Boys are often raised to be 'tough' and indifferent to nurturing and domestic activities, while girls are more often encouraged to cook and clean through their play and in domestic life.

We suspect there are a few reasons for the gender bias. As they have traditionally, women still do most of the grocery shopping, meal planning and much of the cooking and cleaning. Whoever is responsible for the acquiring of single-use items and packaged goods in a household tends to be more aware of its existence and may be more motivated to reduce it. There is also the related phenomena of male privilege, entitlement and social conditioning, which has been shown to extend to perceptions around the environment and reduction of waste.

Boys are often raised to be 'tough' and indifferent to nurturing and domestic activities, while girls are more often encouraged to cook and clean through their play and in domestic life. Men have traditionally dominated industries that create the most waste, such as construction, mining, agriculture and manufacture.

But they also dominate most decision-making processes in government. When processed, packaged and frozen foods first became readily available, it was seen as a boon for women wanting to enter the workforce. Convenience foods enabled women to work, then return home to feed their families. Men seemingly carried on regardless, returning to a cooked meal at the end of the day and perhaps taking out the rubbish at dusk. Aside from taking out the bin, men had very little to do with what went in it. And it looks like not much has changed.

CHANGE

We know everyone is different and that not all men are the same. We don't want to reinforce gender stereotypes. In fact, we want to challenge what we've seen as the persistence of traditional stereotypes by suggesting that more men make a big deal out of waste issues, wherever they see them. Reducing waste is cool. Standing up for the environment demonstrates personal integrity. Men, keep your mates accountable for their waste. Show your children how to grow food, shop, meal plan, cook and mend things. Talk to them about the precious planet we all share and how to nurture it. Show them how real men give a damn about their footprint on the planet. Do it for yourself, your partner and children, and for future generations. A family that works together towards waste-free living is going to find the going easier and more rewarding than when one member is doing all the work alone.

Changing laws and regulations

— Our societies are structured around laws and policies. Some of these legal instruments relate to standards of production, so that our food and other products are safe, and to ensure that workers (and the environment) are treated fairly. Other laws regulate whether certain items are permitted to be sold at all, or how they are to be sold; for example, consider the plain packaging now required for cigarettes. Certain types of laws and policies are particularly relevant to waste, its production and its management. For example, the National Waste Policy was signed by all Australian environment ministers in 2009 and sets out the country's direction for waste management through to 2020.

When we make changes to live with as little waste as possible, we do so within the bounds of what is legal where we live. However, some laws can restrict our capacity to reduce waste as much as we'd like in our homes or community. For example, there may be local laws preventing the household management and composting of human manure waste and greywater, or poor standards around energy efficiency requirements for homes. Bans of certain wasteful and polluting products, which would assist in broad-scale waste reduction, vary from place to place.

Changes to laws and regulations do not happen in a vacuum. They happen due to various motivations, such as when public demand or expectations influence politicians to enact change. In this regard, a single voice is rarely as powerful or effective at prompting positive change as the voices of many. Utilise the networks at your disposal, whether online or in-person, to build a case for positive change and then let decision-makers know what you want and why.

Not all change requires a change in law. Some changes can be policy guidelines or voluntary standards. For example, the Australian Packaging Covenant (APC) is a national program started in 1999, under which businesses (mostly big ones) specify actions to reduce environmental impacts caused by product packaging. Whilst businesses are required to report on actions, there are no thresholds enforced – in this way, the APC demonstrates an instrument of good intent to do better. Whether such good intentions lead to significant positive change is arguable.

Imposing bans can be an effective way to bring about broad-scale elimination of a particular waste stream. Many cities and some countries have passed legislation to ban single-use plastics, to varying degrees of success. Bans are more likely to be successful if the community is informed and consulted about the proposed change well in advance. Otherwise, they may not be receptive to change.

Local businesses and stakeholders should also be consulted, to identify suitable alternatives once the ban is in place. If affected people do not agree with the ban, then there is more likelihood that loop-holes will be found and waste won't be reduced as intended. Where no financially comparable options exist to the banned item, then a system should be devised that subsidises affected businesses or individuals to utilise the lower-waste option.

HERE ARE SOME PRODUCTS THAT WE THINK ARE CLEAR CANDIDATES FOR BANNING UNDER MOST, IF NOT ALL, CIRCUMSTANCES:

plastic bags

polystyrene

single-use takeaway packaging and cutlery

disposable coffee cups that are not 100 per cent compostable at home

various single-use plastic items (e.g. individual soy sauce or tomato sauce dispensers)

plastic and other single-use straws

Increasingly, cities and states (and some countries) are enacting legislation to phase out or ban products that are producing mountains of polluting waste. Write to or speak with your local council representative and explain the bans or other changes you'd like to see in your area. Perhaps you want to see more support for composting of organic waste, or better signage on recycling bins – whatever it is, your voice matters!

CHANGE

Influencing change in business and government

— There is power in your voice. If you see needless waste, you can speak to those responsible for it to encourage positive change. If you can identify less wasteful or harmful ways of doing things, then all the better – it takes speaking out beyond simply complaining and towards problem-solving. Remember, not everyone who creates waste is creating that waste in some sort of malicious, evil-overlord-like fashion. Many are just doing their job and haven't twigged the impacts of their actions.

On one occasion, we were at a local small supermarket and we requested to buy bread from behind the counter. We handed over our cloth bag for the shop assistant to put the loaf into, but the assistant put on a single-use plastic glove, picked up the loaf and put it in our bag. The plastic glove was then discarded. It was clear that there was no awareness of why we were using a cloth bag. Our eldest daughter, who was 12 years old at the time, wrote to the business owner on social media, explaining the situation and offering solutions (e.g. using tongs instead of plastic gloves). After a few weeks the owner responded by saying they would switch to tongs from now on. In this instance the articulate words of a child were enough to potentially avoid the needless consumption of thousands of single-use plastic gloves. There is great power in your voice!

HERE ARE SOME ACTIONS YOU CAN TAKE TO HELP ENACT CHANGE FOR WASTE REDUCTION IN LOCAL BUSINESS OR IN YOUR COMMUNITY:

- Speak with the shopkeeper and discuss waste-free alternatives to their practices.

- Write to local businesses and ask them to offer ways to provide items to you without unnecessary packaging. Suggest that retail outlets establish a cloth bag library (to replace single-use carry bags), or offer reusable options over single-use items (e.g. returnable containers or cups).

- Write to your local council member or elected government representative and highlight the waste problem and propose waste-free solutions.

- Start a petition or a local community-action group to involve others to work collaboratively with you towards solving local area waste problems.

- Identify novel solutions for making use of waste products from businesses and let business owners know about them (e.g. collecting a cafe's spent coffee grounds for home composting).

- Work out where your own skills or talents can be best placed to communicate your message. You may be a quiet introvert but a great social media communicator, so you may wish to stick to online forms of advocacy. Or you may be a great negotiator and public speaker, so look for public forums to voice your concerns. Inevitably, there will be challenges to avoiding waste when you step out into the big wide world, so do the best you can within your own means.

SUPPORT YOUR YOUNG ACTIVISTS

Once waste issues are explained, it is likely that your children will start to notice waste occurring when you are out and about. They may ask questions and those 'real life' situations provide great opportunities to discuss potential solutions. Your older children may even start to suggest solutions to waste problems that they see in shops or other places. Work with them to engage those businesses, to identify those problems and to suggest practical solutions. They will (hopefully) feel empowered that they can enact change in different ways. Have a go at writing letters to local council members, engaging businesses through social media and having a chat with shopkeepers together.

Reflecting on change

— After you and your family have made the conscious decision to reduce your waste, and have made concerted efforts in that direction – what then? We think it's a good idea to take stock and reflect on how far you've come. If you undertook a waste audit, like the one described on page 23, you might like to try another one after making changes and compare both. Are you recycling less, but composting more? Are you producing less waste? How has it changed your health and happiness?

You may notice that you make less waste, but you might notice other things, too. Perhaps you've discovered shorter waiting lines when shopping at the bulk food shop, compared to the chain supermarket. Maybe you're finding a new appreciation for the quality of the clothes you buy and the things you bring into your home.

Maybe you've developed what we call 'waste goggles' – and you find when you're out in public that you see waste everywhere. Maybe you've found a new or renewed appreciation for your grandparents' preserved plums and find yourself preserving the surplus from your garden. Maybe you're reconnecting with your own plot and with others in your community. We live in a time of rapid change. Technological advancements continue to determine how we get our energy supply, how we communicate and how we get from A to B. We can expect to see an increase in innovative technologies that convert different waste products into useful stuff. Hopefully, there will be fancy ways of removing the legacy of our waste from landfill and oceans, to reduce environmental harm. These technological advancements won't change the need to question, or to consider the potential harmful impacts to the environment and social welfare. It is easy to be enamoured with new inventions, including those that are marketed as green and eco. Watch out for greenwashing.

One of the factors that limits broad acceptance of the need to reduce waste lies in complacency and indifference around waste issues. We've known people to argue against reducing waste because 'someone will fix this problem in the future' and 'what's the point, the earth is stuffed anyway', or 'it's only one plastic straw'. We simply don't accept those arguments. The positive changes that are needed can start now and they start with you.

We are optimistic that waste-free living will become broadly accepted in the near future. We have seen positive change occur in our local community, following the effort of only a small number of individuals. We've heard shop owners remark that more people are shopping with cloth bags and our butcher has observed that more people are using reusable containers. We have seen families feel empowered by their own ability to control the footprint that they leave on the planet. We can rally our efforts to elevate those who make a positive difference in the world and support those who want to do better. We can take all the knowledge we've gained from previous generations and design a cleaner way of life. Through the simple waste-free choices we make each day, we can create a resilient future. We look forward to seeing you there.

IN SUMMARY

- Your positive actions to reduce waste will influence those around you. Even small actions can have a great ripple effect.

- Waste-free living becomes easier when others in your community support your efforts to reduce waste and participate in waste-reduction initiatives, too. Lead by example.

- Acting and living locally helps to reduce the waste that comes with long-distance travel. Local food, energy and support systems can improve the ability of your neighbourhood to provide for itself.

- Foster a culture of sharing by pooling skills and belongings. Bring back the finer aspects of village life!

- Consider ways to reduce waste at work and school. Young people can be great problem-solvers, and find novel ways to reduce waste. Support those efforts!

APPENDIX:
Fabric waste considerations

NATURAL FABRICS

These are renewable and compost at end of life.

- **Bamboo** is a very fast-growing and quickly renewable plant that requires no pesticides, herbicides or irrigation to grow. It grows densely and provides great yield for the area of land it uses, slowing deforestation. Bamboo cellulose is often converted into a semi-synthetic rayon or viscose fibre which can use some pretty toxic chemicals, such as sulphuric acid, carbon disulphide or caustic soda. These chemicals are highly polluting and workers are often exposed to them, creating significant health issues. Look for brands of bamboo-derived fibres that use mechanical crushing instead of corrosive chemicals in production.

- **Cotton** requires huge amounts of water for growing and production. Commercially farmed cotton relies heavily on pesticides and herbicides, and is an unethical industry for farmers with many lives lost each year. Certified organic cotton is a better choice, as it tends to be free from chlorine bleaches and synthetic dyes, herbicides and pesticides, and is typically a fairer industry for workers.

- **Hemp** is one of the most ethical fabrics. The hemp plant is productive, water-efficient, easy to cultivate and generally pest-tolerant, needing fewer herbicides or other chemical additions. Growing hemp for textiles in Australia is in its infancy.

- **Leather** is often (but not always) an agricultural by-product of the meat and dairy industry. Durable, reusable and biodegradable. Check the source of the leather as animal welfare in some countries is non-existent. Hazardous chromium can be used in tanning processes.

- **Linen** is derived from flax (a traditional fibre crop) and is usually fairly ethically produced, hard-wearing and long-lasting. It requires fewer pesticides and herbicides, and less water and energy than other conventional crops, such as cotton. It can be more expensive than other fabrics due to the locations where it is easily cultivated and the manual processes required for production.

- **Silk** is a strong, light and durable protein fibre. It is dependent on water and fertiliser to grow the mulberry leaves that silkworms feed on, so the process has a relatively large carbon and water footprint. If you're concerned about ethical treatment of animals then this may not be for you, as traditional silk production may be considered somewhat exploitative towards silkworms in their pupal stage. Look for ethical silk (called peace silk), which utilises empty cocoons of silkworms.

- **Wool** is a strong, long-lasting fibre that aids regulation of body temperature and provides superior warmth to most other renewable fibres. However, wool farming requires high amounts of energy, water and grazing land. Look for organic wool that has been certified according to standards for chemical use, animal welfare and sustainability.

SYNTHETIC FABRICS

These are non-renewable and degrade slowly, leaching toxic monomers into groundwater.

- **Acrylic**. Highly toxic compounds are required in the manufacture of acrylic fabric, which contains carcinogens and is not easily recycled nor readily biodegradable. It also releases microfibres (*see* Polar fleece).

- **Microfibre**. Usually made from polyester and nylon (*see below*).

- **Polar fleece**. A long-time staple for those in cold climates, polar fleece is derived from polyester or recycled plastic bottles (both oil-based materials). Each wash of these synthetic garments can release thousands of harmful microfibres into the marine environment.

- **Polyester and nylon**. These fibres are derived from petrochemicals and use lots of energy and water in production. The fabric degrades into harmful microplastics and is best avoided. Nylon manufacture creates toxic nitrous oxide, a greenhouse gas 310 times more potent than carbon dioxide.

Glossary

Some of the terms used in this book could do with a bit of defining, just so we are all on the same page about what we mean.

BIODEGRADABLE: Materials that are biodegradable have the potential to decompose into compounds found in nature, with the action of animals or bacteria. Biodegradable material should break down into organic matter, carbon dioxide and water. Biodegradable packaging may be made from a variety of materials and these may include fossil fuels.

BIOPLASTIC: Plastics made from plants (as opposed to plastics derived from petroleum-based materials). Bioplastics may or may not be biodegradable or compostable.

CARBON FOOTPRINT: This describes the total carbon dioxide and methane emissions from a particular activity or event. There are online calculators to help determine these for a given situation. Waste-free living provides a useful way of reducing your carbon footprint.

CIRCULAR ECONOMY: A system of production and consumption that minimises waste (of energy, fuel, water, pollutants or other resources). A circular economy can be achieved by closing production loops, shortening supply chains, avoiding non-renewable resources and making more efficient use of inputs (e.g. through better design, reuse of wastes and repairing broken goods). *See also* Linear economy.

CLIMATE CHANGE: Also known as 'global warming' – this refers to the century-scale rise in the earth's average temperature and related effects (e.g. sea level rise, expansion of deserts and changing rainfall patterns), which has been most influenced by humans emitting vast amounts of greenhouse gases since the beginning of the industrial revolution in the 1700s.

COMPOSTABLE: Materials that are able to break down in a compost pile. Australia has standards for industrial/commercial and home composting, which relate to the conditions under which a material should biodegrade into biomass, carbon dioxide, water and inorganic compounds. Commercial composting facilities generally run at higher temperatures than home systems. Once composted, the original item should not be distinguishable.

DEGRADABLE: Materials that disintegrate into small pieces, especially with exposure to light (e.g. photodegradable) or heat. Degradable materials do not compost. For example, most plastics are degradable, breaking up into smaller pieces and microplastics.

DYNAMIC ACCUMULATORS: Plants that gather certain micronutrients, macronutrients and minerals from the soil and store them in their leaves. The leaves can be cut and used as a fertiliser for other plants that lack certain nutrients.

FOOD MILES: These measure the distance that food travels from the start of production until it reaches our plate. It helps convey one aspect of the environmental impact of our food and the potential greenhouse gas emissions from the transport associated with food production. The energy used in production and the social consequences of food production should also be considered.

FOSSIL FUELS: These include petroleum, coal and natural gas, which are formed by natural processes within the earth after decomposition of organisms that lived millions of years ago. The energy in these fuels comes from the ancient photosynthesis that occurred in those long-dead creatures. These fuels take millions of years to produce and are considered non-renewable. Humans are extracting and using fossil fuels much faster than any new ones being made within the earth.

GREENHOUSE GASES: Gases in the atmosphere that emit and absorb radiation. Greenhouse gases include water vapour, carbon dioxide, methane, nitrous oxide and ozone. These regulate the temperature at the earth's surface. Human-influenced increases in some greenhouse gases since the 1700s (particularly carbon dioxide, methane and nitrous oxide) are contributing to a dangerous warming of the earth and to other impacts of climate change.

LINEAR ECONOMY: A 'take, make and dispose' type of production that is common in industrialised societies. This involves taking finite, non-renewable resources from the ground, making 'stuff' with those resources and then having manufactured items go to landfill or incineration after use. *See also* Circular economy.

MICROPLASTICS: Small particles of plastic less than approximately 5 mm in diameter. These may be intentionally produced (e.g. microbeads in some exfoliants) or result from the degradation of plastics exposed to heat and/or light.

MINIMALISM: This is a design approach that involves paring down belongings to the bare necessities. This can involve a process of discarding or re-homing belongings, with the intent of having a more uncluttered and simple life. Minimalism tends to favour quality (of an item) over quantity.

PLANNED OBSOLESCENCE: This is a concept in product design where items are planned or designed to have an artificially limited life. Having shorter life spans on products encourages people to buy new items (e.g. the latest version or gadget) more often, with the aim of generating more revenue for retailers and makers. Items may intentionally lack durability, be non-repairable or have a style that is quickly marketed as undesirable (compared to the latest version).

RECYCLING: A process that involves converting waste into new materials and objects. Whilst recycling of nutrients occurs in nature, we use the term to refer to kerbside recycling (e.g. of cans, bottles, paper and plastic) unless we say otherwise.

UPCYCLING: A process of repurposing waste or unwanted materials or objects. This could be as simple as turning a broken boot into a plant pot, or something more technical, such as turning industrial textile waste into a base for new clothing.

WASTE FREE: This term can be applied to any aspect of one's lifestyle where there is no waste produced from a certain item or action. A waste-free lifestyle is one that involves conscious decisions and actions to minimise waste to as close to zero as possible. Synonymous with the term zero waste.

ZERO WASTE: *See* waste free.

GLOSSARY

References

CHAPTER 1: THE BASICS
Australian Bureau of Statistics census data: http://www.abs.gov.au/census/.

Pickin J. and Randell P. (2017). *Australian National Waste Report 2016.* Department of the Environment and Energy & Blue Environment Pty Ltd.

CHAPTER 2: FOOD
FoodWise. (2018). *Food Waste Fast Facts.* Available at: http://www.foodwise.com.au/foodwaste/food-waste-fast-facts/.

CHAPTER 3: PACKAGING
Absorbent Hygiene Products Manufacturers Association: http://www.ahpma.co.uk/.

Ceccarelli D. M. (2009). *Impacts of plastic debris on Australian marine wildlife.* Report by C&R Consulting for the Department of the Environment, Water, Heritage and the Arts.

Drake, D. (1997). Antibacterial activity of baking soda. *Compendium of Continuing Education in Dentistry Supplement,* 18(21): S17–21.

Hinterthuer A. (2008). Just How Harmful Are Bisphenol A Plastics? *Scientific American.* Available at: https://www.scientificamerican.com/article/just-how-harmful-are-bisphenol-a-plastics/.

Industry Edge. (2018). *Pulp & Paper Industry Outlook seventeen22.* Geelong West, Victoria.

Intergovernmental Panel on Climate Change (IPCC). (2014). *Climate Change 2014 Synthesis Report Summary for Policymakers.* Available at: https://www.ipcc.ch/.

O'Farrell K. (2018). *2016–17 Australian Plastics Recycling Survey National Report.* Envisage Works. Report for the Australian Government.

Rivera X.C.S. et al. (2014). Life cycle environmental impacts of convenience food: Comparison of ready and home-made meals.

Journal of Cleaner Production, 73, pp. 294-309.

Sustainability Victoria: www.sustainability.vic.gov.au/.

Van Oel P.R. and Hoekstra A.Y. (2010). *The green and blue water footprint of paper products: methodological considerations and quantification.* Value of Water Research Report Series No. 46, UNESCO-IHE, Delft, the Netherlands.

World Economic Forum. (2016). Ellen MacArthur Foundation and McKinsey & Company, *The New Plastics Economy – Rethinking the future of plastics.* Available at: http://www.ellenmacarthurfoundation.org/publications/.

Worldwatch Institute: http://www.worldwatch.org/.

CHAPTER 4: AROUND THE HOUSE
Ausgrid: www.ausgrid.com.au/.

Australian Bureau of Statistics: http://www.abs.gov.au/.

Australian Communications and Media Authority: www.acma.gov.au/.

Australian Veterinary Association: www.ava.com.au/.

Dawson T. (2010). Cat Disease Threatens Endangered Monk Seals, *Scientific American.* Available at: https://www.scientificamerican.com/article/cat-disease-threatens-endangered-monk-seals/.

Global Fashion Agenda & The Boston Consulting Group. (2017). *Pulse of the Fashion Industry.* Copenhagen, Denmark.

Hoekstra A.Y. & Chapagain A.K. (2008). *Globalisation and Water.* Blackwell Publishing, Malden, MA, USA.

Koehler A. & Wildbolz C. (2009). Comparing the Environmental Footprints of Home-Care and Personal-Hygiene Products: The Relevance of Different Life-Cycle

Phases. *Environmental Science and Technology,* 43, pp. 8643–8651.

O'Brien K. et al. (2009). *Life Cycle Assessment: Reusable and disposable nappies in Australia.* Australian Life Cycle Assessment Society Conference 2009, 6th Australian Conference on Life Cycle Assessment, Melbourne, (1–14), 17–19 February.

CHAPTER 5: CELEBRATE & VENTURE OUTSIDE
Geng L. et al. (2015). Connections with Nature and Environmental Behaviors. *PLOS One,* 10(5), p.e0127247.

Hardesty B.D., et al. (2014). *Understanding the effects of marine debris on wildlife.* A final report to Earthwatch Australia, CSIRO, Hobart, Tasmania.

The Senate's Environment and Communications References Committee. (2016). *Toxic tide: the threat of marine plastic pollution in Australia.* Commonwealth of Australia, Canberra.

Xiang Dong Li et al. (2003). Waste reduction and recycling strategies for the in-flight services in the airline industry. *Resources Conservation and Recycling* (Volume 37).

CHAPTER 6: CHANGE
Brough A.R. et al. (2016). Is Eco-Friendly Unmanly? The Green-Feminine Stereotype and its Effect on Sustainable Consumption. *Journal of Consumer Research,* 43(4), pp. 567-582.

Pickin J. & Randell P. (2017). *Australian National Waste Report 2016,* Department of the Environment and Energy & Blue Environment Pty Ltd.

Walsh, B. (2014). Your Data Is Dirty: The Carbon Price of Cloud Computing. *Time Magazine.* Available at: http://time.com/46777/your-data-is-dirty-the-carbon-price-of-cloud-computing/.

Acknowledgements

- We would like to acknowledge the traditional and original owners of this land, the Muwinina people. We also acknowledge today's Tasmanian Aboriginal community, who are the custodians of this land upon which we live.

- Thanks to our family and friends who have supported and encouraged our waste-free ways. Hugest love and thanks to our three owlets for your extraordinary patience while we wrote this book and for your constant enthusiasm, understanding and open-mindedness in taking on new challenges. Thanks to Patti (Lauren's mum) for excellent thrifty knowledge and for flying down to keep the girls company while we finished writing, even if it didn't go to plan! Thanks to John (Lauren's dad) for loaning us Patti, for your optimistic outlook on life, and for always being tough on litterers. Thanks to Pat (Oberon's mum) for instilling strong environmental values, and to Stephen (Oberon's dad) for advising to always carry a hanky. Thanks to Lauren's grandmothers, Peg and Doris, for the snippets of kitchen hints and thrifty ways hidden in those notebooks from long ago – we wish we could have chatted to you about them! Thanks to Brian Carter (Oberon's uncle) for your lifetime of advocacy for environmental causes and waste issues.

- Thank you to Hugh and Margaret, for being the best kind of neighbours, who share fresh produce, local knowledge, tools, handfuls of nails and buckets full of lemons whenever we need them.

- Special thanks to the members of Zero Waste Tasmania for all the waste-related conversations and camaraderie.

- We would also like to thank the following Tassie folk for their support and great conversations about waste, food and caring for the earth: Hannah and Anton at Good Life Permaculture, Michelle and Paul at Harvest Feast, all the folks at Elgaar Farm, Marcus and Thea at Vermey's Butcher, Anna at Unpacked, Molly and the folks at the South Hobart Tip Shop, Bill Harvey, Melanie Tait, Robyn Thomas, Maria, Todd and Lissa from Sustainable Living Tasmania, and the lovely peeps at our local zero-waste cafe and meeting spot, the Picnic Basket.

- Thanks to Kay Scarlett, for suggesting that we write a book about our waste-free life. Thanks to Ashley Carr, Clare Marshall and Mary Small at Plum for bringing the book to life, and to Michelle Mackintosh for her amazing design work. Thanks to Natalie Mendham for the wonderful images and for understanding us so well.

- And finally, thank you, reader, for picking up this book, perusing its pages and for entertaining the thought of a waste-free world. We hope you find it useful and, when your family has used it, pass it around until it is useful no more. Then, please find a spot for it in your compost heap – the soil will thank you for it.

INDEX

A Plum book
First published in 2019 by
Pan Macmillan Australia Pty Limited
Level 25, 1 Market Street,
Sydney, NSW 2000, Australia

Level 3, 112 Wellington Parade,
East Melbourne, VIC 3002, Australia

Design and illustration by Michelle Mackintosh
Edited by Emily Rolfe and Lucy Heaver
Index by Helena Holmgren
Photography by Natalie Mendham, with
additional photography by Lauren and Oberon
Carter and Chris Middleton
Typeset by Michelle Mackintosh
Colour reproduction by Splitting Image
Colour Studio
Printed and bound in China by 1010
Printing International Limited

A CIP catalogue record for this book
is available from the National Library
of Australia.

We advise that the information contained in
this book does not negate personal responsibility
on the part of the reader for their own health
and safety. It is recommended that individually
tailored advice is sought from your healthcare or
medical professional. The publishers and their
respective employees, agents and authors are not
liable for injuries or damage occasioned to any
person as a result of reading or following the
information contained in this book.

Inevitably, there was waste generated in the
production and transport of this book, but we
hope that its usefulness will outweigh any harmful
impacts. Care has been taken to ensure that this
book has been produced in the least harmful
way possible, using paper certified by the Forest
Stewardship Council® and other controlled material.

The publisher would like to thank Green Collect
for providing props for the book.

Frances Hodgson Burnett quote on page 8 from
The Secret Garden, 1911.
Joel Salatin quote on page 26 from *Folks, This
Ain't Normal: A Farmer's Advice for Happier Hens,
Healthier People, and a Better World*, copyright ©
2011, 2012. Reprinted by permission of Center
Street, a subsidiary of Hachette Book Group, Inc.
Kurt Vonnegut quote on page 76 from a panel
discussion at the Conneticut Forum, 2006.
Vivienne Westwood quote on page 162 from
a Guardian Live event, 2014.
Henry David Thoreau quote on page 218 from
Walden and Other Writings, 1937.
Margaret Mead quote on page 274 from
source unknown.

MIX
Paper from
responsible sources
FSC® C016973
www.fsc.org

10 9 8 7 6 5 4 3 2 1